Pearls

Pearls

Their History, Sources, Types and Qualities

Renée Newman, GG

Firefly Books

Published by Firefly Books Ltd. 2025

First printing

Library of Congress Control Number: 2025936120

Library and Archives Canada Cataloguing in Publication
Title: Pearls : their history, sources, types and qualities / Renée Newman, GG.
Names: Newman, Renée, 1948- author
Description: Includes bibliographical references and index.
Identifiers: Canadiana 20250188902 | ISBN 9780228105749 (hardcover)
Subjects: LCSH: Pearls. | LCSH: Pearls—Pictorial works. | LCGFT: Illustrated works.
Classification: LCC NK7680 .N49 2025 | DDC 739.27—dc23

Published in the United States by
Firefly Books (U.S.) Inc.
P.O. Box 1338, Ellicott Station
Buffalo, New York 14205

Published in Canada by
Firefly Books Ltd.
50 Staples Avenue, Unit 1
Richmond Hill, Ontario L4B 0A7

Cover and interior design: Hartley Millson

Printed in China | DC

Front cover: (top left) Natural spiny oyster pearl and spinel ring by Assael. *Photo courtesy of Assael*; (top right) Natural color bubble Tahitian pearl ring by Sean Gilson for Assael. *Photo courtesy of Assael*; (bottom) South Sea keshi cultured pearl and diamond yin-yang ring by Assael. *Photo courtesy of Assael.*

Back cover: (top) A retro cultured pearl, diamond and synthetic ruby 18-karat gold brooch depicting a Spanish dancer. *Photo © Heritage Auctions (HA.com)*; (bottom) Cleopatra Collection earrings by Yoko London, featuring turquoise, mother-of-pearl, diamonds and cultured freshwater pearls. *Photo courtesy of Yoko London.*

Frontispiece: An Autore cultured South Sea and colored gem angel fish brooch from the Oceania Collection, inspired by Australian underwater creatures. *Photo courtesy of Autore Pearls.*

ACKNOWLEDGMENTS

I would like to express my appreciation to the following people for their contributions to *Pearls: Their History, Sources, Types and Qualities.*

The staff at Firefly Books responsible for producing this beautiful, high-quality book: Lionel Koffler, president; Julie Takasaki, managing editor; Gillian Watts, freelance copy editor; George A. Walker, map illustrator; and Hartley Millson, designer. I have greatly appreciated the opportunity to create this book with such dedicated and talented professionals.

The following people who have made valuable suggestions, corrections and comments regarding the portions of this book and/or the editions of my *Pearl Buying Guide* (much of this book's information on value factors, pearl types, imitation pearls and treatments is from my previous *Pearl Buying Guide*): Eve Alfillé, Francisco Adame, Mohamed Alslaise, Enrique Arizmendi, Albert Asher, Blaire Beavers, K.C. Bell, Charles Carmona, Sarah Canizzaro, Pin P. Chen, Shane Elan, Prof. Dr. Henry A. Hänni, Jeff Hunter, Susan B. Johnson, Betty Sue King, Chien Lin, Peter Malnekoff, Henri Masliah, Rick Matsui, Douglas McLaurin, Lynn Marie Nakamura, Wes and Tish Rankin, Avi Raz, Jeremy Shepherd, Charles Ueng, Fuji Voll, and Richard Wan. They are not responsible for any possible errors, nor do they necessarily endorse the material contained in this book.

The following people and companies allowed me to use their pearls, jewelry or mollusks for some of the photographs: A & Z Pearls, Inc., Atlantic University Harbor Branch Oceanographic Institute, Blue River Gems & Jewelry Co., Florida Atlantic University, Grace Pearl Co., Inter World Trading, Jye Luxury Collection, KCB Natural Pearls, King Plutarco, Inc., Kojima Company, Stephen Metzler, Pacific Coast Pearls, James Peach, Pearl Concepts, Pearl Exporting Company, Pearl Paradise, Shima Pearl Company, Shinyu Inc., Somewhere in the Rainbow Collection, T. Stern Collection, Tibarumal Jewellery, Yee On Gems & Jewellery, and Kiyoshi Yoneguchi.

The following people and companies allowed me to reproduce photos or diagrams in this book: A & A Jewelry Supply, A & Z Pearls, Adin Fine Antique Jewellery, Adore Adorn, Alishan, Eve J. Alfillé, Enrique Arizmendi, ASBA USA, Assael International, Atacama Pearls, Autore Pearls, K.C. Bell Natural Pearls, Blair Beavers, Bialonczyk Gemstones & Melopearls, Busatti, Columbia Gem House, Angela Conty, Paula Crevoshay, Cultured Pearl Associations of America and Japan, Cynthia Renée, Divina Pearls, Doyle Auctioneers & Appraisers, GAAJ Research Lab, Galatea, Gem A, GeorgianJewelry.com, GIA, J. Grahl Design, Prof. Dr. Henry A. Hänni, Matt Harris Designs, Robyn Hawk, Barbara Heinrich Studio, Heritage Auctions, Alan Hodgkinson, Hubert Jewelry, J. Hunter Pearls Fiji, Inter World Trading, Jewelmer, Kamoka Pearls, K.C. Bell, Dawn King, King Plutarco, King's Ransom, Kojima Pearl Company, Lang Antiques, Le Vian, Linnean Society of London, Lupino Jewelry, Lyon & Turnbull Auctioneers, Douglas McLaurin, Stephen Metzler, Mikimoto (America) Co., Daniel Moesker, Pacific Coast Pearls, Pala International, Pearl Exporting Co, Pearl Paradise, Linda K. Quinn Designs, Pacific Pearls, Paka's Pearls, Paspaley Pearling Co. Pty. Ltd., Fred and Kate Pearce, Pearl Concepts, King Plutarco, Pearl Society Collection, Perlas del Mar de Cortez, Rainforest Design, Rio Pearl, Naomi Sarna, Mark Schneider Design, Sea Hunt Pearls, Sarah Senzer, Senzerina Virtuous Jewelry, Hisano Shepherd, Jeremy Shepherd, Shogun Pearl Co., Brenda Smith, SSEF Swiss Gemmological Institute, T. Stern, Robert Wan, Yoko London, and Zaffiro.

Ernie and Regina Goldberger of the Josam Diamond Trading Corporation. I will forever be grateful to them for hiring me to sort and oversee their diamonds, pearls and jewelry production. This book could not have been written without the experience and knowledge I gained from working with them.

CONTENTS

CHAPTER 1

Why Are Pearls So Prized? 8

Persian Gulf Region 9
India and Sri Lanka 12
Basic Pearl Terminology 14
Venezuela and Panama 15
Mexico 16
China 18
Europe 19
Australia 22
Japan 23
United States 23

CHAPTER 2

Natural Versus Cultured Pearls 26

How Are Natural Blisters and Pearls Formed? 27
The History of Culturing Blisters and Pearls 30
How Are Whole Pearls Cultured? 32
How Pearl Farming Helps the Environment and Communities 35
Tests a Layperson Can Do to Identify Cultured Pearls 36
Gem Lab Tests Used to Identify Natural and Cultured Pearls 38
Main Sources of Natural Oyster Pearls 41

CHAPTER 3

Pearl Value Factors 46

Luster 46
Surface Quality 51
Shape 57
Nacre Thickness 60
Color 62
Size 66
Matching 69

CHAPTER 4

Akoya Cultured Pearls 72

Sources of Akoya Cultured Pearls 72
Keshi Pearls 78
Price Factors 80

CHAPTER 5

South Sea Pearls 84

Sources of South Sea Pearls 85
South Sea Cultured Keshi 92
Price Factors 93

CHAPTER 6

Black Pearls 102

Sources of Black Pearls 102
Price Factors 111

CHAPTER 7

Freshwater Pearls 116
Sources of Freshwater Pearls 116
Changes in Chinese Freshwater Cultured Pearls from 1978 until the Early 2000s 124
Price Factors 134

CHAPTER 8

Pearls Produced by Sea Snails 138
Abalone Pearls 138
Nacreous Versus Non-Nacreous Pearls 143
Conch Pearls 144
Melo Pearls 148
Helmet Pearls 150

CHAPTER 9

Pearls from Scallops, Clams, Saltwater Mussels and Nautiluses 152
Scallop Pearls 152
Clam Pearls 155
Saltwater Mussel Pearls 160
Nautilus Pearls 161

CHAPTER 10

Imitation Pearls 162
Types of Imitation Pearls 162
Observation Tests that Require No Special Equipment 163
Drill Holes of Cultured and Imitation Pearls 166

CHAPTER 11

Pearl Processing and Treatments 172
Pearl Treatments 172
Simple Tests for Detecting Treatments 179
Specialized Tests for Detecting Treatments 180

CHAPTER 12

Creating Unique Pearl Jewelry with Colored Gems 182
Period Jewelry (European and American) 183
Georgian (1714–1837) 184
Victorian (1837–1901) 186
Art Nouveau (1890–1914) 192
Belle Époque (1890–1914) 194
Edwardian (1901–15) 196
Art Deco (1915–40) 197
Retro (1939–50) 198
Mid-Century (1950–70) 199
Modern (1970–Present) 200

CHAPTER 13

Style and Care Tips for Pearl Jewelry 216
Versatile Ways to Wear a Strand of Pearls 216
Versatile Ways to Wear Pearl Studs 221
Caring for Your Pearl Jewelry 222

Appendix 228
Glossary 229
Bibliography 233
Index 236

1 Why Are Pearls So Prized?

> *The topmost rank of all things of price is held by pearls.*
>
> — Pliny the Elder, *Historia naturalis (The Natural History)*, Book IX

Pearls are naturally beautiful and rare. They do not need to be cut or polished to bring out their luster. Their resemblance to the moon and raindrops led ancient cultures to believe that pearls had supernatural powers that could protect their owner. This in turn helped pearls become symbols of purity, love, fertility, wealth, power, authority and status. As a result, they are often called the "Queen of Gems."

The virtues of pearls were particularly well described by George Kunz and Charles Stevenson in *The Book of the Pearl* (1908):

> Unlike other gems, the pearl comes to us perfect and beautiful, direct from the hand of nature. Other precious stones receive careful treatment from the lapidary, and owe much to his art. The pearl, however, owes nothing to man ... . It is absolutely a gift of nature, on which man cannot improve. We turn from the brilliant, dazzling ornament of diamonds or emeralds to a necklace of pearls with a sense of relief, and the eye rests upon it with quiet, satisfied repose and is delighted with its modest splendor, its soft gleam, borrowed from its home in the depths of the sea. It seems truly to typify steady and abiding affection, which needs no accessory or adornment to make it more attractive. And there is a purity and sweetness about it which makes it especially suitable for the maiden.

The importance of pearls has varied depending on the culture and the period. This chapter will explore their significance to various societies through time.

PERSIAN GULF REGION

Archaeological records indicate that pearling (diving and fishing for pearls) has occurred for thousands of years throughout the Persian Gulf area. Countries with a coastline in this region include Iran, Oman, the United Arab Emirates (UAE), Saudi Arabia, Qatar, Bahrain, Kuwait and Iraq. The oldest recorded Gulf pearl was discovered in 2017 on Marawah Island, off the coast of UAE, and dates back 7,800 years. Named the "Abu Dhabi Pearl" after the UAE capital, it is light pink, nacreous and about 3 millimeters in diameter. It was found at a Neolithic site dating to between 5800 and 5600 BCE (the Neolithic period was the last stage of the Stone Age).

As time passed, pearls became a valuable commodity in the Persian Gulf, not only because of their natural beauty and the resulting demand for them as adornment, but also because the Gulf was the primary source of natural pearls. Unlike bulkier products, pearls were a luxury item and easy to transport, and they did not spoil like perishable goods; small quantities could yield enormous profits. Basra, Iraq's main port, was an important trading center for pearls.

Early portraits of Arab royalty show them adorned lavishly with pearls, which were a symbol of power and wealth. Women who wanted to win favor with a ruler would offer him pearls. In 1901 a pearl necklace dating back to before 300 BCE was found in Iran, in the stone coffin of a person assumed to be a princess or queen, considering the gem-encrusted gold ornaments adorning the skeleton. The necklace was added to the Persian Gallery of the Louvre in 1908.

For centuries the Kingdom of Bahrain, an island with freshwater springs, has played a major role in the development of the pearl trade in the Persian Gulf. Its massive, dense pearl oyster beds and prime location in the middle of the trade route from Iraq to India made it an ideal pearling center. Increased demand for natural pearls in the 1800s and early 1900s turned Bahrain into a single-product economy—and that product was pearls.

A portrait of Nader Shah (Shah of Persia, 1736–47) wearing strands of pearls. *Wikimedia Commons.*

This pearl necklace, which is more than 2,300 years old, was found in a stone coffin in Iran. *Photo © RMN, Musée du Louvre/Mathieu Rabeau.*

Persian Gulf Region.

The Cartier store in Manhattan, New York. The Fifth Avenue mansion was acquired by Pierre Cartier in 1917 in exchange for $100 and a double-stranded necklace of natural pearls worth $1 million. *Shutterstock/DW labs Incorporated.*

Natural pearls were so highly valued that in 1917, Pierre Cartier was able to trade two strands of natural pearls—worth $1 million—for a building in Manhattan, New York. However, their value took a downward turn after the introduction of cultured pearls into the market in 1918. Prices dropped further during and after the Great Depression (1929–39). Then oil was discovered in 1932 by the Bahrain Petroleum Company, and it became the country's most important commodity.

In 1957 Cartier's pearls were sold at auction for only $157,000, but eventually natural pearl prices were on the rise again. A double-stranded necklace with natural pearls ranging in size from 6.5 to 12.25 millimeters sold for $3.7 million at Christie's in 2012, demonstrating that natural pearls have since regained their previous prestige.

In 2012 UNESCO declared the Bahraini pearl oyster beds and 17 nearby buildings a World Heritage Site. According to UNESCO's website, the designation was made because the "site is the last remaining complete example of the cultural tradition of pearling and the wealth it generated at a time when the trade dominated the Gulf economy (2nd century to the 1930s). It also constitutes an outstanding example of traditional utilization of the sea's resources and human interaction with the environment, which shaped both the economy and the cultural identity of the island's society."

Bahrain wants to restore itself as the global center for sustainable natural pearls. In 2017 the Bahrain Institute for Pearls and Gemstones (DANAT) was established to support a national plan to revive the natural pearl sector. The health of the pearl beds is monitored by DANAT, the Coast Guard and the Supreme Council for the Environment. Licensed divers carefully gather the oysters by hand, and sometimes diving is suspended in certain areas to allow for the growth of the oysters. Other functions of the institute include testing and certifying pearls and offering hands-on pearl-grading education. DANAT's efforts have been effective. In January 2022 the Rapaport Group announced the launch of a new market for ethical natural pearls in collaboration with DANAT.

An image of Krishna, a beloved Hindu god often associated with pearls. *Dinodia Photos/ Alamy Stock Photo.*

INDIA AND SRI LANKA

In India pearls are not only viewed as valuable gems but also have cultural and spiritual significance. Hinduism often associates pearls with Krishna, one of its most popular and revered gods. According to one legend, Krishna retrieved a pearl from the sea to adorn his daughter on her wedding day. Thus pearls are considered ideal wedding gifts because they symbolize purity, innocence, prosperity and good luck.

The link between pearls and weddings extends even to the Western world, where they are as much a wedding jewel as diamonds. Just have a look at a bridal shop or wedding catalog. You will find pearls—both imitation and real—decorating wedding gowns, veils, tiaras, gloves, purses, ring-bearer pillows, cake toppers and party favors.

Many of India's natural pearls were sourced from oysters in the shallow waters along the Gulf of Mannar and Palk Strait, which separate India from the island of Sri Lanka (formerly Ceylon). The exportation of pearls became a main source of foreign exchange for Sri Lanka, and when Sri Lankan officials wanted to impress foreign dignitaries, they gave them gifts of pearls. The island's ideal environment for pearl fisheries and its favorable location near India, on the trade route from East Asia to the Middle East, helped it become famous for both natural pearls and high-quality gems.

Unfortunately, overfishing caused pearl oyster stocks to decline significantly, leading India's Central Marine Fisheries Research Institute (CMFRI) to ban pearl oyster fishing in 1962. The Institute's 1961 annual report stated: "More than 1,500 divers were engaged in pearl fishery and an average of 3 lakh (300,000) oysters were fished every day." According to a September 2022 article in the *New Indian Express*, the CMFRI has taken steps to replenish the pearl oyster population in the Gulf of Mannar, releasing more than 500,000 hatchery-produced Indian pearl oyster spats into the Gulf of Mannar to help replenish its population.

Hyderabad, the capital of the Indian state of Telangana, is known as the "City of Pearls"; it is one of the largest pearl-trading centers and a major pearl-drilling location. The most notable area is the village of Chandanpet, just outside Hyderabad, where almost the entire population is involved in drilling pearls, a skill they have practiced for generations. Pearls traded in Hyderabad have not only been part of traditional royal regalia but are also believed to have healing and beautifying properties.

Hyderabad and Diamonds

Historically, Hyderabad was also a notable trading center for Golconda diamonds, mined in the present-day southern Indian states of Telangana and Andhra Pradesh. Famous diamonds from this region include the Hope, the Koh-i-Noor, the Regent, the Dresden Green and the Orlov. Today, Surat and Mumbai are India's main diamond centers.

India and Sri Lanka.

Basic Pearl Terminology

Pearl: an organic gem that forms inside a living one-shelled or two-shelled mollusk, such as an abalone, conch, oyster, mussel, clam or scallop.

Nacre: a hard, iridescent substance secreted by a mollusk. It is called mother-of-pearl when it lines the inside of the mollusk's shell and nacre when it is a component of pearls.

Mother-of-pearl: the smooth, hard, iridescent coating on the inner shell surface of mollusks.

Natural pearls: pearls formed inside saltwater and freshwater mollusks in the wild without human intervention.

Cultured pearls: pearls that are formed after a mantle tissue graft from a donor mollusk is inserted by a human into a live mollusk, with or without a bead.

Oriental pearls: an old trade name for natural saltwater pearls mainly from the Middle East.

Saltwater pearls: pearls that grow in mollusks found in oceans, seas and gulfs. They can be natural or cultured.

Freshwater pearls: pearls that grow in mollusks found in rivers, lakes and streams. They can be natural or cultured.

South Sea pearls: pearls from the silver-lipped and gold-lipped *Pinctada maxima* oysters. They are cultivated in Australia, Indonesia, the Philippines, Myanmar, Vietnam and Thailand.

Tahitian pearls: pearls from the black-lipped *Pinctada margaritifera* oyster, found in French Polynesia. They are marketed in Tahiti but cultivated elsewhere in French Polynesia.

Mantle: the tissue that lines the inner shell surface and encloses the soft inner body of the mollusk.

Shell blisters: natural or cultured dome-shaped formations that grow on the inner surface of a mollusk shell. They are also called "blisters."

Mabe pearls: the trade term for assembled cultured blisters. They are composed of a shell blister; a wax, resin or paste filling in the blister cavity; and a backing, usually made of mother-of-pearl.

Whole pearls (also known as free, loose or cyst pearls): pearls formed in the interior of a mollusk instead of being attached to the inner surface of its shell.

Blister pearls: whole pearls that become attached to the shell, according to the World Jewellery Confederation definition. This term is also used in the American trade to mean shell blisters.

Pre- to early Columbus-era pearls found in a clay pot on an island off the coast of Venezuela. *Photo by Douglas McLaurin.*

What's in a Name?

Incidentally, if you go by Margaret, Peggy, Marjorie, Margo, Maggie, Gretchen, Gretel or Rita, your name also means "pearl," which in turn signifies purity, innocence, humility and sweetness.

VENEZUELA AND PANAMA

During the 1500s, oyster beds in the Gulf of Panama and off the coast of Venezuela became major sources of pearls for Europe. This was the result of discoveries by Spanish explorers such as Christopher Columbus and Vasco Núñez de Balboa. Pearls and gold were two of the main treasures Columbus had hoped to find when he set sail westward, but it was not until his third trip, in 1498, that he found natives wearing pearls, along the coast of present-day Venezuela. News of pearls in the Americas spread and encouraged other Spaniards to explore the New World.

One reminder of what an important source of pearls this area once was is the name of an island off the Venezuelan coast: Isla de Margarita. *Margarita* means "pearls" in Latin, derived from the Greek word *margaritēs.*

By 1513 Balboa had also found pearls in Panama. According to Kunz and Stevenson in *The Book of the Pearl*, "From the point of view of the Spaniards of his day, the greatest result of Balboa's immortal journey in 1513 across the Isthmus of Panama in the broad waters of the Pacific, was the discovery of the pearl resources in the Gulf of Saint Michael, now known as the Gulf of Panama."

It was there that the famous 50.56-carat pear-shaped La Peregrina pearl may have been found. It was presented to Philip II of Spain (1527–98) and later owned by various other European monarchs. In 1969 the pearl pendant was sold at auction for $37,000 to Richard Burton, who bought it as a Valentine's Day gift for his wife, Elizabeth Taylor. In collaboration with Alfred Durante of Cartier, Taylor designed a necklace for the pearl that used 56 more natural pearls, four cultured pearls, rubies and diamonds. The authenticity of the pearls was confirmed by the Swiss Gemmological Institute (SSEF). In 2011 the necklace fetched US$11.8 million at a Christie's auction.

La Peregrina is famous for its history, huge size and perfect symmetry. It weighs 50.56 carats (0.36 ounces) and measures about 25.5 mm (1 in.) in length. *Photo courtesy of SSEF.*

Two of the pearl necklaces found in Oaxaca at the Monte Albán archaeological site. *Photo by Douglas McLaurin.*

MEXICO

Mexico is the source of the world's oldest known pearls. An August 2019 article in *Latin American Antiquity* reported that 15 pearls had been discovered on Espíritu Santo Island in the Gulf of California, also known as the Sea of Cortez. The island is near the city of La Paz in Baja California, Mexico. Accelerator mass spectrometry (AMS) radiocarbon dating indicated that the pearls were at least 8,500 years old. They showed signs of having been gently smoked or heated and had grooves suggesting they had been strung and used as jewelry.

Evidence for the historical importance of pearls in Mexico was also provided by the 1932 discovery of the Monte Albán archaeological site in the present-day state of Oaxaca. Pearl necklaces and pendants were found at the site, which was inhabited from 500 BCE to 850 CE.

In 1535 Hernán Cortés landed north of La Paz and saw local natives wearing necklaces with pearls of different colors. This was an important discovery; for the next 400 years the Sea of Cortez became a major source of natural pearls for Europe, especially during the 1600s.

According to Enrique Arizmendi, owner of Perlas del Mar de Cortez, the pearls of Baja California became New Spain's most important export product, with a value even greater than the combined extraction of silver and gold, for the first 50 years after the Spanish conquest of Mexico in 1521. Local natives were put to work either by force or with promises of payment as divers in the pearling armadas of the Spanish Crown. These armadas consisted of a sailboat (the "flagship") that could pull several smaller boats or canoes. Each canoe had two or three occupants, a sailor and two divers. The divers started diving for oysters early in the morning and would plunge into the water repeatedly until noon. They would rest for three hours and then start diving again for another three or four hours. Bags of oysters were transported to the flagship for harvest, where the shells were cleaned and inspected for pearls. These activities continued, mostly unchanged, for several centuries.

The island of Espiritu Santo became the location of the world's first commercial pearl oyster hatchery in 1903, when Gastón Vivès founded the Compañía Criadora de Concha y Perla de la Baja California, S.A. This was his response to the declining number of pearl oyster beds, caused by

Natural Mexican oyster pearls from Pacific Coast Pearls. *Photo by Tish Rankin.*

overfishing. Vivès was a partner in one of the pearl armadas, so he knew about the decline firsthand. His pearl farm became a huge success; it had more than 8 million *Pinctada mazatlanica* oysters under the care of 500 workers—6 percent of the population of La Paz. The company's main product was mother-of-pearl; it was able to ship up to 10 million shells per year to Europe and the United States; even more important, it exported between 200 and 500 natural pearls (non-nucleated) of superior quality every year.

In 1914, during the Mexican Revolution, the company's pearl oyster farm was destroyed and its facilities were looted. The sustainable cultivation of oysters that Gastón Vivès had developed ended, and soon the beds were exhausted. By 1939 the federal government had placed a permanent ban on pearl oyster fishing, but it came too late: recovery at that point was almost impossible. The government would have to wait seven decades before it was safe to issue new permits to fish pearl oysters.

Thanks to the development of pearl culturing in Mexico, as well as government efforts to stop overfishing, wild oysters have become more plentiful. As a result, natural pearls in a variety of colors and shapes are being found again in Mexico.

Two cultured blisters in a *Pteria sterna* shell. *Photo by Douglas McLaurin.*

CHINA

In her classic book *Pearls,* Elisabeth Strack states that 3,000 years ago the Chinese considered pearls to be the "Queen of Gems." They were first used for idols and religious statues, but later they were possessed by people in power. The *Book of Documents* (*Shujing*), the oldest Chinese history book, describes a string of pearls dating as far back as 2300 BCE. Although natural saltwater pearls are found along China's coast, the area is more noted for its freshwater pearls. The record auction price for a freshwater pearl necklace was a Qing Dynasty emperor's court necklace, a strand of 108 freshwater pearls and colored gemstone beads. It sold for 67,860,000 HKD (US$8.66 million) at a Sotheby's Hong Kong auction in April 2010.

The Chinese were the first to culture shell blisters. Evidence of Buddha images overgrown with nacre dates to graves from the Han Dynasty, around 100 BCE. According to a 2014 article about the history of cultured pearls on the Gemological Institute of America (GIA) website, Chinese pearl farmers began cultivating shell blisters in freshwater mussels as early as the 13th century, sometimes using small molds shaped like the Buddha. These cultured shell blisters were hollow and flat.

The Chinese believed that pearls had healing powers and were probably the first to use them as medicine. Pearl powder remains a part of traditional Chinese medicine today. It is used as an antacid and anti-inflammatory agent and is believed to eliminate toxins from the body. Pearl powder is also a popular ingredient in skincare products. The Japanese also believe that pearls have health benefits. At the age of 94, Kokichi Mikimoto, founder of the cultured pearl industry, said, "I owe my fine health and long life to the two pearls I have swallowed every morning of my life since I was 20."

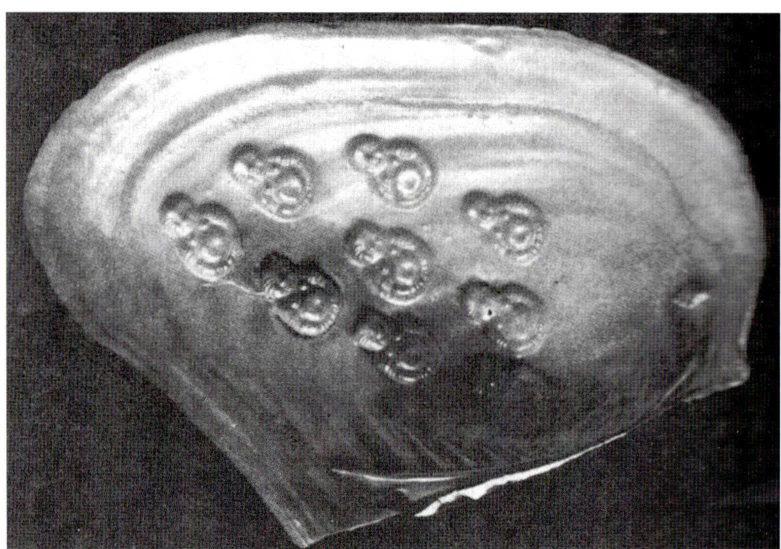

Buddha images on a cockscomb mussel (*Cristaria plicata*) shell. Image from George Kunz and Charles Stevenson, *The Book of the Pearl* (1908).

A first-century mosaic of a Pompeian matron wearing a pearl necklace and earrings. *Mondadori Portfolio/Getty Images.*

EUROPE

Ancient Greek culture associated pearls with Aphrodite, the goddess of love, who rose from the water out of a shell. The Greek word for pearl, *margaritēs*, is used in scientific names, such as *Margaritifera margaritifera*, the European freshwater pearl mussel.

Rome experienced a pearl craze around 61 BCE, after the Roman general Pompey the Great returned from military campaigns in Asia Minor and Armenia. According to Kunz and Stevenson, Pompey's triumphal procession included 33 crowns of pearls, a pearl-decorated shrine and a portrait of the general adorned with pearls. Afterward pearls became the gem most esteemed by the Romans, and huge prices were paid for single pearls if they were large and perfect. The general Aulus Vitellius was said to have financed an entire military campaign by selling one pearl from his mother's ear.

Pearls were dedicated to Venus, the Roman goddess of love and fertility. Some people slept on pearl-inlaid beds and wore pearls at night,

so that even while sleeping they would be aware of possessing beautiful gems that were the ultimate symbol of status.

The value of pearls was acknowledged even in the New Testament. In Matthew 13:45–46 Jesus says, "The kingdom of heaven is like unto a merchant man seeking goodly pearls, who, when he had found one pearl of great price, went and sold all that he had and bought it."

After their discovery in Venezuela, Central America and Mexico by Spanish explorers, pearls became a lucrative source of income for Spain during the 1500s and 1600s. They adorned not only Spanish rulers but also monarchs of other countries. Queen Elizabeth I (1533–1603) loved pearls so much that she almost always wore several strands of them, and her gowns were covered with pearls that had to be removed whenever the fabric was cleaned.

Marie Antoinette (1755–93), the last queen of France, was known for her extravagant jewelry and her love of fine things. However, those tastes would be to her detriment. In 1793 she was convicted of depleting the national treasury, one of the charges that led to her execution. One notable piece of jewelry owned by Marie Antoinette spurred record prices in November 2018. Her diamond-and-pearl pendant sold at a Geneva Sotheby's auction for 36,427,000 Swiss francs (approximately US$43 million)—a world record for a natural pearl. The pendant is believed to have been among the jewels that were packed up as the king and queen prepared to escape from the Tuileries Palace in 1791 as armed revolutionaries surrounded them.

Before the mid-1900s, Europe was an important source of natural freshwater pearls. However, overfishing and the impact of industrial and agricultural pollution led to a major decline of pearl mussels. As a result, freshwater pearl fishing in Europe is now prohibited or strongly regulated. Some of Europe's freshwater pearls ended up in the British Crown Jewels, together with saltwater pearls. (Since pearls were traditional for queens, their beauty was more important than their source.)

Pearls have remained a popular choice for more contemporary royalty. Queen Elizabeth II wore pearls on her wedding day in 1947, and she was rarely seen in public during the day without a pearl necklace, usually of three strands.

According to Evelyne Poumellec, who was a lead designer at Garrard between 1996 and 1998, pearls were Princess Diana's favorite gem, which is evident from the many photos of her wearing them. Together, she and

A portrait of Queen Elizabeth I of England adorned lavishly with pearls. *Print Collector/Getty Images.*

Opposite page: The world's most expensive pearl, in Marie Antoinette's diamond-and-pearl pendant, which sold for 36,427,000 Swiss francs (approximately US$43 million) at a Geneva Sotheby's auction in 2018. *Photo courtesy of SSEF.*

Poumellec designed a necklace featuring five South Sea pearls, based on a reversed tiara. This piece was important to the princess because the necklace would be hers as an independent woman, rather than borrowed from the Crown. Photographs of the recently divorced Diana wearing the necklace to the opening of the ballet *Swan Lake* on June 3, 1997, were seen in newspapers around the world and on the front cover of *People* magazine. The Swan Lake necklace and earrings would be among her final jewelry purchases. On August 31, 1997, she died following a car crash.

Princess Diana wearing her pearl necklace at the opening of Swan Lake on June 3, 1997. *Julian Parker/Getty Images.*

AUSTRALIA

The Aboriginal peoples of Australia were among the first in the world to appreciate mother-of-pearl and to use pearl shells in ceremonies and art and as a medium of exchange. According to the Western Australia Museum, the oldest evidence of this is a 22,000-year-old piece of shell found in a West Kimberley rock shelter, 200 kilometers (over 124 miles) from the shoreline. The shells of the large *Pinctada maxima* pearl oyster were some of the most commonly traded items in pre-European Australia and were more highly valued than pearls.

In the late 1800s and early 1900s, Australia was the main supplier of pearl oyster shell to Europe and the United States. By 1914, the coastal town of Broome in Western Australia was supplying about 80 percent of the world's pearl shell. It was used for manufacturing mother-of-pearl products such as buttons, inlays and other decorative items, making it a valuable commodity until more affordable plastic substitutes replaced it in the 1940s.

Australia is noted for having played a major role in the development of cultured saltwater pearls. Beginning in 1889, William Saville-Kent (1845–1908), a British marine biologist, conducted experiments on Thursday Island in Queensland, and by 1891 he had succeeded in culturing South Sea oyster shell blisters, which were exhibited in London. This was two years before Kokichi Mikimoto cultured his first akoya shell blisters. According to the May 2023 issue of *Facette*, the SSEF magazine, at the end of the 19th century Saville-Kent became the first person to successfully culture loose pearls. His pioneering experiments influenced the development of pearl cultivation techniques in Japan.

Australia's first South Sea pearl farm was established in 1956 in Kuri Bay, Western Australia, as a joint venture between American and Japanese partners. Today Australian South Sea cultured pearls are a major asset to Australia's economy.

William Saville-Kent, a pioneer of the concept of sustainable fisheries and the first person on record to produce cultured saltwater shell blisters and loose pearls. *The Natural History Museum/Alamy Stock Photo.*

JAPAN

In Japan, pearls have been associated for centuries with purity, wisdom and spiritual transformation. They are considered sacred and have been used in imperial regalia and ceremonial attire.

Japan is famous for its cultured saltwater akoya pearls. In 1893 Kokichi Mikimoto (1858–1954) harvested his first cultured blister, which at the time was called a half-pearl. In 1908 Tatsuhei Mise (1880–1924) and Tokichi Nishikawa (1874–1909) signed an agreement of joint ownership of the Mise-Nishikawa method of culturing round pearls with tissue implantation, a process each had accomplished separately. Mikimoto was granted a patent for cultured round pearls in 1916 and started mass-producing them using nuclei cut from American mussel shells—unlike Mise and Nishikawa, who had used metal beads. Mikimoto proved to be the most successful at commercializing and promoting cultured pearls.

According to the May 2023 *Facette* article, after 1918 Mikimoto sold round cultured pearls in London for 75 percent of the price of natural pearls. In 1922 *The New York Times* reported that cultured pearls were selling for 30 percent less than natural ones. By 1928 cultured pearls were about one-tenth the value of natural pearls, which had also lost value as more and more cultured pearls entered the market.

In 1925 at Lake Biwa, the Japanese became the first to cultivate whole freshwater pearls. These pearls had a shell-bead nucleus, similar to akoya pearls, and by the 1930s, they were being sold overseas. Pearl farming at Lake Biwa ended in the mid-1980s because of pollution from agricultural fertilizers and pesticides. Today cultured akoya pearls are Japan's main pearl product.

Kokichi Mikimoto, the founder of the cultured pearl industry. *Gainew Gallery/Alamy Stock Photo.*

UNITED STATES

Before the Europeans arrived, Native Americans used freshwater pearls as trade commodities and for ceremonial celebrations. They considered pearls to be symbols of beauty for both men and women. When British and French colonizers arrived in North America, they saw Native Americans wearing pearls and offered them goods such as tools and knives in exchange for the gems, which they then took back to Europe.

North America provides an ideal habitat for pearl mollusks, especially within the Mississippi River drainage basin, because of its large limestone riverbeds. Limestone is composed mainly of calcium carbonate, the same material that makes up pearl nacre and shell. According to Elisabeth Strack in her book *Pearls*, the rivers and streams of North America were once paved with layers of mussels stacked on top of one another.

Joc Pederson wearing his signature pearl necklace at an Atlanta Braves baseball game. *AP Photo/Ben Margot.*

In 1857 a "pearl rush" ensued after Jacob Quackenbush found a 15-millimeter pink pearl in a mussel in Notch Brook, New Jersey, and sold it to Tiffany & Co. for $1,500. In *The Book of the Pearl,* Kunz and Stevenson recount how a French dealer bought it for 12,500 francs and then sold it to Empress Eugénie, the wife of Emperor Napoleon III. Many local people in New Jersey then quit their jobs and started searching for pearls. The fever spread to other states, and pearls were discovered in New York, Connecticut, Pennsylvania, Ohio, Wisconsin, Mississippi, Tennessee, Arkansas and Texas.

Natural pearl prices soared during the pearl boom of the late 19th and early 20th centuries. At a 1982 GIA symposium, gem dealer Maurice Shire said that natural pearls were so important at the end of the 19th century that many fine jewelers earned most of their income—as much as 80 percent—from the sale of pearls. Elisabeth Strack explains their popularity: "For a certain time, American pearls held second place on the world market, after pearls from the Persian Gulf. Victorian jewellers preferred the pearls because they were larger than European river pearls and easier to obtain. Moreover, prices were lower than for oriental pearls. Art Nouveau jewellery also preferred American river pearls of irregular shapes."

Considering the demand for pearls in the United States during the late 1800s, it is not surprising that in 1885 the famous baseball player John Ward of the New York Giants wore a pearl necklace during a game. Since then, pearls have been a symbol of success and professionalism in the sport. Joc Pederson of the Atlanta Braves made headlines when he wore a pearl necklace during the 2021 World Series. The pearls ended up being a good luck charm for Pederson: the Braves won the Series. His pearl necklace was displayed at the Baseball Hall of Fame.

The 1800s pearl rush led to the development of the mother-of-pearl industry in America. In 1891 John Boepple, a German button maker, established the first mother-of-pearl factory in Muscatine, Iowa. By 1900 Muscatine had become the "Pearl Button Capital" of the world. Mother-of-pearl buttons replaced porcelain, ivory and glass buttons imported from Europe. However, the industry declined during the 1920s as mother-of-pearl buttons went out of style. The cause was the invention of the washing machine, which damaged them. Plastic buttons replaced mother-of-pearl buttons in the 1930s.

The mother-of-pearl button business ended in the 1950s but the commercial shell industry continued, because the Japanese needed American freshwater mussel shells for the nuclei of their cultured pearls. American shells were considered superior because they could provide white beads that were free of colored banding and did not crack when the pearl was drilled. Thousands of tons of freshwater mussel shells were exported to Japan each year. From the 1960s to the 1990s, Tennessee's commercial mussel shell business employed about 2,000 people, and according to a GIA field report, during that time almost 90 percent of the cultured pearls produced worldwide had American freshwater mussel shell nuclei.

John Latendresse, founder of the American Pearl Company in Camden, Tennessee, was involved in the mussel shell and pearl trade in Japan when he was challenged by his Japanese friends to culture freshwater pearls in the United States. From 1963 until 1983, he and his wife, Chessy, experimented with pearl culturing until they succeeded in harvesting their first bead-nucleated American freshwater pearl. By 1985 the American Pearl Company had become the first and only commercial producer of American freshwater cultured pearls. Their Tennessee farm produced cultured pearls for retailers until 2000, when John passed away. His family has stopped culturing pearls but still runs a pearl business in Nashville.

Pearls of all types have become a hot fashion item for men. *Necklaces by Senzerina Virtuous Jewelry; photo courtesy Sarah Senzer.*

During the 1900s, advertisers of cultured pearls usually showcased their jewelry on female models. This created the perception that pearls were solely a woman's accessory. Photos of European queens and American First Ladies wearing pearl necklaces and earrings reinforced this belief. But pearls are no longer just for mothers and grandmothers. Today pearls of all types have become popular with younger generations, and male pop stars, actors and athletes have all been photographed wearing the gems.

Centuries ago, only royalty and the very wealthy could afford pearls. Persian shahs and European kings and queens wore them as a symbol of power, authority and wealth. Fortunately, pearls are no longer restricted to the rich. Today anyone can wear them as part of their personal style or as an expression of individuality. Ordinary men and women can now afford to enjoy them in a wide variety of price ranges, types, colors and styles. Thanks to their natural beauty, pearls are just as prized today as they were when first discovered.

2 Natural Versus Cultured Pearls

The term *pearl* has different meanings depending on the user and context. It generally refers to an organic gem composed of calcium carbonate ($CaCO_3$), protein material and water that forms within a mollusk such as an oyster, mussel, clam, scallop, abalone or conch. This chapter focuses on oyster pearls. The World Jewellery Confederation (CIBJO) limits the use of the term *pearl* to natural pearls formed within a sac inside a mollusk. If the gem is attached to the inner shell when it forms, it is called a blister, not a pearl. If it forms with human intervention, it is called a cultured pearl.

The calcium carbonate in pearls and shells consists of two distinct minerals with different crystal structures: aragonite and calcite. The first form of calcium carbonate secreted by a mollusk is columnar calcite. After that, brick-like layers of microscopic aragonite platelets are secreted. These layers form the pearly substance called *nacre* when it is a component of pearls and *mother-of-pearl* when it lines the inside of the mollusk. The mantle of the

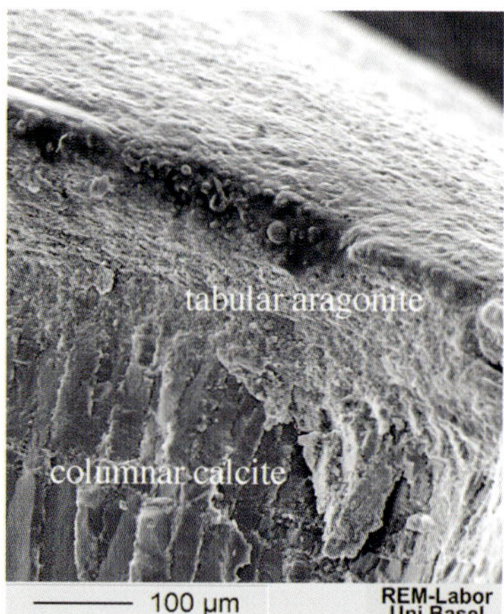

Left: Aragonite platelets of pearl nacre magnified approximately 5,000 times.

Right: This scanning electron microscopic (SEM) photo shows tabular aragonite and columnar calcite in a cross section of a natural pearl.

Photos © REM-Labor, Basel University; information provided by Prof. Dr. H.A. Hänni, SSEF.

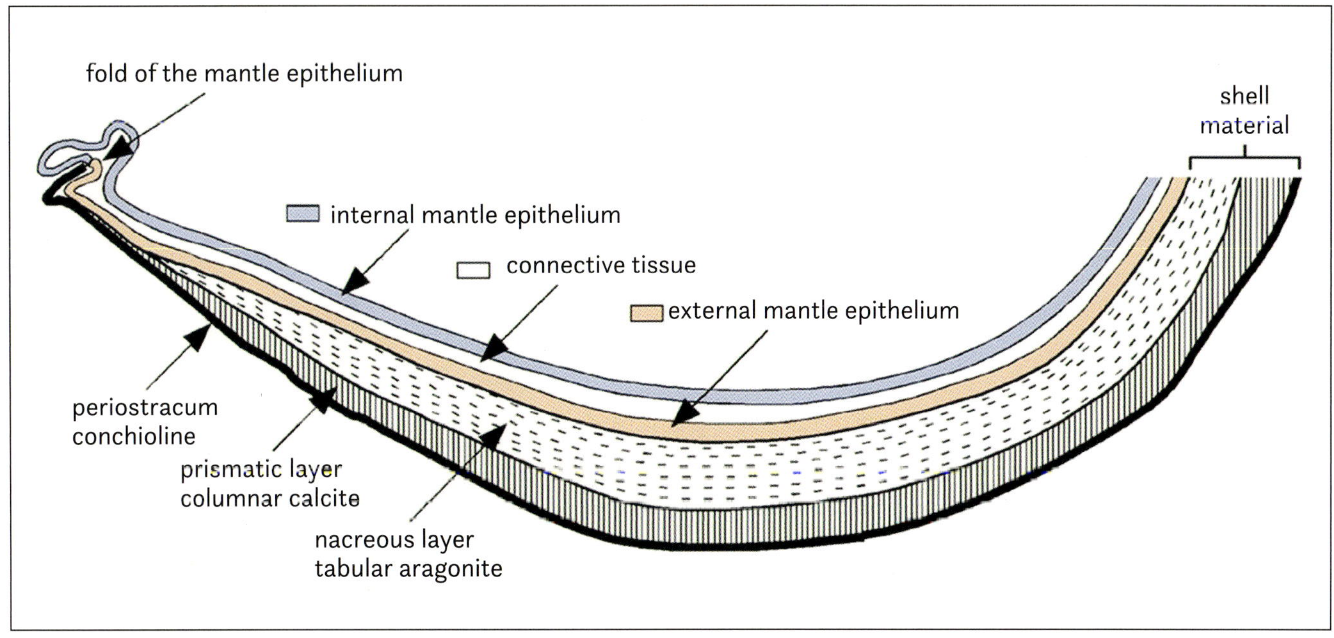

A schematic cross section of a shell. *Diagram © Prof. Dr. H.A. Hänni, SSEF.*

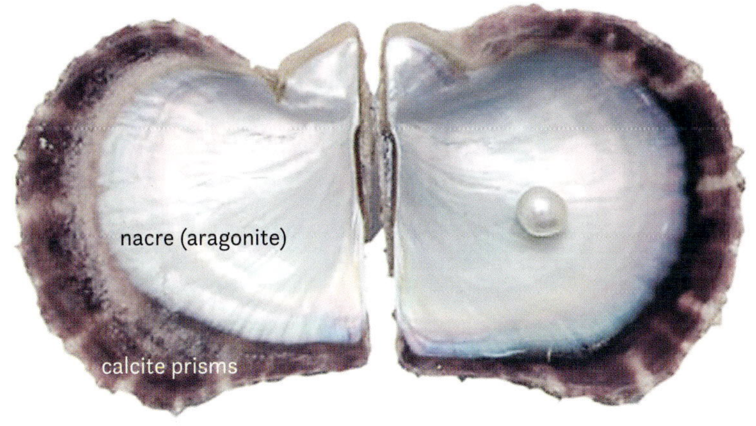

The inner shell of a *Pinctada radiata* oyster from Bahrain, showing the two growth sections: brown columnar calcite (the mantle's first calcium carbonate formation) and silvery, iridescent mother-of-pearl (the aragonite nacre product precipitated by older mantle cells). *Photo © Prof. Dr. H.A. Hänni, SSEF & GemExpert.*

mollusk is tissue that lines the inner shell surface and encloses the creature's soft inner body. The cells of the external mantle layer, or epithelium, are responsible for producing nacre and the shell.

Shells have the same structure as natural pearls, which have a core of calcite prisms and an overgrowth of aragonite platelets—the nacre that corresponds to the mother-of-pearl layer in the shell.

What Causes Pearl Iridescence?

When light waves pass through layers of aragonite, they interfere with each other by both reflecting and penetrating deeper into the layers. The result is the iridescence and play of color that you see in both mother-of-pearl and pearls.

HOW ARE NATURAL BLISTERS AND PEARLS FORMED?

Natural blisters can form when marine invaders such as parasites, worms, fish, crabs or other creatures penetrate the oyster's shell. They are then covered with nacre and organic material as a defense mechanism. If the intruder is not trapped between the mantle and the shell and reaches the

A cluster of natural blisters in a wild rainbow-lipped *Pteria sterna* oyster from Perlas del Mar de Cortez. *Photo by Enrique Arizmendi.*

A worm embedded in the nacre of a wild *Malleus malleus* oyster shell. *Photo © Prof. Dr. H.A. Hänni, SSEF & GemExpert.*

inner part of the mollusk, it can be ejected by the movement of water under pressure, created by the animal when filtering water for food.

Natural whole pearls are formed spontaneously as the mantle's reaction to an injury caused by an attack from a marine invader. The injury and healing process produce a pearl sac, or cyst, made up of displaced external mantle cells. The pearl sac forms in the connective tissue of the mantle where the injury occurred.

This explanation is at odds with how many people believe natural pearls are formed. Sources often claim that a loose natural pearl is created when a foreign object, such as a grain of sand or a parasite, gets trapped in the mollusk's mantle and the mollusk covers it in nacre to isolate it. However, Elisabeth Strack explains in her book *Pearls* that in "1912/13, the German zoologist Friedrich Alverdes proved that the formation of pearls is not caused by a foreign object, but is only caused when epithelium cells of the upper mantle layer are transferred into the connective tissue of the mantle where they form a so-called epithelium sac or pearl sac." Furthermore, when natural loose pearls have been cut open, no creatures or grains of sand have been found inside them. Mollusks can easily eject irritants such as sand with water as they filter feed, although marine invaders are found in blisters.

Examination of X-ray photographs by Kenneth Scarratt, a specialist who has worked at the Gemological Institute of America (GIA) and the Bahrain Institute for Pearls and Gemstones (DANAT), also indicates that pearls are not formed by encasing an irritant with nacre. Hubert Bari and David Lam, in their book *Pearls*, state that Scarratt found only 20 cases in millions of X-rays that indicated the presence of a foreign body at the center of a natural pearl.

A loose natural pearl grows in the same sequence as its shell. The core may contain an organic protein substance that is involved in the growth and binding of the pearl. Calcite prisms usually form with the organic material. The final stage in the formation of the pearl (in other words, its outer layer) is composed primarily of aragonite tablets (nacre), the same lustrous material that lines the mollusk's shell. The physical structure of pearls can vary to some extent among different species.

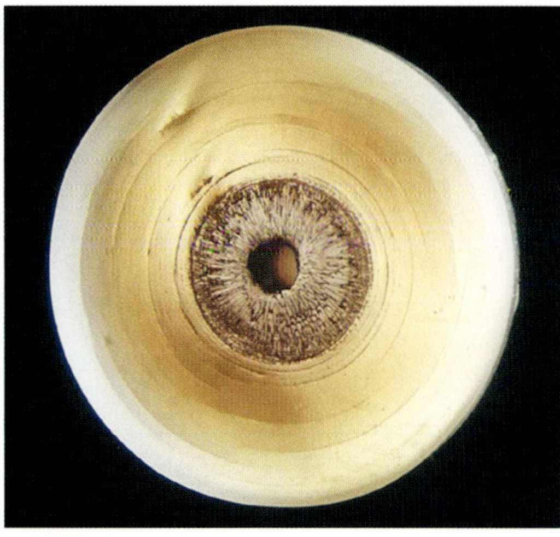

The cross section of a drilled natural pearl (approximately 5 mm). The inner part is rich in organic material and shows a columnar structure made of calcite prisms. The outer part shows fine concentric rings and is made of nacre, aragonite in submicroscopic tablets. *Photo © Prof. Dr. H.A. Hänni, SSEF & GemExpert.*

A cultured blister in the form of the Buddha in a shell at the Robert Wan Pearl Museum. *Photo courtesy of Robert Wan.*

THE HISTORY OF CULTURING BLISTERS AND PEARLS

The term *cultured pearl* refers to pearls that are formed after a human inserts a mantle tissue graft from a donor mollusk into a live mollusk, with or without a bead nucleus. Cultured blisters, however, do not require a mantle tissue graft because they grow next to the external mantle epithelium.

The first attempts to culture pearls were made by the Chinese, when they placed Buddha figures on the inner shell walls of large freshwater pearl mussels. CIBJO identifies the resulting nacre-coated Buddhas as "cultured blisters" to distinguish them from "cultured blister pearls." The latter form when a whole cultured pearl that has grown inside the body of the mollusk adheres to the inside of its shell and is then further covered by nacre. Many American gemologists and pearl sellers use the term "blister pearl" for both types of blisters.

If the nucleus of a shell blister is removed and the opening is filled with resin and then sealed with mother-of-pearl or another type of backing, it is called an assembled cultured blister, a cultured mabe blister, a

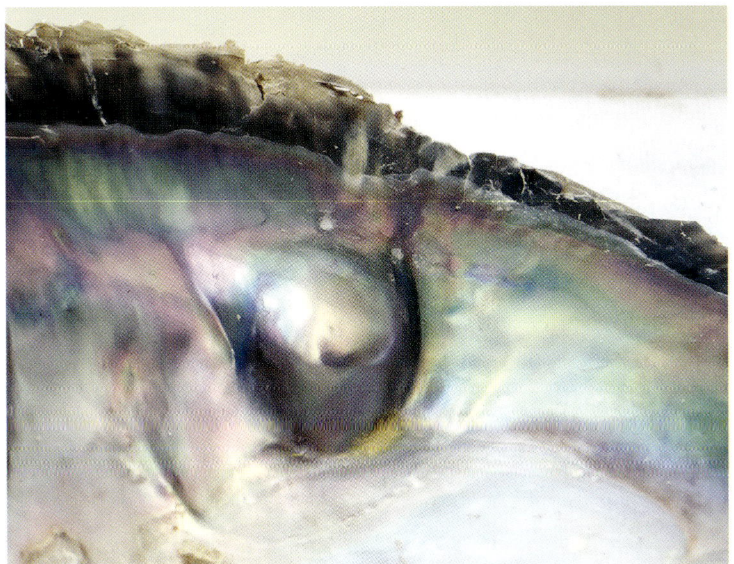

Left: A cultured blister in a rainbow-lipped *Pteria sterna* oyster shell from Perlas del Mar de Cortez. It was formed around a plastic hemisphere cemented to the inner part of the shell, below the mantle. *Photo by Enrique Arizmendi.*

Right: Cultured mabe blister from a *Pinctada mazatlanica* oyster. *Photo by Douglas McLaurin.*

cultured mabe or a cultured mabe pearl. Americans usually prefer to call it simply a mabe pearl, with the assumption that it is cultured. The term (pronounced *mah-bay*) originated from *mabe gai*, the Japanese name for the *Pteria penguin* oyster. This species, known also by its common name penguin's wing oyster, has often been used for culturing mabe blisters.

Chinese mass production of Buddha blisters began as early as 1100 CE, but according to Strack, the first example of Buddha figures overgrown with nacre was found in graves dating to the Han Dynasty, around 100 BCE.

As described in chapter 1, in 1891 William Saville-Kent, a British marine biologist, successfully produced several saltwater cultured blisters in Queensland, Australia, and exhibited them in London. According to Strack, he was the first person on record to culture loose pearls. Kokichi Mikimoto produced his first cultured blisters in Japan in 1893 and patented the procedure in 1896, making him the first person to receive a patent for a pearl-culturing process.

Several years later, in 1904, the Japanese carpenter Tatsuhei Mise successfully harvested small, round akoya pearls from a *Pinctada fucata* oyster by using lead and silver nuclei. He received a patent in 1907 for the needle he used in the operation. Around the same time, government biologist Tokichi Nishikawa was developing a similar approach. He successfully produced small, round akoya pearls in 1907 by using gold and silver nuclei and was granted a patent for the transplantation process. Because of the similarities between their procedures, in 1908 Mise and Nishikawa signed an agreement making them co-owners of the akoya round pearl cultivation method.

Mikimoto Pearls

Today Mikimoto is a brand name for pearls produced and marketed by Mikimoto & Company Limited. But if you want to purchase Mikimoto pearls, be aware that the name is misrepresented in some jewelry and discount stores. Therefore, you should not assume that pearls labeled "Mikimoto" are in fact Mikimoto pearls. Experts recommend that you look at the necklace clasp. Only pearls with an 18-karat-gold signature clasp with a pearl or diamond in the center are true Mikimoto pearls. Also, when you buy Mikimoto pearls, ask the jeweler for the certificate of authenticity that should come with them.

A verified Mikimoto clasp. *Photo courtesy of Mikimoto America Ltd.*

Mikimoto received a patent for whole cultured pearls in 1916 and afterward became their most successful promoter. This is why he is the person most often associated with the introduction of cultured pearls to the market. Since he spent so much time educating the jewelry trade and the public worldwide about the pearls, Mikimoto eventually came to be regarded as the founder of the cultured pearl industry.

HOW ARE WHOLE PEARLS CULTURED?

Whole pearls (also known as free, loose or cyst pearls) are cultured by inserting a mantle tissue graft from a donor mollusk into a live mollusk, either in the connective tissue of its mantle or in the gonad (sex organ). Without the transplanted mantle tissue, no cultured pearl will form; adding a bead nucleus is optional. Saltwater cultured pearls usually contain a shell bead nucleus to grow around; these are called bead-nucleated pearls, beaded cultured pearls or, simply, beaded pearls.

Cultured pearls are grown in both saltwater oysters and freshwater mussels, and both types of mollusks can create beadless or beaded pearls. With saltwater oysters, beaded pearls are typically grown in the gonad (except when the oyster rejects the bead, resulting in a "keshi" pearl). With freshwater mussels, beadless pearls are usually grown in the mantle

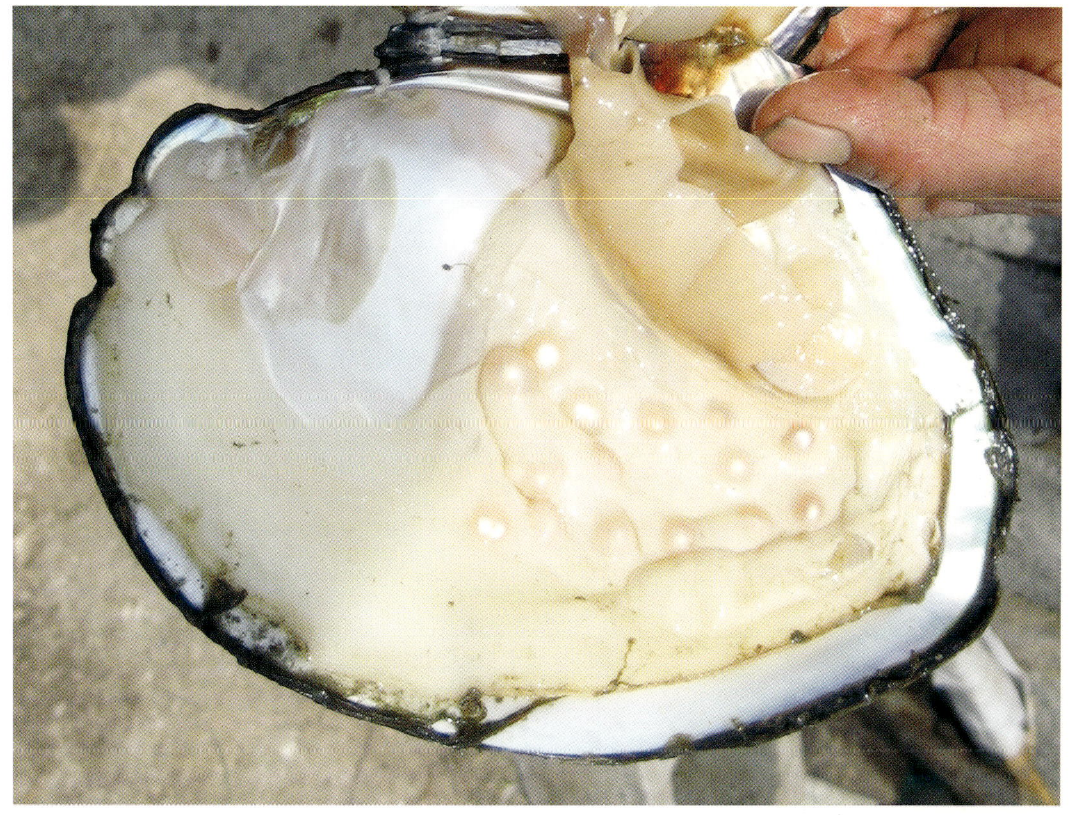

The mantle tissue of a freshwater mussel containing beadless cultured pearls formed in individual pearl sacs within its connective tissue, after the mussel received multiple tissue grafts. The outer epithelial layer of the implanted mantle tissue survived the graft, but the inner epithelial layer and connective tissue have dissolved. The external epithelial cells were transformed into long, elastic cells that formed the pearl sac. *Photo © Renée Newman.*

A freshly opened silver-lipped *Pinctada maxima* oyster from the Paspaley Pearling Company, with a cultured pearl that formed after a bead and a tissue graft from a donor mussel were inserted into the gonad of the oyster. The white mantle lies next to the inner surface of the shell. *Photo © Blaire Beavers.*

CULTURED PEARLS

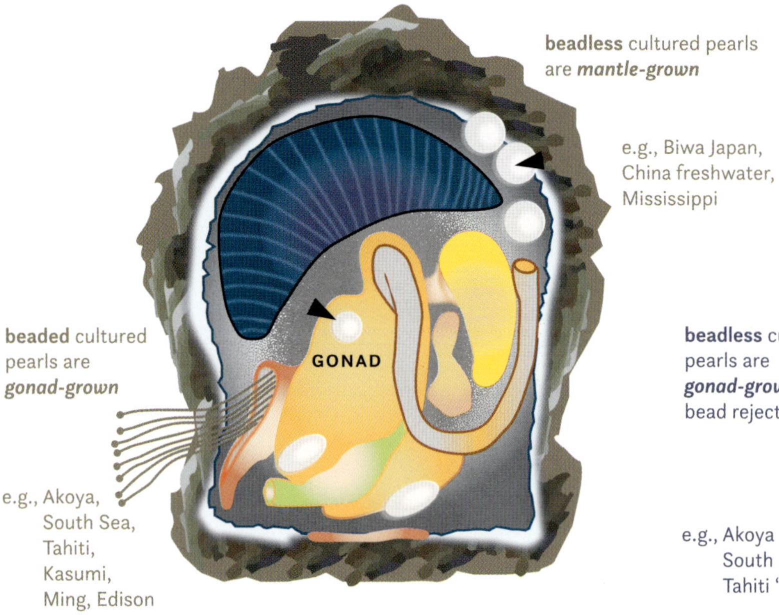

General rule

beadless cultured pearls are ***mantle-grown***

e.g., Biwa Japan, China freshwater, Mississippi

beaded cultured pearls are ***gonad-grown***

GONAD

e.g., Akoya, South Sea, Tahiti, Kasumi, Ming, Edison

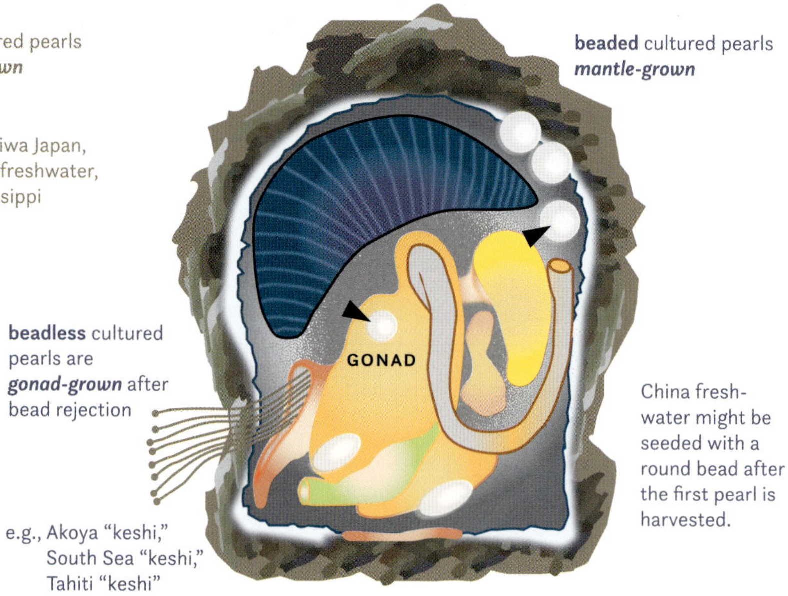

Exceptions

beaded cultured pearls ***mantle-grown***

beadless cultured pearls are ***gonad-grown*** after bead rejection

GONAD

e.g., Akoya "keshi," South Sea "keshi," Tahiti "keshi"

China freshwater might be seeded with a round bead after the first pearl is harvested.

Left: This diagram shows the two basic methods of cultivating whole pearls: (1) inserting donor mantle tissue in the connective tissue of the mantle and (2) inserting donor mantle tissue plus a bead nucleus in the gonad. The blue and gray areas are the mantle.

Right: This diagram explains modified methods of cultivating pearls. If a bead nucleus is rejected by the oyster, a beadless pearl may form in the gonad. This type of pearl is often called a "keshi" pearl in the trade. Freshwater pearls that are bead-nucleated are also grown in the mantle.

Oyster diagrams by Schöffel, 1996, modified by Hänni and adapted by the publisher; slide by Prof. Dr. H.A. Hänni © GemExpert.

and beaded pearls are grown in both the mantle and the gonad. The two diagrams above summarize the different methods of creating cultured pearls in the mantle and gonad of mollusks.

Freshwater cultured pearls may be bead-nucleated in the mantle or in the gonad. The shape and size of the resulting pearls depend to a large degree on the shape and size of the implanted piece of mantle tissue and/or bead. The choice of mantle tissue can also affect the color and luster of the pearl. The brighter the tissue, the brighter the pearl can be. The appearance of a pearl is also governed by the area in which the mantle tissue and/or bead are placed.

Wild saltwater and freshwater mollusks can produce several natural pearls per mollusk, but cultivated saltwater oysters are generally nucleated with only one bead, so they produce only one pearl per harvest. Afterward, the oyster can be renucleated one or two more times. However, with each successive implantation, the quality of the resulting pearl usually decreases.

Freshwater mussels can produce as many as 30 to 50 mantle-grown pearls per harvest, because the mantle is a large organ that can accommodate up to 25 tissue grafts on either wing. This is one reason why cultured freshwater pearls typically cost less than cultured saltwater pearls of similar quality.

How Pearl Farming Helps the Environment and Communities

Most pearl oyster farming involves growing oysters in hatcheries by collecting the sperm and eggs of high-quality oysters to create a new generation of oyster larvae. However, in Australia there is still a sustainable wild fishery. Unlike many other economic activities, pearl farming has a positive effect on the environment and society:

Fish attracted by the Jewelmer company's oyster baskets, which also act as miniature artificial reefs, providing a structure for plankton and the floating larvae of other marine organisms to settle on as they are carried along by the currents. *Photo by Gutsy Tuason.*

- It motivates communities to take strong action to protect the ocean and avoid polluting the waters, because oysters need clean water to produce pearls. Pearl farmers are at the forefront of lobbying against water pollution and fishing with cyanide or dynamite.
- Pearl oysters and mussels help purify water by filtering it and by eating phytoplankton (microscopic algae) and the by-products of fish and coral reefs.
- Pearl farming creates jobs and reduces the need to rely on fishing as a source of income.
- Unlike farm animals, which add large amounts of carbon dioxide to the atmosphere, oysters and mussels absorb carbon dioxide from their surroundings, as they rely on steady carbonate ion concentrations to produce the calcium carbonate needed to develop their shells.
- Farmed oysters and mussels provide a good source of protein and do not need antibiotics to stay healthy.
- Pearl farming helps prevent the extinction of mollusk species by reducing the overfishing of wild mollusks and by providing oyster baskets, on which the floating larvae of other marine organisms can settle and grow.
- Pearl oysters help increase the diversity of fish in the surrounding area: Fish eat organisms on their shells, and small fish can hide between the shells in the baskets to avoid predators. According to fishers in the Philippines, their catch has increased three to four times compared to what it was in the pre-farming era.

Responsibly produced oceanic pearls are not just beautiful but an investment in healthy oceans.

— J. Hunter, Fiji Pearls

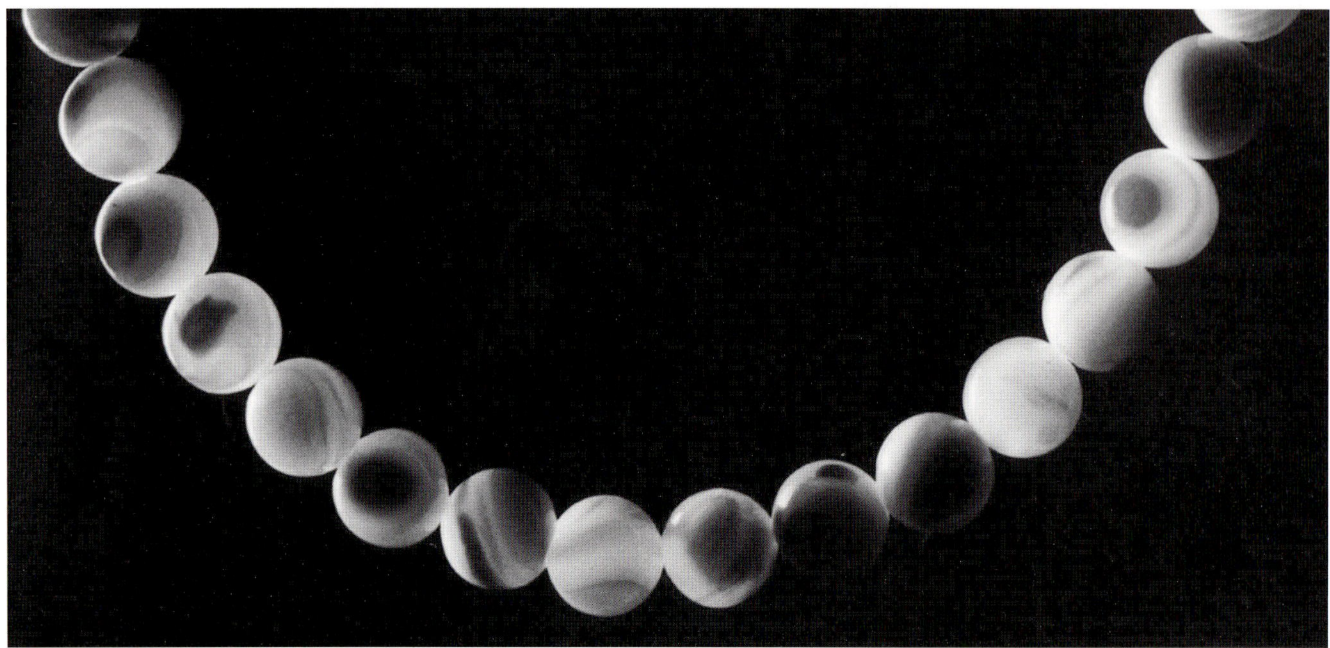

Mother-of-pearl shell beads (the cores of cultured pearls) seen with transmitted light. If you turn these pearls, some will blink from light to dark. *Photo © Renée Newman.*

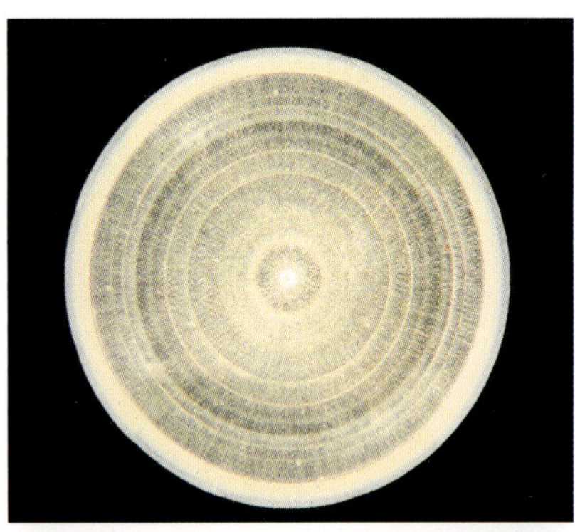

Above: Cross section of a natural saltwater pearl, showing growth rings.

Below: Cross section of a cultured pearl with shell bead and nacre overgrowth.

Photos © Gem-A, London.

TESTS A LAYPERSON CAN DO TO IDENTIFY CULTURED PEARLS

Because of their inherent rarity, natural pearls are usually worth considerably more than their cultured counterparts; therefore, it is important to be able to distinguish between them. Advanced X-ray testing is typically required to prove that a pearl is natural, but this can be costly. Fortunately, less expensive tests can help determine if a pearl is cultured or not. Keep in mind that most of the pearls produced today are cultured. You are more likely to find natural pearls in antique pieces, since whole pearls were not cultured before the 1900s. However, keep in mind that the natural pearls in antique jewelry may have been replaced with cultured ones.

Blink Test

Hold a strand of pearls in front of a strong desk lamp; the light should shine through the pearls but not into your eyes. Rotate the strand. If the pearls blink from light to dark as they are turned, this indicates they are cultured and have only a thin coating of nacre. (Imitation pearls with mother-of-pearl shell-bead centers may also blink.) The dark areas are the dense mother-of-pearl layers on the shell bead, which block the light. However, cultured pearls with a thin nacre layer may not necessarily blink when rotated.

Stripe Test

As you rotate the pearls with the strong light shining through them, look for curved lines and stripes. These are the growth layers of the shell beads. If they are visible, the nacre layer is very thin and the pearls are cultured.

Dark and light views of pearls with thin nacre in transmitted light. Note the curved bands, which indicate the growth layers of the shell-bead nucleus. *Photo © Renée Newman.*

Not all shell-bead nuclei show stripes, though. Keep in mind that imitation pearls with shell-bead centers can also display this banded effect. Natural pearls and beadless cultured pearls, however, will not appear striped.

Color Test

Examine the color. Cultured pearls, unlike natural pearls, often have a faint greenish tint. Some dealers find that natural pearls have a greater potential for brightness than cultured pearls. Their color can only suggest that a pearl might be cultured; again, it is not proof.

Drill-Hole Test

Look inside the drill hole with a 10-power magnifying loupe. If you can see a dark line separating the nacre from a bright bead nucleus, the pearl is cultured. This dark line is the organic material that binds the nacre to the bead. Natural pearls may show a series of growth lines that become more yellow or brown toward the center of the pearl. According to B.W. Anderson in *Gem Testing*, a black deposit at the center of a white pearl—which corresponds to the columnar calcite core—can be a sign that the pearl is natural. Natural pearls are valued partly by carat weight, so the drill holes are made as narrow as possible to minimize weight loss.

Matching Test

Because of their rarity, it is difficult to find natural pearls that match. Consequently, natural strands will not appear as well matched for color, shape, luster and size as those that are cultured.

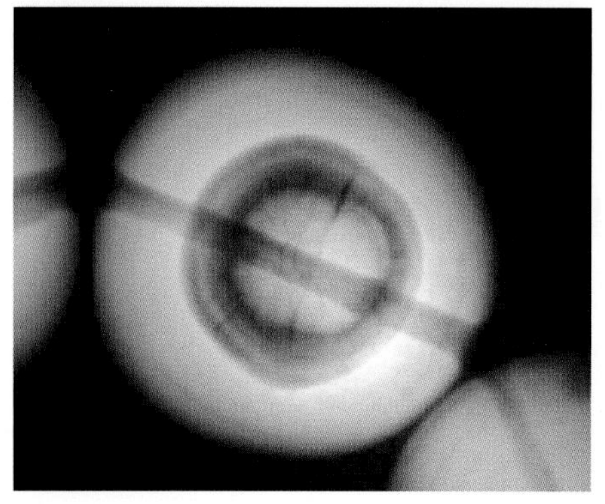

Radiograph of a natural saltwater pearl. *Photo © Prof. Dr. H.A. Hänni, SSEF & GemExpert.*

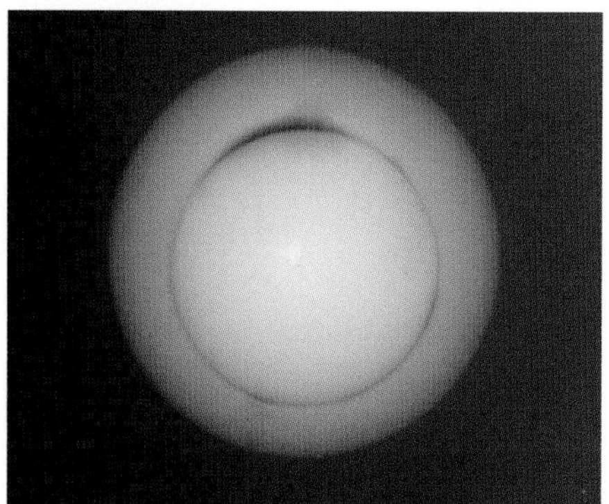

Left: Radiograph of a beaded cultured pearl. **Right:** Radiograph of a non-beaded cultured freshwater pearl. *Photos © Prof. Dr. H.A. Hänni, SSEF & GemExpert.*

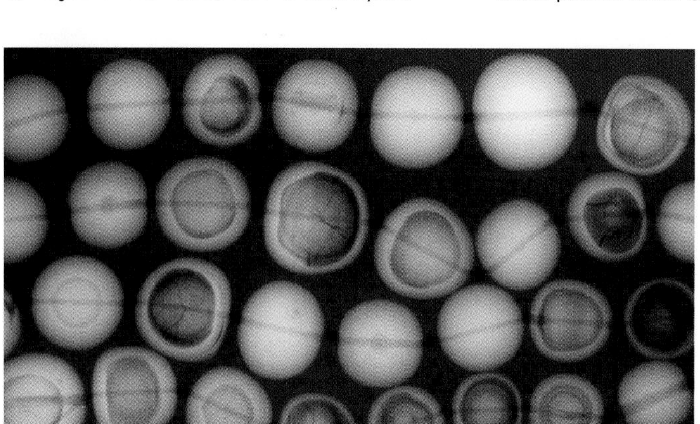

Radiograph of a multistrand natural pearl necklace. Notice how irregular and different the pearls look compared to those of a cultured pearl necklace. *Photo © Prof. Dr. H.A. Hänni, SSEF & GemExpert.*

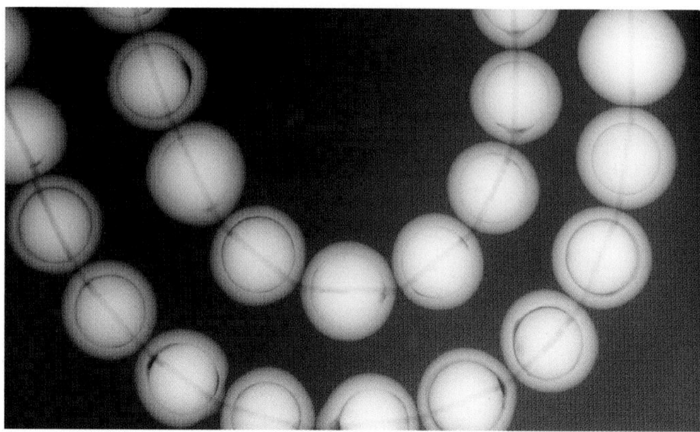

Radiograph of a section of a beaded Tahitian cultured pearl necklace. *Photo © Prof. Dr. H.A. Hänni, SSEF & GemExpert.*

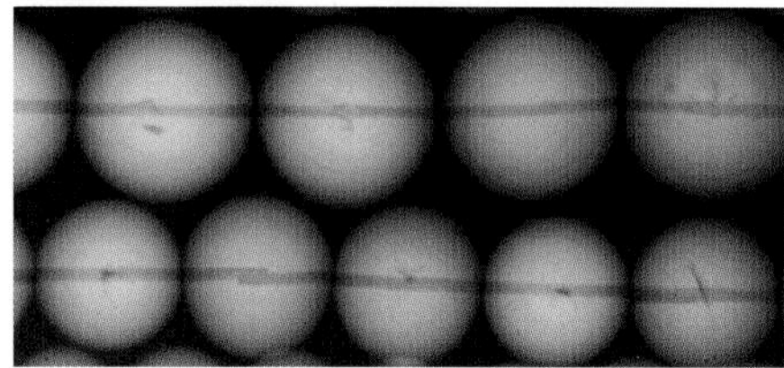

Radiograph of two strands of Chinese freshwater non-beaded cultured pearls (note the small cavities in the centers). *Photo © Prof. Dr. H.A. Hänni, SSEF & GemExpert.*

GEM LAB TESTS USED TO IDENTIFY NATURAL AND CULTURED PEARLS

There are several tests that gem labs can use to identify natural pearls.

X-Radiography

X-rays are the most reliable way to distinguish between natural and cultured pearls. On an X-radiograph negative, beaded cultured pearls usually show a clear separation between the core and nacre. In addition, the cores of akoya and Australian beaded cultured pearls normally look lighter than their nacre coatings. X-rays of natural pearls tend to either present the same tone throughout or get darker in the center, because the core contains more organic components and corresponds to columnar calcite growth, if present. Sometimes, however, part of the central area may look bright.

The disadvantage of X-ray tests is that they can cost from $100 to $500 or more, and not many gem labs have the required equipment.

You can achieve a better understanding of pearls and their X-ray images by analyzing images of pearls sliced in half and comparing what they look like to the X-rays.

A variety of sliced natural pearls. An "unripe" pearl has no nacre on top of its columnar calcite core. *Photo © Prof. Dr. H.A. Hänni, SSEF & GemExpert.*

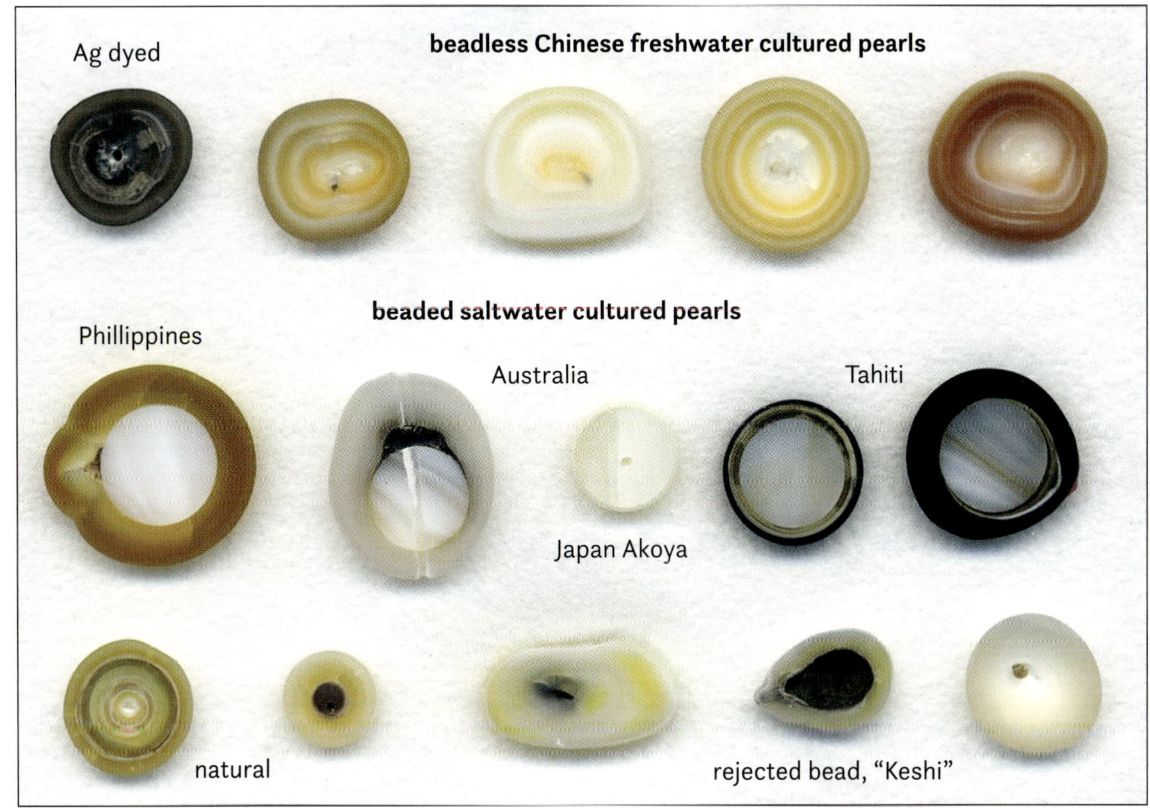

A variety of sliced cultured pearls. The "Ag dyed" pearl was dyed with a silver nitrate solution. *Photo © Prof. Dr. H.A. Hänni, SSEF & GemExpert.*

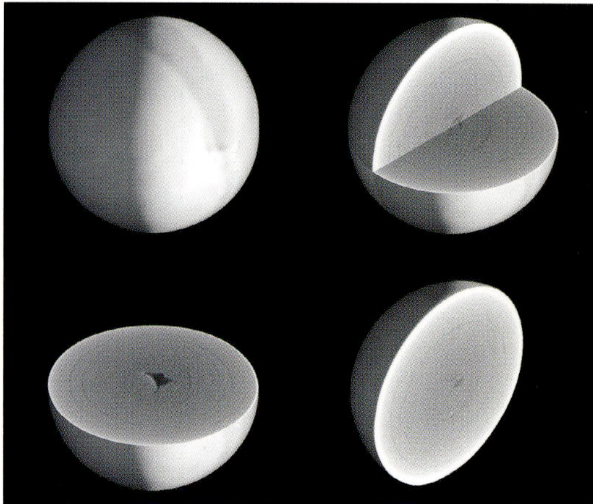

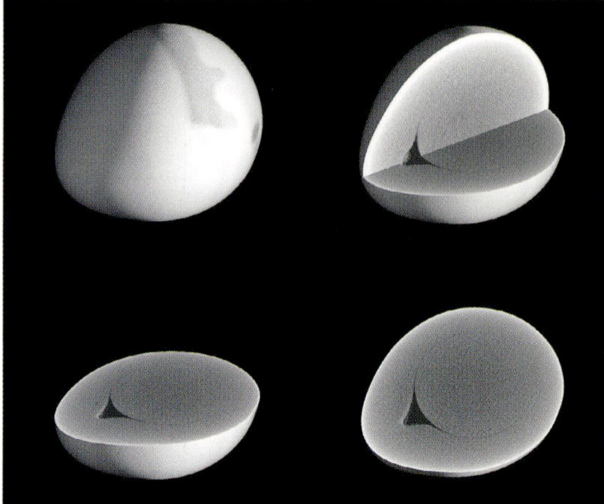

Above: Three-dimensional CT images of a non-beaded freshwater cultured pearl.

Below: Three-dimensional CT images of a drop-shaped bead-nucleated South Sea silver-lipped *Pinctada maxima* oyster pearl.

Images courtesy of GAAJ-Zenhokyo Laboratory.

X-Ray Computed Tomography

A CT scan reveals the internal structure of a pearl in three dimensions by taking radiographs at various angles and then assembling the figure on a computer. It allows for a more detailed analysis of the irregularities within a pearl than an X-radiograph.

Phase-Contrast and Scattering X-Ray Imaging

A new pearl-testing method has been used by the Swiss Gemmological Institute (SSEF) since 2015. Compared to conventional radiography, X-ray phase-contrast imaging and scattering provide more detail and improve contrast, especially for biological samples. Additional information about these imaging techniques is available in the February 2016 issue of *Facette*, the SSEF's annual publication.

Ultraviolet Fluorescence

In UV fluorescence testing, pearls are placed under long-wave ultraviolet light and compared to known samples of cultured and natural pearls. In his book *Gemstones*, G.F. Herbert Smith mentions how cultured pearls can display a peculiar greenish fluorescence that differs markedly from the sky-blue effect of many natural pearls. He points out that this is not an infallible test, however, because natural pearls can also have a greenish fluorescence, particularly if they are from waters adjacent to those of cultured pearls. Gem labs with X-ray equipment do not use this test, but it may be helpful for those without X-ray machines. Seeing a unique sky-blue fluorescence under long-wave UV light instead of a greenish-yellow glow may serve as an incentive for clients to pay for an X-ray to test for natural origins. Cultured pearl strands tend to show greater uniformity in their intensity of color.

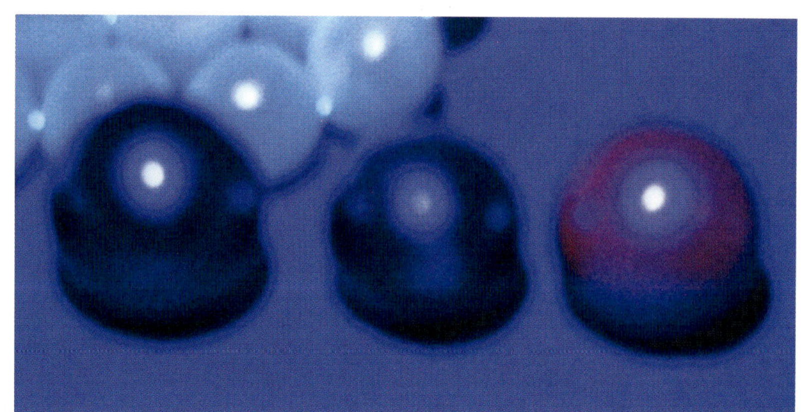

On the right, the unique red long-wave fluorescence of a cultured saltwater Cortez® *Pteria sterna* pearl. A cultured Tahitian pearl is on the left and a natural Mexican black pearl from the *Pinctada mazatlanica* oyster is at the center. *Pearls from Columbia Gem House; photo by Douglas McLaurin.*

Most pearls from the rainbow-lipped *Pteria sterna* oyster have a distinctive red-to-pink long-wave fluorescence that distinguishes them from other species of dark pearls. The test, however, does not differentiate natural *Pteria sterna* pearls from those that are cultured.

If pearls are of good quality and preliminary tests suggest they may be natural, it is advisable to have them X-rayed. Jewelers and appraisers can send them to the appropriate lab for you. A list of independent appraisers and appraisal organizations is available at www.reneenewman.com (click on "Appraisers").

MAIN SOURCES OF NATURAL OYSTER PEARLS

Natural oyster pearls have been found worldwide, but historically the most important source areas extended from the Persian Gulf to the saltwater regions of Southeast Asia, and from the saltwater areas of Mexico to those of Central America and Venezuela.

Oyster pearls were one of the most important commodities in the Middle East and India, as well as the ultimate symbol of luxury and status. Surprisingly, many of these pearls ended up in Hyderabad, the "City of Pearls," which is 320 kilometers (about 200 miles) from the sea. Even today it is famous for its impressive pearl jewelry. Nearly all the natural and cultured seed pearls and tiny akoya keshi are drilled in the nearby village of Chandanpet.

A pearl driller in the village of Chandanpet, near Hyderabad, India. *Frédéric Soltan/Corbis via Getty Images.*

A natural oyster pearl and diamond necklace displayed at the 2024 Hong Kong International Jewellery Show by Tibarumal Jewellery, which is based in Hyderabad. Notice how the pearls vary in shape and size, which is typical of natural pearl jewelry, especially when the gems are as large as these. *Photo © Renée Newman.*

During the 20th century, natural pearls became less in demand for a couple of reasons. To start with, there were simply fewer being found. Overfishing in the Gulf of Mannar, which lies between India and Sri Lanka, reduced the quantity of natural pearls available, prompting India's Central Marine Fisheries Research Institute (CMFRI) to ban pearl oyster fishing in 1962. Since 2022 the CMFRI has taken steps to replenish the pearl oyster population in this region. Many other countries also had to ban pearl fishing after 1900 because of overfishing. Since natural pearls were less available for sale, their promotion declined.

However, the biggest reason why people lost interest in natural pearls in the 20th century was the introduction of cultured pearls to the market by Kokichi Mikimoto. Prices of natural pearls plunged because people could not tell the difference between them and the cultured variety. The Great Depression and World War II caused further declines in the sales of natural pearls. But the industry's situation started improving around 2000, and now there is a renewed interest in natural pearls. Most natural oyster pearls today come from antique jewelry and old collections, and they usually attain higher prices than their cultured counterparts.

Be careful when buying natural pearls. Sometimes Australian South Sea cultured pearls are incorrectly identified on websites and social media posts as natural South Sea pearls because suppliers have told retailers that they are of "natural color." When Australian South Sea cultured pearl wholesalers say their pearls are "all natural" and "only washed," it simply means they have not undergone the bleaching and other types of treatments used in Japan for akoya cultured pearls. Natural Australian pearls do exist, but they are rare, expensive and very difficult to match. Do not expect large, clean, well-matched round Australian pearls to be of natural origin. They are likely cultured, even if the seller does not say they are. As of the publication date of this book, most new natural oyster pearls come from Bahrain, Mexico and the Indo-Pacific region.

Kingdom of Bahrain

Before the discovery of oil in the island country of Bahrain, a high percentage of families there were involved in some way in the pearling trade, whether as free divers, dealers, pearl drillers, ship's crew members or merchants of pearling goods. Because of its dense oyster beds and the increased demand for natural pearls in the 1800s and early 1900s, Bahrain became a single-product economy based on pearls. However, after the lower-cost cultured pearls were introduced to the market, it became easier to sell oil than pearls.

In the 1930s Bahrain established a regulation prohibiting anyone from selling or owning cultured pearls for trading, because natural pearls had been so integral to the kingdom's economy and culture. The law still exists today.

The renewed interest in natural pearls after 2000 motivated Bahrain's government in 2017 to launch a campaign to revive its pearling industry and to establish the Bahrain Institute for Pearls and Gemstones (DANAT). The institute tests and certifies the pearls and offers hands-on education in pearl grading.

Licensed divers gather the oysters by hand, and the health of the pearl beds is monitored by DANAT, the Supreme Council for the Environment, and the Coast Guard. Sometimes diving is suspended in certain areas to allow for replenishment of the oyster beds. The government's efforts have been successful. In January 2022 the Rapaport Group announced that it was launching a new market for ethical natural pearls in collaboration with DANAT. Besides being available online, Bahraini pearls are sold at Rapaport booths at the Las Vegas and Tucson gem shows.

Most of the pearls that come from Bahrain are from the *Pinctada radiata* oyster and range from 2 millimeters to 8 millimeters in size, with a few rare larger pearls. The average length of the oyster's shell is 5 to 7 centimeters (about 2 to 2¾ inches), but they can grow up to 10 centimeters (about 4 inches). The majority of the pearls range in color from cream to light yellow, but they can also be white, pink, blue, purple, light brown and or gold. Their shapes are as varied as the pearls from South Sea oysters.

DANAT indicates the carat weight of the natural pearls it documents, but some dealers in the Arabian Gulf and India still sell pearls by *chaw*, which is a system of converting weight into volume. The formula for calculating the weight in chaw is to multiply the carat weight by itself and then multiply that number by 0.6518.

Bahraini natural pearls gathered by one diver during a single season of pearl diving. These pearls were displayed by the Rapaport Group booth at the American Gem Trade Association show. Only one pearl is perfectly round. *Photo by Sarah Senzer.*

A natural pearl and diamond pendant that sold at auction for $3,365,000 at a Doyle Auction in April 2014. The SSEF appendix to the pearl report stated that a "matching pair of natural pearls of this size and quality is very rare and exceptional, and thus this pair of pearls can be considered a very exceptional treasure of nature." This pair of natural pearls is believed to have belonged to Empress Eugénie; they were sold at an 1887 auction of the French Crown Jewels. The SSEF report described the color of the pearls as slightly brownish gray. *Photo © Doyle Auctioneers & Appraisers.*

Mexico

The coastlines of Baja California were a major source of natural pearls for 400 years after Hernán Cortés landed north of La Paz in 1535 and was one of the first Europeans to discover pearls there. Gray pearls from Baja California were often worn by European royalty; Empress Eugénie, the wife of Napoleon III, was especially fond of them.

However, Mexico's oyster beds gradually became depleted by overfishing, so in 1939 the government placed a ban on pearl fishing for the next 70 years. Thanks to the development of pearl culturing in Mexico, as well as government efforts to stop the overfishing of oysters, wild rainbow-lipped *Pteria sterna* oysters and *Pinctada mazatlanica* oysters have since become more plentiful. As a result, the government now issues some permits to fish wild pearl oysters, and natural pearls in a variety of colors and shapes are being found again. In addition, pearls are being cultured in the Sea of Cortez near Guaymas, unlike in Bahrain, where cultured pearls are banned.

Natural wild oyster (*Pteria sterna*) pearls from Mexico. *Pearls from Kojima Pearl Company; photo by Sarah Canizzaro.*

Indo-Pacific Region

The Indo-Pacific region is famous for its white, black and golden natural and cultured South Sea pearls from *Pinctada maxima* and *Pinctada margaritifera* oysters (discussed in chapters 5 and 6). Also found in the Indo-Pacific is the *Pteria penguin* oyster, known for its cultured mabe blisters.

One oyster pearl from the Indo-Pacific that is not cultured is the pipi pearl from the *Pinctada maculata* oyster, the smallest species in the *Pinctada* mollusk genus. Most are found around French Polynesia and the Cook Islands. According to an article in the spring 2014 edition of GIA's *Gems & Gemology*, several unsuccessful attempts were made in the 1950s to produce cultured specimens, but today all pipi pearls are considered natural. The authors of a winter 2018 *Gems & Gemology* article agreed, stating: "Given the limited documentation of *Pinctada maculata* cultured pearls, it is almost certain that all pearls currently fished from the species are natural pearls." They added that "no definitive information can be gleaned from the spectra of *Pinctada maculata* pearls that will guarantee their separation from other mollusk species, so other factors such as external appearance and internal structures must also be considered."

Pipi means "tiny" in Polynesia, an appropriate name for the pearls from this small oyster, which averages 2.5 to 5 centimeters (1 to 2 inches) in width across its adult shell. Its pearls average from 3 to 3.5 millimeters in diameter and rarely exceed 7 millimeters. Most of the pearls are in the cream-to-gold color range, but they can also be white, gray, red, orange, brown or black. A deep golden color is the most prized. Near-round shapes are common.

Because of their rarity, pipi pearls are more of a collector's item than a commercial product. However, buyers do not just keep them in safety deposit boxes. They are used to create rare pearl jewelry and unique, one-of-a-kind jewelry pieces, sometimes with other types of natural pearls. The best places to find pipi pearls are at gem shows and in Fiji and French Polynesia.

Natural pipi pearl necklace from Lupino Jewelry that required 10 years of collecting. The pearls range in size from 3 mm to 5.6 mm. *Photo by Andrea Shipley.*

A natural abalone and pipi pearl pin designed for Steve Metzler by Bergman and Sons. *Photo by Blaire Beavers.*

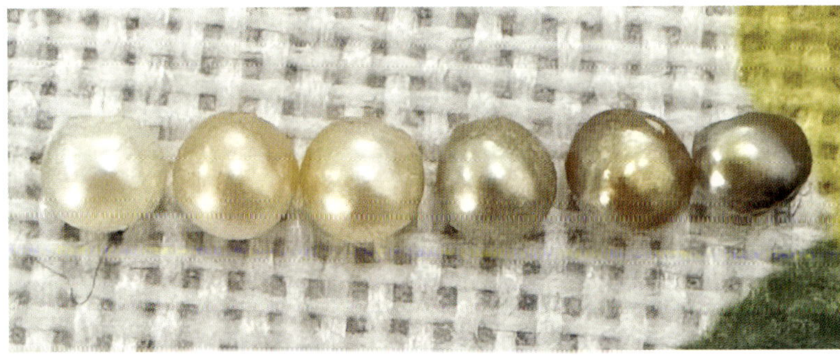

Examples of the color range of natural pipi pearls measuring 3–4 mm, from Lupino Jewelry. *Photo by Andrea Shipley.*

Pinctada maculata shells from Lupino Jewelry. *Photo by Andrea Shipley.*

3 Pearl Value Factors

The Gemological Institute of America (GIA) has developed seven value factors for cultured pearls: luster, surface quality, shape, nacre thickness, color, size and matching. These factors establish a standard terminology for judging the quality of akoya, South Sea, Tahitian and freshwater cultured pearls. This chapter describes how each factor is evaluated. The size category includes the measurements (in millimeters), weight and strand length.

LUSTER

The noted gemologist Robert Webster defines luster as the surface brilliance of a gemstone. Luster depends on the quality and quantity of the light reflected off its surface. When the term is applied to pearls, it tends to have a broader meaning: it also refers to light reflected off the internal layers of nacre. In other words, a lustrous pearl has more than just a shiny reflective surface; it also has a glow from within.

For example, compare a pearl to a highly polished gold bead. The bead will have sharper surface reflections than the pearl, but that does not mean it is more lustrous. In fact, it is more conventional to describe gold as shiny, bright or metallic. On the other hand, pearls with very high luster will generally show these characteristics when viewed under naked light with the naked eye:

- strong light reflections
- sharp light reflections
- good contrast between the bright and darker areas of the pearl

Many pearl experts also list iridescence as a characteristic of luster, because lustrous pearls not only reflect light but also break it up into different colors. On round pearls, the iridescence tends to be very subtle, and a pinkish tone may result. On high-luster baroque pearls, you may see flashes of a rainbow of colors. Since iridescence is a color phenomenon, this chapter lists it as a quality factor in the section on color.

What Determines Luster?

The luster of a pearl depends on the quality of the nacre: its transparency, smoothness and overall thickness, as well as the thickness of each of its microscopic layers. Under an electron microscope, the nacre crystals of lustrous pearls have a strong hexagonal form and are regularly distributed, whereas the crystals forming the nacre of lifeless-looking pearls lack a clear outline, are thinly scattered or are irregularly deposited, according to Kenneth Blakemore in *The Retail Jeweller's Guide*.

The quality of the nacre and, in turn, the luster is affected by a variety of factors, including:

- cultivation techniques
- the health of the mother oyster
- the length of time the pearl is in the oyster
- the time of year when the pearl is harvested
- variations in temperature
- pollution
- natural disasters such as earthquakes or typhoons
- the type of oyster. For example, the *Pteria penguin* oyster, found mainly in the tropical seas of Southeast Asia, can produce pearls with a higher luster than those of the silver-lipped *Pinctada maxima* oyster. The *Pinctada fucata* (akoya) oyster is also noted for its capacity to produce pearls of high luster.

But high luster is not merely the result of leaving a pearl in an oyster for an adequate length of time. In fact, cultivating a lustrous pearl is a complex process that involves both skill and chance.

Luster comparison of akoya cultured pearls viewed against black and light backgrounds. From top to bottom, these examples show pearls with very good, good, fair and poor luster. *Photos © Renée Newman.*

Luster Categories

If all the pearls in the world were lined up according to the quality of their luster, from high to low, the degree of luster would change very gradually and there would be no distinct categories. The line of pearls could be divided into any number of ranges or categories of luster. The GIA pearl description system lists five such categories:

- **Excellent:** Reflections are bright, sharp and distinct.
- **Very good:** Reflections are bright and near sharp.
- **Good:** Reflections are bright but not sharp.
- **Fair:** Reflections are weak, hazy and blurred.
- **Poor:** Reflections are dim and diffused.

Pearls with an excellent luster have sharp, intense, almost mirror-like light reflections, and there is a high contrast between their bright and dark areas. Such pearls are not always easy to find; you will be lucky if you can find a store in your area that has them in stock. Expect to pay premium prices for these pearls, although the final cost of a strand will be determined by a variety of other factors.

Poor-luster pearls are easy to spot. They look milky or chalky, more like a white bead than a pearl. This is a result of low contrast between the light and dark areas. Some jewelers will not stock this type of pearl, but others will. This is also the type of pearl a mail-order retailer might be tempted to sell, since the customers cannot see what they are getting—they see only the super-low prices listed in the catalog.

Most pearls sold in stores probably fall in the very good to fair luster ranges. Many fine-quality jewelry stores also stock high-luster pearls.

The best way to learn to recognize the luster quality of pearls is to look at strands representing the high, medium and low ranges. Some jewelers may show you short master strands illustrating these or similar categories, although they may use different category names, such as "bright" or "commercial." Top-quality pearl salespeople are eager to help you recognize luster differences so you will know what you are getting for your money. They do not want their prices unfairly compared to those of stores offering low-quality "bargain" pearls.

As you shop for pearls and examine them for luster, keep in mind that their descriptions can vary from one jeweler to another. Therefore, do not rely only on verbal or written descriptions of pearls. What you see is what counts most. Verbal descriptions are merely guides. If you have any strands of pearls at home, it is a good idea to take them along and use them as a basis for comparison. Even dealers rely on comparison strands when buying pearls.

Tips for Judging Luster

- Examine the strands on a flat white surface such as cloth, board or paper. Luster can be hard to judge when pearls are on a dark surface or suspended.
- Look at light reflections on the pearls. Usually the less sharp and intense they are, the lower the luster. Sometimes, however, a lack of sharpness is caused by surface blemishes rather than inferior luster.
- If possible, examine the pearls both directly under a light and away from the light. Lighting is discussed in more detail in the next section.
- Look for the brightest and darkest areas of the pearls, then compare the contrast between the two. The lower the contrast and the milkier looking the pearl, the lower the luster. This is one of the quickest and easiest ways to spot low or very low luster. Milky-looking pearls are sometimes sold in "high-quality" stores, but be aware that they have low luster.
- Compare the luster of individual pearls on a strand—they will almost always vary somewhat. The luster quality of a strand is determined by its overall appearance, not just by one pearl. High-luster strands, however, should not contain low- or very-low-luster pearls.

- Roll the pearls so you can see all their surfaces. Luster varies not only from pearl to pearl but also on each individual pearl.
- Try on the pearls and check whether you can see highlighted spots on them from a distance of, say, 3 meters (10 feet). You should be able to see those bright spots if the pearls are of good quality.
- If possible, lay the pearls alongside other strands and compare their luster. This is most effective when you already know the quality of the comparison strands. Keep in mind that your impression of a strand will be affected by the pearls it is compared to. A strand will look better next to lower-luster strands than next to those of higher luster.

Sometimes buyers get so involved in examining the shapes and blemishes of pearls that they overlook their luster. The Japan Pearl Exporters' Association would consider this a big mistake. According to its booklet *Cultured Pearls*, "The most important value point in pearls of equal size is luster because that is what gives a pearl its beauty."

How Lighting Affects Luster

Gemologists and appraisers normally grade pearls under standardized lighting conditions. When shopping for pearls, you will encounter various lighting situations, so it is important to understand how lighting affects the appearance of pearls in order to avoid being misled.

The stronger and more direct the light, the more lustrous the pearls will look. Ask yourself the following questions:

- Is the lighting diffused? For example, does the light fixture have a white shade? Is the light coming through clouds, curtains or translucent glass? Is there fluorescent lighting instead of bare bulbs? The more diffused the light is, the lower the luster will appear to be. Bare lights or direct sunlight, on the other hand, will bring out the luster of pearls.
- How intense is the light? In the case of sunlight, is it early morning or midday? Midday sunlight will bring out the luster more. In the case of light bulbs, what is their wattage? The higher the wattage, the more lustrous your pearls will look.

Mabe pearls in decreasing order of luster from left to right, viewed under a lamp with an undiffused 100-watt light bulb. *Photo © Renée Newman.*

The same pearls viewed under a 100-watt light bulb diffused with paper. *Photo © Renée Newman.*

- How close is the light to the pearls? The farther away it is, the smaller and less intense the reflections become and the less the pearls will seem to glow. If it is possible for you to carry or wear comparison strands of pearls, do so. You will be able to compare known strands with unknown ones under the same conditions, and it will be easier for you to gauge the effect of the lighting on both.

SURFACE QUALITY

Imagine that you are buying a bouquet of roses for a special friend. If you were to look closely at each rose, you would probably notice some brown spots, small holes or torn edges. Yet it is doubtful that any of these flaws would keep you from getting the bouquet. You would select it based on its overall attractiveness. However, if you were buying just one rose, you would most likely examine it more closely and expect it to have fewer flaws than the roses in a bouquet. Judging pearls is much the same. Our standards of perfection for a single pearl are normally higher than for a strand. But whether we are dealing with roses or pearls, we should expect nature to leave some sort of autograph.

When discussing flaws in diamonds or colored gems, the jewelry trade uses the term *clarity*—the degree to which a stone is flawed. In the pearl industry, a variety of terms are used, such as *spotting, cleanness, surface quality, purity* and *texture*. In the United States, *surface quality* (or simply *surface*) is the term most frequently selected to denote pearl clarity.

There are also many synonyms for the term *flaw*. They include *blemish, imperfection, irregularity, spot, surface characteristic, surface mark* and *marking*. When dealing with diamonds and colored gems, gemologists limit *blemish* to surface flaws such as scratches and bumps. *Inclusion* refers to flaws that extend below the surface, such as cracks and holes.

Surface quality is determined by the size, number, nature, location, visibility and type of surface characteristics of a pearl. These are cultured pearls with surface qualities ranging, from left to right, from clean to heavily spotted. *Photo © Renée Newman.*

Blemish takes on a different meaning when used with pearls. It means any kind of flaw, internal or external. Ironically, flaws can be positive features. They serve as identifying marks that indicate a gem is yours and not somebody else's. They help prove that the pearl is real and not an imitation. Flaws can lower the price of gems without affecting their overall beauty.

Perfection does not seem to be a goal of nature. In fact, the longer a pearl is in an oyster, the more likely it is that irregularities will occur. Therefore, when shopping for pearls, there is no need to look for flawless ones; you just need to know which types of imperfections to avoid.

Types of Pearl Blemishes

A standardized terminology for pearl blemishes has not yet been developed. The following terms are based primarily on those listed in the GIA pearl-grading course. These imperfections are usually judged without magnification.

A group of tiny welts. *Photo © Renée Newman.*

A group of minor pits. *Photo © Renée Newman.*

- **Dull spots:** areas of very low luster caused by variations in nacre quality or contact with chemicals, cosmetics or skin secretions.
- **Bumps and welts:** raised areas found alone or in groups. Sometimes they may even cover most of the surface area of the pearl. If the bumps or welts are very large, they can put the pearl into the off-round category. Occasionally pearls have a wrinkled appearance that is caused by groups of welts.
- **Discolorations:** spotty areas often caused by concentrations of a protein substance that holds nacre crystals together. Discolorations are not frequently seen because pearls are typically bleached to even out their color.
- **Scratches:** straight or crooked lines scraped on the surface. These are not serious unless the pearl is so badly scratched that its luster and beauty are affected.
- **Pits and pinpoints:** tiny holes on the surface that are normally hardly noticeable and therefore not serious. *Pinpoints* may also refer to tiny bumps, since from a distance they look similar to tiny pits.
- **Dimples:** circular depressions or indentations that are often found in groups.

- **Cracks:** breaks in the nacre and/or bead nucleus. Small cracks in the bead may look like little hairs trapped under the nacre. Cracks, even when not visible, can compromise the durability of a pearl.
- **Chips, gaps and patches of missing nacre:** blemishes that may occur on any type of pearl but are particularly common in those with thin nacre.

Determining Whether Blemishes Are Acceptable or Unacceptable

The presence of flaws is not as important as the type, quantity and prominence of those flaws. Listed here are blemishes that would normally be considered unacceptable:

- **Patches of missing nacre:** Just as diamonds with big chips are considered unacceptable, so too are pearls with missing chunks of nacre. Both the beauty and the durability of the pearl are affected.
- **Obvious discolorations throughout:** For the sake of beauty, try to select pearls with a uniform color; plenty of them are available.
- **Cracks throughout:** Thick nacre does not crack easily, while thin nacre does. Even if the cracks are not noticeable, they are a sign that the nacre is too thin and that the pearls will not wear well over time.
- **Prominent flaws on a single pearl:** When buying pearl earrings, pendants, pins or rings, pay close attention to the flaws. For example, a pearl with a large visible bump would not be acceptable as the featured gem of a jewelry piece, but it would be acceptable in a strand. If you are buying an expensive pearl and you want to compromise on price, try selecting one whose imperfections can be hidden by the setting.
- **Blemishes that cover the majority of the surface:** A pearl that is covered in flaws can direct attention more to the blemishes than to the pearl itself.

Missing nacre around the drill hole. *Photo © Renée Newman.*

Cracks and a hole on an abalone mabe cultured pearl with thin nacre. *Photo by Enrique Arizmendi*

Despite the undesirability of blemishes, if you had to choose between heavily flawed lustrous pearls and nearly flawless pearls with thin nacre and low luster, you would be better off with the flawed ones. At least you would be getting more pearl for your money! Keep in mind when buying

Typical pearl blemishes: pits, bumps, welts, pinpoints, holes and a dull white area. *Photo © Renée Newman.*

pearls that it is not just their inherent quality that determines their acceptability—your needs and desires also count.

If you are looking for a high-quality necklace, you will want to avoid strands with noticeable flaws. If your budget is limited, you will probably be glad that blemished pearls are available at reduced prices. You have the final say as to what is acceptable and what is not.

Grading Surface Quality

The diamond industry has a standardized system for grading clarity based on a system developed by GIA. Ten-power magnification is used. The advantage of this system is that buyers can communicate what they are looking for anywhere in the world. In addition, written appraisals and quality reports are more meaningful. GIA has established a surface-grading system for pearls with four levels, but it is not as commonly used as the diamond grading system. The association defines its four surface grades as follows:

Surface comparison of three strands of pearls. The top strand is graded clean, the middle strand is lightly spotted with a couple of moderately spotted pearls, and the bottom strand is heavily spotted. *Photo © Renée Newman.*

- **Clean:** Pearls are blemish-free or may have minute surface characteristics that are difficult to see.
- **Lightly spotted:** Pearls show minor visible surface irregularities.
- **Moderately spotted:** Pearls show noticeable surface characteristics.
- **Heavily spotted:** Pearls show obvious surface irregularities that may impact their durability.

Most pearl dealers have their own systems for grading surface quality. Occasionally you will encounter grades such as AAA, AA and A. Depending on the supplier or the store, these grades may refer to luster, blemishes or a combination of these two factors, or they may include other factors such as shape and nacre thickness. In essence, pearl grades have no meaning other than what the seller assigns to them. Therefore, do not rely on grades to compare pearl prices. Examine the pearls yourself, use your own judgment, and consider these points:

- **The prominence of the blemishes:** Visible flaws distant from drill holes are more serious than those near the holes. Prominent bumps can be more noticeable than small pits or low bumps.
- **The type of flaws:** Chipped or missing nacre is usually more serious than bumps, even though it may be less noticeable.
- **The percentage of the pearl surface that is flawed:** It is a lot more serious if 80 percent of the surface of a pearl is flawed than if only 10 percent is. You need to roll the pearls to check for this factor.
- **The percentage of pearls on a strand that are flawed, and to what degree:** This is a factor that does not exist in diamond

grading. Pearl grading is more complex because you are often judging a strand, not just a single pearl. It is much harder to develop consistent grades for sets of gems than for single gems.

Tips for Judging Surface Quality

When you shop for diamonds, the salespeople may suggest that you look at the stone under magnification so you can observe its clarity. This will not happen when you shop for pearls. The reason jewelers do not suggest you view them under a microscope is that pearls are usually valued based on how they look to the naked eye, not under magnification. Nacre thickness is an exception to this rule.

When dealing with knowledgeable salespeople who have your interests at heart, you will not need to look at pearls with a magnifier loupe. They will point out the imperfections and other quality factors and show you how to compare pearls. But sometimes it is advisable to use a loupe, such as in the following situations:

- **When dealing with people you do not know or who may not be trustworthy:** Suppose you are at a flea market or an antique show and you see a pearl piece you love that you would never find in a jewelry store. Or suppose you are on vacation abroad and you want to buy a souvenir, but you do not know any jewelers and none have been recommended to you. In both cases it is advisable to use a loupe to check for flaws, thin nacre, dye and imitations. The more experienced you become at examining a pearl's surface and drill holes with a loupe, the easier it will be for you to identify pearls and judge their quality.
- **When the lighting is poor:** Suppose you are at an antique shop or pawnbroker's where the lighting is not ideal, and suppose you must make a quick decision about whether to buy some pearls and how much to offer. Poor lighting will make it harder to judge surface quality and detect imitations. Use a loupe to compensate for the lack of proper lighting.
- **When pearls are being offered at a price that seems too good to be true:** There is usually a catch somewhere. It will probably be easier to discover any issues with a loupe than with the unaided eye, especially if you do not deal with pearls on a regular basis.

Here are a few other pointers for judging imperfections:

- Besides looking at the pearls against a white background, look at them against a dark one as well. Certain flaws show up better against black or other dark colors. Also, hold the pearls up in the air to examine them for flaws (do not judge luster or color in this way, however).
- Roll the pearls. Otherwise you may not see some serious flaws and you will not know what percentage of each pearl is flawed.
- Examine the pearls under a strong light. The more intense the light, the easier it is to see details. When judging blemishes, it is also a good idea to look at pearls under different types of lighting: direct and diffused, fluorescent and incandescent, close and distant. Each type may bring out different details.
- Keep in mind that it is normal for pearls to have a few blemishes.

SHAPE

Shape can play a major role in determining the price of pearls. Throughout history, round (i.e., spherical) has generally been considered the most valuable shape for a pearl. Perhaps this was because pearls were considered a symbol of the moon. Nevertheless, the most famous and valuable pearls are often not round. That is because factors such as size, luster, nacre quality and origin are also important.

Round natural pearls are rare because they do not have a round bead nucleus like cultured pearls. Finding a round natural pearl above 6 millimeters in diameter is a major challenge. Natural symmetrical drop shapes like La Peregrina (see chapter 1) are also rare and highly valued.

Akoya cultured pearls have the least variation in shape and are commonly round or near round. Perfectly round South Sea cultured pearls are far rarer, since they come in a wider variety of shapes. Many South Sea and Tahitian pearls are irregular or freeform, described as "baroque" shapes. Designers like baroque pearls because each one is unique, and they are usually more affordable than round and symmetrical pearls of similar quality. When you need to cut down on the price, shape is a good category to compromise on. In fact, baroque shapes often make more interesting jewelry pieces than round pearls.

A very rare round 14 mm natural pearl from the Mississippi River. It weighs 16.84 carats (3.37 grams). *Pearl courtesy of Pala Gems; photo by Wimon Manorutkul.*

Tips on Judging Pearl Shape

When judging pearls for shape, take into consideration the type of pearl you are looking at. For example, expensive natural pearls are typically baroque, whereas inexpensive cultured pearls with thin nacre are generally round, since they contain a round bead nucleus, and beads that are barely coated with nacre do not have much of a chance to grow into irregular shapes. The typical shapes of five pearl types are described here to help you learn the degree of roundness to expect from pearls. They are listed from the most commonly round to the most commonly baroque.

Akoya cultured pearls with thin nacre: often round.
Akoya cultured pearls with thick nacre: frequently near round, but round ones are available too. Baroque akoya pearl strands are usually considered low quality, but exceptions can occur if the pearls have high luster and interesting shapes.
South Sea cultured pearls: rarely perfectly round. The larger the pearl, the more it tends to deviate from round. Baroque pearls are often regarded as a good alternative to the more expensive symmetrical shapes when one's budget is limited.
Natural freshwater and saltwater pearls: often baroque or semi-baroque. Round ones are very rare.
Cultured mantle-grown, second-harvest freshwater pearls: frequently baroque. Baroque freshwater pearls are considered desirable. Cultured round freshwater pearls are also readily available. They are normally much more affordable than saltwater pearls of similar quality and size.

Another grading factor to consider when judging near-round and especially semi-baroque pearls is their degree of symmetry. Perfectly round pearls are always symmetrical, and baroque pearls are, by definition, asymmetrical. If, for example, you are buying a teardrop pearl pendant for someone special, one with equal sides would probably be the most desirable. Lopsided pearls can be interesting, but they are considered less valuable than those that are symmetrical.

Even though dealers agree that round is the most expensive shape, there is no standardized system for determining how shape affects prices. How pearls are discounted for shape variation can differ from one dealer to another. Do not let this lack of standardization lead you to ignore pearl shape as a value factor. Consider it important, and keep in mind when judging pearl prices that it is best to compare pearls of the same shape as well as of the same size, color, type and luster.

Aquamarines and Tahitian pearls with good symmetry. *Earrings by Assael; photo courtesy of Assael.*

Opposite page: Baroque cultured pearls are ideal for one-of-a-kind designer jewelry. *Earrings by Hubert Jewelry; photo by Diamond Graphics.*

NACRE THICKNESS

If you were to cut a 7 millimeter akoya cultured pearl in half, you would see a large core inside. That would be a bead, probably cut from an American mussel shell. The outside of the bead would be encircled with a pearly layer of nacre. If the pearl had been left in the oyster for just six months, that layer would be very thin—too thin to be very durable or lustrous.

Before about 1960, Japanese akoya pearl farmers left pearls in their oysters for at least two and a half years. Mikimoto left his in for more than three years, for maximum nacre thickness. Then many farmers dropped the time to one and a half years, and around 1979 pearl harvesting started happening after just six to eight months. This practice resulted in many inexpensive, low-quality pearls coming onto the market. And they are still out there, offered at rock-bottom prices. Their buyers end up with mostly shell beads and hardly any pearl. Fortunately, better pearls with thicker nacre are also available, but rarely as thick as those cultured before the 1960s. The goal of this section is to help you determine if the nacre thickness of the pearls you are looking at is acceptable or not.

Above: Pearl with nacre so thin that it is peeling off.

Below: Pearl with very thin nacre peeling near the drill hole.

Photos © Renée Newman.

Tips on Judging Nacre Thickness

Nacre that is only 0.1 to 0.2 millimeter thick is considered too thin, because it will eventually peel, leaving only the bead core. According to the "Pearls as One" course offered by the Cultured Pearl Association of America, adequate thickness is considered to be 0.4 millimeter or more. The nacre thickness of good-quality South Sea and Tahitian pearls is generally greater than that of Japanese akoya pearls, because the waters around Japan are colder. This slows the metabolism of the oysters, causing them to deposit nacre at a slower rate, but this leads to a denser and more compact nacre than that of South Sea pearls.

Pearl dealers and buyers do not need to measure the nacre to determine if it is thin or very thin. They can tell by looking at the pearls. Here are some clues:

- The pearls usually have low or very low luster and may look milky. Some thinly coated pearls, however, may show a decent medium luster.
- The nacre coating has cracks.

Light and dark views of thinly coated pearls with light shining through them. Note the curved stripes, which indicate the growth layers of the shell bead. *Photo © Renée Newman.*

- Areas are visible where the nacre has peeled.
- The layers of the shell beads are slightly visible when the pearls are suspended with light shining through them. These layers can look like curved lines, stripes or wood grain. Usually the thinner the nacre, the easier it is to see the lines. Keep in mind that, even if you cannot see any shell layers, this does not mean the nacre is thick. Many thinly coated pearls do not show these layers. However, if you can see them, the nacre is probably too thin.
- As the beads are rolled, some may look light and then dark as the light shines through them. This is because the shell beads may have mother-of-pearl layers that block the light. This phenomenon is called blinking and can sometimes be seen in thinly coated pearls. When rotated, each thinly coated pearl "blinks," while pearls with thick nacre should not.

A more accurate way of judging nacre thickness is by examining the drill holes of the pearls, preferably with a 10-power magnifier, such as a jeweler's hand loupe. Examining drill holes with a loupe will also help you detect dyeing and imitations. The drill-hole method is too slow to be practical for dealers, but it is a good way for less skilled people to estimate nacre thickness. It also allows appraisers to establish a more objective measure of nacre thickness.

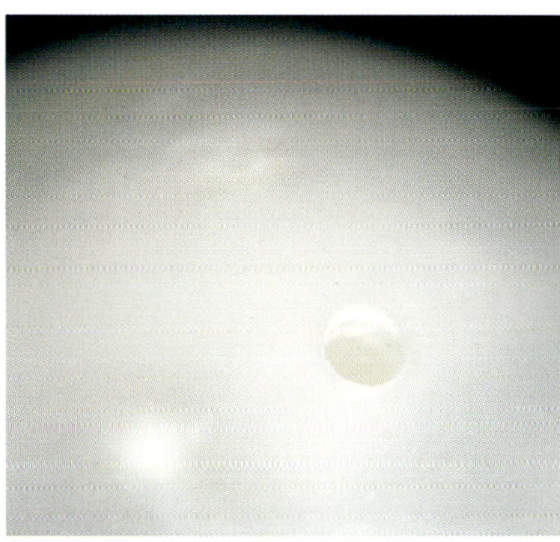

Drill hole showing acceptable nacre thickness. *Photo © Renée Newman.*

If you have some pearls at home, try examining their drill holes with a loupe under good lighting. Find the dividing line between the nacre and the bead. Then look at a millimeter ruler with the loupe to get an idea of 0.4 millimeter thickness. Compare this thickness to that of the nacre. Viewing actual examples of thin, medium and thick nacre is an effective way to learn to tell the difference. Of course, there must be a drill hole or other opening on a pearl for an accurate estimate of nacre thickness to be made visually.

Often the effect of nacre thickness on price is linked to that of luster. Thicker nacre usually means higher luster, and both contribute to higher prices. It naturally costs a farmer progressively more to culture pearls for six months, one year or one and a half years. The additional cost is passed on to the buyers.

COLOR

Pearl color is a complex topic. It is a combination of these factors:

Body color: the predominant basic color of the pearl.
Overtone: one or more colors that overlie the body color. On black pearls these colors are usually easiest to see in the lighter areas of the pearl. On white pearls they are easier to see in the darker areas. For example, lay some white pearls on something white and look at them under a strong, direct light (midday sun is ideal but a bare light bulb will do). The outer rims of the pearls, reflecting the white background, will be lighter than the centers if they are of decent quality (except for the bright reflection of the light). If you look closely, you should see a slight pink, green, blue and/or silver color in the central dark areas of the pearls. This is the overtone. Generally you will see more than one overtone color in a strand of pearls. You may also see more than one overtone color on the same pearl.
Iridescence: a play of lustrous colors. They may be like a rainbow or they may be a subtle combination of colors such as pink, blue, green and silver. The colors change when you move the pearls around. *Orient* is another term that is used to refer to pearl iridescence. Some dealers, however, employ the term more loosely to also mean a combination of overtone

Green and purple overtones on Tahitian cultured pearls with a dark gray body color. *Rings by Linda Quinn; photo by Chris Rockafellow.*

Iridescence on natural-color cultured Chinese freshwater pearls. *Earrings by Naomi Sarna; photo courtesy of Naomi Sarna.*

colors. In its book *Splendour and Science of Pearls,* GIA defines *orient* as "an iridescent rainbow of colours shimmering on, or just below, a pearl's surface ... A pearl is also described as having orient when it shows more than one overtone colour." Other dealers and many books written in the past use the term to refer to luster, because iridescence and luster are interconnected. Since *orient* may be interpreted in various ways, this book primarily uses the term *iridescence.*

Pearls come in a variety of colors. When deciding what color pearls to buy, your primary concern should be what looks best on you. But you will also want to know how the color affects their price. The overall body color can play a significant role in determining the price of pearls.

What Causes Pearl Color?

A variety of factors are responsible for pearl colors. These include:

- **Type of host oyster:** Oysters vary in their potential to produce certain colors of pearls. For example, black pearls are cultivated in the black-lipped *Pinctada margaritifera* oyster because other oysters do not produce pearls of the same type.
- **Quality of nacre:** If the nacre is very thin, the color will look milky and lack overtone tints. Besides being affected by the number of layers of nacre, pearl color is also affected by the thickness of each layer. In *Pearls of the World,* researcher Koji Wada states: "The reason why the pearl made by the akoya pearl-oyster has a better pink tone than pearls made by other mollusks is that it has layers of equal thickness."
- **Environment in which the pearls are grown:** It is theorized that trace elements in the water surrounding the oysters may affect the color of their pearls. For example, a cream color is typical of natural pearls from the Ohio River, but not of those found in other American rivers.
- **Color of the tissue inserted with the bead nucleus:** Tissue from a donor oyster's mantle—the part of the oyster that secretes pearl nacre—must be implanted with the shell bead in a host oyster for a cultured pearl to grow. Pearl researcher Dr. Koji Wada has found that if the tissue inserted into akoya oysters is yellow, cream-colored pearls tend to form. If it is white, white pearls result. Black pearl specialist and farmer Josh Humbert agrees; his Kamoka Pearls website states that the mantle of the donor oyster creates the eventual color of the pearl.

Natural and cultured pearls of various colors from Kojima Company. *Photo by Sarah Canizzaro.*

Tips for Judging Color

- Judge the color of pearls against a non-reflective white background. Pearls not only reflect the color of their background, they also absorb it. Then hold the pearls in your hand or place them around your neck to see how they look on you.
- Take into consideration the lighting (see next page). If possible, look at the pearls under different types of light: daylight near a window, fluorescent bulbs, incandescent lights. The pearls will probably be worn under a variety of lighting conditions.
- If possible, wear or take along some comparison pearls. Otherwise, compare the color to other pearls in the store. Even using white and cream-colored paper as color references is better than relying on your memory; it is a lot easier to compare colors than to remember them.
- When pearl strands are right next to each other, their colors may seem to bleed from one strand to another. Therefore, also compare them slightly separated.
- Every now and then, look away from the pearls at other objects. When you focus on one color for too long, your perception of it becomes distorted.
- Consider how evenly distributed the color is, especially if you are looking at one major pearl in a ring or pendant. A uniform color is usually more highly valued than a blotchy one.
- Make sure you are alert and feeling good when examining pearls. If you are tired, sick or under the influence of alcohol or drugs, your perception of color could be impaired.

How Lighting Affects Color

When buying pearls, consider the lighting, because it has a strong impact on your impressions of color and luster. An indirect neutral light such as noon daylight is often recommended for grading pearls. Its color temperature ranges from about 5,000 to 5,500 kelvins and it does not favor either end of the spectrum. Incandescent light bulbs, battery-powered flashlights and some halogen spotlights will shift the color balance from neutral toward the yellow or warm end of the spectrum, intensifying the appearance of reds and oranges. Daylight fluorescent lights and overcast skies produce light spectra that contain more blue wavelengths; this strengthens blue colors and makes reds look more purplish and greens and purples more bluish.

When you shop for pearls, your choice of lighting will probably be limited. However, try to view the gems under different sources, such as slightly bluish fluorescent lights, slightly yellowish halogen lights, LED lamps and daylight near a window. Keep in mind that each of these light sources can have different color temperatures. For example, fluorescent lights can lean toward the blue or yellow end of the spectrum or may have a neutral 5,000 to 5,500 kelvin color temperature. The color temperature of light outdoors varies throughout the day, tending toward yellow at sunrise and sunset, toward blue under clouds or blue skies, and toward neutral at noon.

SIZE

The size of round saltwater cultured pearls is expressed in terms of their diameter measured in millimeters (1 millimeter is about 1/32 inch). Since pearl sizes vary within a strand, variances of half a millimeter are usually indicated, for example, 7 to 7.5 millimeters. Occasionally a few of the pearls may fall slightly above or below the size indicated. Usually, the larger the size, the higher the price.

The size of non-round pearls can be expressed in terms of their greatest width, length and, in some cases, depth. These measurements are generally rounded to the nearest half or whole millimeter.

When determining the effect of size on price, keep these points in mind:

- Price jumps between pearl sizes are often uneven. As sizes reach the 8 or 9 millimeter mark, pearl prices tend to jump higher.
- Price/size relationships can vary from one dealer to another.

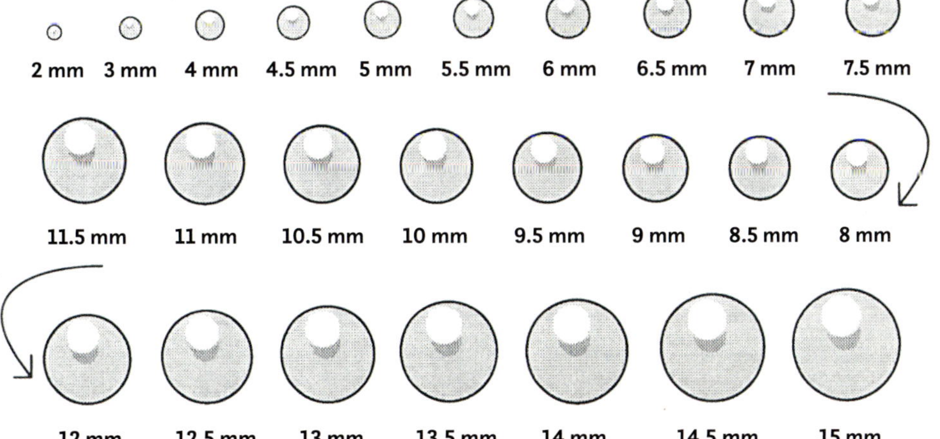

Sizes in Millimeters.
Illustration by Dawn King.

- The effect of size on price varies from one harvest to another. If too many pearls of one size are harvested, their price will decrease.
- Demand can have an important impact on the way size affects price. If there is a high demand for a specific size, the price for those pearls tends to increase. This explains why smaller pearls occasionally sell for more than larger ones of the same quality.

Weight

When pearl wholesalers buy large lots of cultured pearls, they are often charged according to the weight of the pearls. The measure generally used is the *momme* (m), an ancient Japanese unit that equals 3.75 grams (0.13 ounce) or 18.75 carats. *Kan* is a Japanese unit of weight equaling 1,000 momme. However, pearls are not sold by the momme or kan in retail stores.

The weight of natural pearls is often expressed in pearl grains (p grain), with one grain equaling 0.25 carat (ct). Natural pearls may be sold according to their carat weight. Grams are commonly used to express the weight of cultured freshwater pearls, although carat weight is also used. One carat equals 0.2 gram; in other words, 5 carats equals 1 gram. Weight equivalences are summarized in the table below.

WEIGHT CONVERSIONS

UNIT	EQUIVALENTS				
1 carat (ct)		0.20 g	0.007 oz av	4 p grains	0.053 m
1 gram (g)	5.00 ct		0.035 oz av	20 p grains	0.266 m
1 ounce avoirdupois (oz av)	141.75 ct	28.3495 g		565 p grains	7.56 m
1 pearl grain (p grain)	0.25 ct	0.05 g	0.0017 oz av		0.013 m
1 momme (m)	18.75 ct	3.75 g	0.131 oz av	75 p grains	

Image courtesy of Mikimoto Company.

Strand Length

When pricing pearls, you should take into consideration the length of the strand as well as the size of the pearls in millimeters. The pearl trade has specific names for different necklace lengths:

Choker: a 35 to 40 centimeter (14 to 16 inches) necklace whose central pearl normally lies in the hollow of the throat or just below. It looks especially attractive with V-neck blouses and dresses.

Princess: a 40 to 50 centimeter (16 to 20 inches) necklace. This slightly longer length is well suited for pearl enhancers (detachable pendants) and can slenderize the neck.

Matinee: a 50 to 66 centimeter (20 to 26 inches) necklace. Some people like to wear a matinee length along with a choker. Or they have it strung with two hidden ("mystery") clasps so it can also be worn as a bracelet and a shorter necklace.

Opera: a necklace about twice the length of a choker, 70 to 91 centimeters (28 to 36 inches).

Rope: a necklace measuring 1 meter (40 inches) or longer. The definition of its length will vary according to the jeweler or the company using the term.

STRAND LENGTH

TYPE OF NECKLACE	INCHES	CENTIMETERS
Choker	14–16	35–40
Princess	16–20	40–50
Matinee	20–26	50–66
Opera	28–36	70–91
Rope	40+	100 (1 meter)+

The preceding lengths are approximate. Definitions of necklace lengths can vary from one jeweler to another. Keep in mind that pearl strands become slightly longer (about 5 centimeters/2 inches) when they are knotted and strung with a clasp to form a necklace.

Here are some other terms related to pearl necklaces that consumers might not be familiar with:

Bib: A necklace of three or more concentric strands. The lowest strand normally does not fall below matinee length.
Dog collar: A multi-strand choker length necklace. The strands may be held together with a single clasp. Dog collars help conceal neck wrinkles.
Torsade: A multi-strand necklace formed by twisting strands around each other. This is a popular way to wear freshwater pearls.
Uniform strand: A strand whose pearls are all about the same size.
Graduated strand: A strand with pearls of different sizes that gradually get larger toward the center. Graduated strands provide a big pearl look at a lower price than uniform strands.

A dog collar necklace. *Photo courtesy of the Cultured Pearl Associations of America and Japan.*

MATCHING

Matching (or "make") describes the uniformity of pearls in a pair, a strand or a piece of jewelry. It is a combination of these factors:

- how well the pearls match or blend together in terms of color, shape, luster, size and surface perfection;
- how centered the drill holes are; and
- how seamless the transition of pearl size is in graduated strands.

Make has a definite impact on price. Some dealers charge a premium that may range from 1 percent to 15 percent for akoya strands that are of very fine make. Others may discount strands if the pearls do not match very well. Premiums of up to 30 percent or more can be charged for well-matched pairs of large, high-quality natural or South Sea cultured pearls. This is because it can take a great deal of time and luck to find pearls that match.

Fine make is relative, though, and buyers should be flexible about their expectations. For example, one should not expect natural or South Sea pearls to be as round and match as well as cultured akoya pearls.

The definitions of what constitutes good, fair and poor make in akoya pearl strands can vary from one dealer to another. Some may emphasize

Well-matched South Sea pearls from A & Z Pearls. *Photo by Diamond Graphics.*

color, while uniform luster, size and/or shape may be more important to others. All dealers, however, probably agree that overall appearance is what counts most when judging make.

GIA uses the term *matching* to denote make. According to the Institute's guidelines, "Matching describes the uniformity of pearls in jewelry. It is judged by the consistency of size, shape, color, luster, surface quality, and luster quality. For pearls that are intentionally mismatched, harmonious design and balanced effect are also considered applicable factors."

The GIA pearl-grading system lists the following matching categories:

- **Excellent:** pearls are uniform in appearance and drilled on-center.
- **Very good:** very minor variations in uniformity.
- **Good:** minor variations in uniformity.
- **Fair:** noticeable variations in uniformity.
- **Poor:** significant variations in uniformity.
- **Not applicable:** "N/A" is used for single pearls and certain intentionally mismatched items.

Tips for Judging Make

As mentioned earlier, it is important to consider the availability of the pearls being graded when judging make. This means:

- Dyed and non dyed strands should not be graded alike, because it is much easier to match dyed pearls than those that are not.
- Pearls with very thick nacre should not be discounted as much for shape variations as thin- and medium-nacre pearls, because pearls that are in the oyster longer have a greater chance of growing into irregular shapes.
- Natural pearls should not be graded as strictly for make as cultured pearls.

In general, buyers should be careful not to become so concerned about perfect matching that they end up downplaying other quality factors. It is important to keep expectations realistic.

The author recalls being in Tokyo after taking a pearl-grading seminar. She looked at some of the highest-priced akoya strands in some of the most exclusive stores in Tokyo, and she was quite surprised to find not a single strand whose overtones matched. They all seemed to have a combination of green, pink and silver overtones, but the strands varied in the percentage of each color. Finally she realized that she was being unrealistic, and that as long as the body color looked uniform, the overtones blended together well and their differences were not obvious, there was nothing wrong with the pearls.

Judging make requires a balanced perspective. On the one hand, we should not be so lax that we let shoddy workmanship become the norm. On the other, we should not be such perfectionists that no pearls can meet our standards. When you look at a strand, consider its overall impact. Your attention should not be distracted by obviously mismatched pearls. Neither is it desirable for the pearls to be perfectly matched but lackluster. Look at as many strands of pearls and different qualities as possible. You will gradually develop a sense of what is acceptable, and eventually you will have an appreciation for truly fine make.

4 Akoya Cultured Pearls

A newly opened akoya pearl oyster, *Pinctada fucata martensii. Eddie Gerald/ Alamy Stock Photo.*

Originally the word *akoya* was used as a trade term for Japanese cultured saltwater pearls. However, when it was discovered that akoya oysters were also used to culture pearls outside of Japan, the meaning expanded to refer to any pearl from an akoya-type oyster found anywhere, including China, Korea, Vietnam, Thailand and Australia. Akoya cultured pearls are produced by the *Pinctada fucata martensii* oyster and are relatively small. They average 7 millimeters in diameter and are usually less than 11 millimeters, because they come from a small oyster. Akoya oysters live for about eight years and grow to a maximum size of 8 centimeters (just over 3 inches) across. The interior mother-of-pearl tends to be white, with strong silver tones and occasional flashes of pink.

The optimal growth time for producing akoya pearls with fine nacre and high luster is 18 to 24 months after inserting a bead nucleus. The minimum growth time is 10 months, but those pearls generally have thin nacre and low luster.

SOURCES OF AKOYA CULTURED PEARLS

Japan

As we learned in chapter 2, natural blisters form when invaders such as parasites, worms, fish, crabs or other creatures penetrate a mollusk's shell and are covered by organic material and nacre as a defense mechanism. Cultured blisters grow after a nucleus is placed on the inner surface of the shell under the mantle. When the shell is returned to the water, nacre grows over the nucleus, creating a blister.

Side view of a natural blister that was formed on the inner surface of an oyster shell. *Photo © Prof. Dr. H. A. Hänni & GemExpert.*

In July 1893, two years after William Saville-Kent cultured shell blisters in Australia, Kokichi Mikimoto and his wife, Ume, produced their first cultured blisters in *Pinctada fucata martensii* oysters on Benten-shima Island in Japan. At harvest time the blister was cut away from the shell, filled with a hardening substance and then capped on the backside with mother-of-pearl, creating what today is called a mabe pearl in America and an assembled cultured blister in Europe. Initially they were sold as "half-pearls." Mikimoto did not receive a patent for his blister-culturing procedure until January 27, 1896. By 1900, his half-pearls were being mass produced and sold as "Mikimoto Pearls" in his shop in the Ginza district of Tokyo. Later they were sold throughout Japan, China, Europe and America.

Between 1902 and 1907, two other people were experimenting with culturing round akoya pearls: Tatsuhei Mise and Dr. Tokichi Nishikawa. Mise started his pearl-culturing project in 1902 and by 1904 had produced his first small round pearls, but he did not receive a patent for the needle he used until 1907. Nishikawa began his experiments in 1905; in 1907 he harvested his first small round pearls with gold and silver nuclei and received a patent for the implantation process. In 1908 the two signed a joint ownership agreement for the "Mise-Nishikawa method" of culturing whole round pearls.

Mikimoto applied for a patent for producing round pearls in 1914, which was granted in 1916. He then began to mass-produce pearls at several pearl farms, using nuclei cut from American mussel shells—unlike Mise and Nishikawa, who used metal beads that could not be drilled.

Traditional pearl divers, or *ama*, demonstrate pearl-diving techniques at Mikimoto Pearl Island. *Photo courtesy of Mikimoto Pearl Island.*

Dealers in natural pearls were upset about the sales of cultured pearls because they led to the devaluation of their own products. Debates ensued on what to call the cultivated pearls. In 1926, at the first International Jewellers' Congress, the international trade adopted the term *cultured pearls*.

The "Pearls as One" course, supported by the Cultured Pearl Association of America, sheds light on the immense size of Mikimoto's business and pearl culturing in Japan generally: "By 1931, Mikimoto had stores around the world, all supplied by the 51 farms he owned in Japan. By 1938, over 360 pearl farms were operating in Japan, reaching a production peak of nearly 11,000,000 pearls." Mikimoto spent a great deal of time educating the jewelry trade and the general public worldwide about cultured pearls. As a result, the pearls became a desirable commodity and were no longer considered imitations. This earned him recognition as the founder of the cultured pearl industry.

After World War II, General Douglas MacArthur's administration urged Japan to resume producing pearls, with the condition that cultured pearls could be sold only to the Central Office of American Supplies. As a result, the pearls were either sold to American GIs and their families in Japan or exported to the United States. Today Japan sells its cultured pearls all over the world.

A statue of Kokichi Mikimoto at Mikimoto Pearl Island, located in Ise Bay, near Toba, Mie Prefecture, Japan. *Various images/ Shutterstock.*

Akoya pearl farms still operate in Ago Bay in Mie Prefecture, where Mikimoto began his pearl farming. Two other important Japanese pearl-producing sites are Omura Bay, in Nagasaki Prefecture, and Uwajima, in Ehime Prefecture, the latter being the most important pearl-cultivation area in Japan today. Pearl farmers lease their land from the government, and the leases are usually passed from generation to generation. They use oysters that are bred and grown in hatcheries, unlike Mikimoto, who initially used wild shells for cultivating his pearls. Wild spat (baby oysters) are collected only to introduce genetic diversity into hatchery stock when necessary.

The pearls are harvested in the coldest season of the year because the metabolism of the akoya oyster is at its lowest then, resulting in slow, tight nacre deposition. That gradual nacre formation has helped Japanese pearls earn their reputation for unusually high luster compared to cultured pearls from other countries, where the water is not as cold. Japan remains the world's largest producer of akoya cultured pearls.

Other Sources of Cultured Pearls

Japan is no longer the sole producer of cultured akoya pearls. China has been culturing these pearls since 1958, but most were sold to Japan until the 1990s, when China began selling pearls internationally. Chinese production

An akoya pearl farm in Ha Long Bay, Vietnam.
Photo © Prof. Dr. H.A. Hänni & GemExpert.

Young akoya pearl oysters (*Pinctada fucata*) in Vietnam ready to receive a bead nucleus or donate mantle tissue. They will not grow much bigger while the bead is being coated with nacre. *Photo © Prof. Dr. H.A. Hänni & GemExpert.*

Assorted natural colors of unbleached beaded pearls freshly harvested from local *Pinctada radiata* oysters at the RAK Pearl Farm in Ras al Khaimah, UAE. *Photo © Prof. Dr. H.A. Hänni & GemExpert*

reached a peak in 2006, bringing down the price of akoya pearls. However, in 2007 strong tropical storms destroyed almost every Chinese pearl farm. The country still has a few operating akoya pearl farms, but China currently imports more pearls from Japan than it exports.

Vietnam started culturing pearls around 1967 and has been producing them commercially since the 1990s. Most of the akoya pearl farms are in Ha Long Bay, in northern Vietnam, and are a mixture of independent operations and joint ventures with the Vietnamese government. Some farms are located in southern Vietnam, at Nha Trang. According to a *Gems & Gemology* field report from 2020, most of the production is akoya pearls, with a smaller quantity of *Pinctada maxima* pearls; much of the product is exported to China, Japan, India and the United States.

Australia is famous for its large South Sea cultured pearls from the *Pinctada maxima* oyster, but it also produces some akoya pearls. In 2004 the Broken Bay Pearl Farm, on the central coast of New South Wales, harvested its first akoya pearls from the *Pinctada fucata* oyster. The site is about the same distance from the equator as the southern Japanese pearl farms, so the climate and seasonal water temperatures are well suited to cultivating akoya pearls. Pearls of Australia is the company that operates Broken Bay, the only pearl farm in New South Wales, in addition to cultivating South Sea pearls at its Cygnet Bay Pearl Farm, on the Kimberley coast of Western Australia.

The United Arab Emirates (UAE) used to be known only for its natural pearls. However, in 2005 Abdulla Al Suwaidi, the grandson of one of the last natural pearl divers in the UAE, established a pearl farm in Al Rams, Ras Al Khaimah. Suwaidi wants to restore the UAE's place in the world market by producing the best cultured pearls from the *Pinctada radiata* oyster, also known as the Gulf pearl oyster. This small saltwater oyster produces cultured pearls that resemble akoya cultured pearls.

Keshi Pearls

The term *keshi* has been used for several types of pearls:

- **Natural akoya seed pearls:** Seed pearls are tiny natural pearls that measure less than 2 millimeters. *Keshi* was a trade term used for these types of pearls before cultured pearls ever existed. Chien Lin, president of Inter World Trading, says that when he lived in Kobe, Japan, older-generation pearl traders told him that *keshi* was initially used to refer to natural seed pearls, found when harvesting wild akoya oysters. The word in Japanese refers to something very small, such as a poppy seed. The seed pearls resembled poppy seeds—hence the name. Lin verified this use of the term with a specialist at the Pearl Museum on Mikimoto Pearl Island in Japan.

- **Beadless cultured pearls formed as by-products of the Japanese akoya pearl-culturing process:** These keshi pearls result from the formation of a cultured pearl sac, either following injury to the mantle rim by handling or from a partial piece of transplanted mantle tissue. If the bead is rejected, the inserted tissue can create a keshi cultured pearl. Since keshi pearls have no bead nucleus, they are composed entirely of nacre. Akoya cultured keshis can range from small, seed-sized pearls to skinny pearls as long as 14 millimeters.

- **Tiny, beadless, seed-like cultured pearls formed as by-products of the Chinese freshwater pearl culturing process:** Saltwater pearl dealers do not consider such pearls

Above: Cultured akoya keshi pearls from the Pearl Exporting Company. *Photo © Renée Newman.*

Below: Freshwater cultured keshi pearls (bottom) and beadless second-harvest freshwater cultured pearls (top). *Pearls and photo courtesy of Inter World Trading.*

Saltwater cultured keshi pearls. *Pearls and photo courtesy of the Pearl Exporting Company.*

to be keshi pearls, since many beadless freshwater pearls are intentionally cultivated with only a tissue graft. Nevertheless, some freshwater pearl dealers believe they should be able to call tiny beadless freshwater pearls keshi because they resemble poppy seeds—especially since saltwater pearl dealers have extended the meaning of the term to include large South Sea and Tahitian beadless cultured pearls that in no way look like poppy seeds or the original Japanese keshi pearls.

- **Beadless second-harvest Chinese freshwater cultured pearls:** These have been sold as freshwater cultured keshi or keshi-type pearls. They have also been called "reborn" pearls. After freshwater coin pearls are harvested, the mussels can be returned to the water without undergoing a grafting process. Within the empty pearl sac once occupied by the coin pearl, another pearl may be spontaneously produced. Freshwater pearl dealers identify this as a reborn, second-generation, second-harvest or keshi-type pearl.

- **Beadless cultured pearls formed as by-products of the South Sea and black-lipped oyster culturing process:** Like other cultured keshi, South Sea and Tahitian keshi cultured pearls are by-products of the culturing process. Some are hollow or contain a relatively large amount of organic matter.

In February 2010 the World Jewellery Confederation (CIBJO) defined *keshi* as the trade term for a beadless cultured pearl formed accidentally or intentionally by human intervention in marine (saltwater) pearl oysters such as the akoya, silver-lipped, gold-lipped and black-lipped oysters. However, as we have learned, the term is still used by some freshwater pearl dealers to distinguish beadless second-harvest cultured pearls and seed-sized freshwater pearls from other types of freshwater cultured pearls.

Keshi-type pearls also form in American mussels. The American Pearl Company uses the term *lagniappe* pearls to refer to the extra, non-beaded cultured pearls that form in American freshwater pearl mussels as a result of the freshwater culturing process.

Because of the confusing use of the term *keshi* and the fact that the origins of pearls cannot be proved, gem labs such as the Swiss Gemmological Institute (SSEF) and GIA's Gem Trade Laboratory do not identify keshi in their lab reports. They simply call them "cultured pearls" or "beadless cultured pearls" and indicate whether they are saltwater or freshwater.

PRICE FACTORS

Shape and color are discussed in greater detail in this chapter. To understand the other price factors for akoya pearls—such as luster, surface quality, nacre thickness and matching—refer to chapter 3, where you will also find images of akoya pearls to illustrate the different qualities within a specific price factor.

Shape

Akoya pearls are generally cultured with spherical nuclei, so they are usually round and have the least variation in shape. They can be divided into four basic shape categories:

- **Round:** so symmetrical that the pearl will roll in a straight line on a flat, inclined surface. Normally this is the most expensive shape, provided that the pearl has an adequate nacre coating.
- **Near-round:** slightly flattened or elongated.
- **Semi-baroque:** obviously irregular and not round; may appear slightly pear-shaped.
- **Baroque:** very distorted and irregular in shape. Frequently the surface is uneven.

Akoya cultured pearl prices are generally based on round pearls. When pearls deviate from the round shape, they are discounted. Baroque pearls, for example, may be sold for 55 to 80 percent less than round ones. Of course, pearl pricing varies from one dealer to another.

From top to bottom, akoya cultured pearls that are round, near round, semi-baroque and baroque. *Photo © Renée Newman.*

Unbleached natural-color cultured akoya pearls from Vietnam, courtesy of King's Ransom. *Photo by Betty Sue King.*

Natural-color cultured blue akoya pearls from Vietnam, courtesy of Pearl Paradise. *Photo by Jeremy Shepherd.*

Color

Most akoya pearls are white because they are commonly bleached. Their natural, unbleached body colors show more variation; they can be light yellow, orangey yellow, blue, lavender or light gray. Bleaching pearls with chemicals and intense light made it easier to create matched strands and to fulfill the demand for white pearls, so it became a common practice with akoya pearls, especially in Japan.

In recent years, however, multicolored strands have become popular. As a result, Vietnamese akoya farmers decided to offer natural-color akoya pearls to their customers. It was a good way to get their pearls noticed by Western dealers, since their akoya strands look distinctly different from those sold by the Japanese.

The color of some blue cultured akoyas is caused by foreign contaminants in the nacre or between the nacre and the shell bead nucleus, unlike Tahitian black pearls, whose color is an inherent characteristic of the pearl nacre. Occasionally akoya pearls are blue with silver and pink overtones, but those colors are extremely rare. Akoya pearls are never naturally black; black akoya pearls have either been irradiated or treated with an organic dye.

Cultured akoya pearl strands with varying body colors and overtones. *Pearls courtesy of Shima Pearl; photo © Renée Newman.*

Their overall body color can play a significant role in determining the price of akoya pearls. The main body-color categories are:

- **Light pink or white:** These are the highest-priced akoya colors. Some dealers used to charge more for light pink pearls, but now white pearls with high luster sell for about the same as those that are light pink. Most pinkish akoya pearls on the market have been tinted, particularly those with a strong pink color; as a result, they do not merit a higher price than white pearls.
- **Cream:** Cream-colored pearls generally cost less than white pearls. The higher the quality of the pearls, the greater the probable price difference will be between cream and white. If the pearls are of low quality, there may be no difference.
- **Dark cream or yellow:** Pearls in these colors are usually priced much lower than white akoya pearls. The darker the cream or yellow color, the greater the price difference can be.

Pink and blue overtones—a rare and desirable pearl characteristic. *Photo © Renée Newman.*

When judging color, keep in mind that there is no standardized system for grading or communicating color in the pearl industry. Nevertheless, there is an awareness of cream and yellow colors and general agreement that cream-colored or yellow akoya pearls tend to cost less than those that are pink or white.

Overtones on any type of pearl are desirable because they add color and indicate that the nacre is of sufficient thickness. Their absence may be a sign of low luster and thin nacre. The three most common overtones are pink, green and silver. A combination of blue and pink overtones is associated with top-quality pearls. Combined overtones are often called orient or iridescence (see chapter 3, page 62).

Some Japanese dealers have described the color of the most valued akoya pearls as bluish pink, which in essence is a light pink or white body color with blue and pink overtones. These pearls are extremely rare and almost impossible to find in North America.

Hanadama Cultured Pearls

Hanadama was the term Kokichi Mikimoto used to describe his finest akoya cultured pearls—the ones that were naturally beautiful when they were harvested and did not require any bleaching or other form of treatment. *Hana* means "flower" in Japanese, and to Mikimoto his top pearls were like flowers. Often *hanadama* is translated as "flower pearl," although the Japanese word for pearl is *shinju*.

Hanadama (top-grade) natural-color white akoya cultured pearls ranging from 7.5 to 8 mm, from Pearl Paradise. *Photo courtesy of Jeremy Shepherd.*

The Pearl Science Laboratory (PSL) of Japan uses the term *hanadama* too. The PSL was established in 1978 in order to conduct research on pearl cultivation and, in later years, on pearl identification and pearl-cleaning equipment. In 2000 the PSL announced a pearl-grading system in which *hanadama* refers to the best-quality white akoya pearls of 6 millimeters or more that have these qualities:

- a blemish grade of not lower than very slightly blemished;
- a minimum nacre thickness of 0.4 millimeter; and
- a very strong luster.

Both brilliance and interference colors (the aurora effect) are also checked according to PSL standards. The aurora effect is determined by placing pearls on a diffused light source.

The PSL uses 10-power magnification to inspect surface quality. Inner inspection of the pearls is done by using optical fibers to test nacre depth at random intervals throughout the strand and verify that they have a minimum thickness of 0.4 millimeter per side. Soft X-ray apparatus is also used to verify nacre depth. An aurora viewer is used to observe and display iridescent colors and brightness.

Originally *hanadama* was a term used only for top-quality untreated akoya cultured pearls. However, today it is also used for high-quality treated cultured pearls, although the definition of high quality can vary from one dealer and lab to another. If a seller does not specify that their hanadama pearls are natural-color white pearls, they have probably been bleached, which is customary for akoya pearls. Since the meaning of *hanadama* is variable, it is best to ask sellers to describe what they mean by the term when they use it.

5 South Sea Pearls

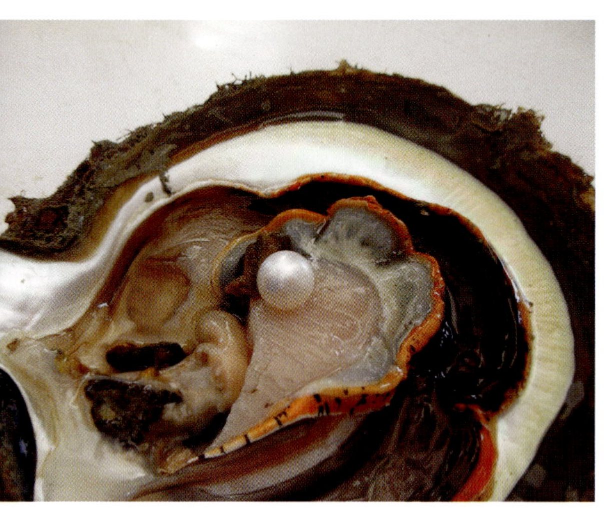

A South Sea cultured pearl in a freshly opened silver-lipped *Pinctada maxima* oyster from the Paspaley Pearling Co. *Photo © Blaire Beavers.*

Koichi Mikimoto called all saltwater pearls cultivated south of Japan "South Sea pearls." Today the term usually refers to pearls from the silver-lipped and gold-lipped *Pinctada maxima* oysters. They command the highest prices for cultured pearls and attain the largest size, usually ranging from 9 to 20 millimeters. The silver-lipped oyster can grow up to 30.5 centimeters (12 inches) across and produces mostly white and cream-colored pearls, whereas most pearls from the gold-lipped oyster have a cream to golden color but are sometimes white.

South Sea oysters that are unsuitable for producing whole pearls or that reject the bead nucleus are used to culture shell blisters, which afterward are used to make the assembled cultured blisters known in America as mabe pearls.

South Sea cultured blisters on the inside shell of a *Pinctada maxima* oyster, surrounded by cultured mabe pearls, at the Yee On Gems & Jewellery booth at the Hong Kong International Diamond, Gem and Pearl Show. *Photo © Renée Newman.*

Various shapes and sizes of South Sea cultured pearls in a necklace from the Autore Orchid Collection. *Photo courtesy of Autore Pearls.*

SOURCES OF SOUTH SEA PEARLS

Indonesia

The first commercial production of South Sea cultured pearls was carried out in 1928 in Buton, Sulawesi (Celebes), Indonesia, under the direction of Dr. Sukeo Fujita. The Buton project was financed and managed by the Japanese company Mitsubishi, so the results were often called Mitsubishi pearls. Gem dealer Andy Müller writes in *Cultured Pearls: The First Hundred Years* that they were 8 to 10 millimeters in size, which amazed the pearl trade because the average size of akoya pearls at the time was 3 to 4 millimeters.

From 1928 until 1932 the Buton project produced 8,000 to 10,000 pearls a year. Unfortunately, Fujita became ill and died in 1931, but he had trained five Japanese pearl-oyster technicians to carry on, and some of them helped develop the South Sea pearl industry in Indonesia, Australia and Burma (Myanmar) after World War II.

In 1945 a revolutionary statesman named Sukarno was appointed president of Indonesia after leading the country in its struggle for independence from the Dutch. Sukarno was opposed to Japanese involvement in either the government or the pearl industry. According to Elisabeth Strack in *Pearls*, it was not until the late 1970s that the Indonesian government began to approve official Japanese ventures within the republic. By the 1990s it was readily issuing pearl-farming licenses to foreign companies, and in 1999 Indonesia was supplying more than a third of the world's South Sea cultured pearls.

Indonesia, which lies between the Indian and Pacific Oceans, has more than 13,400 islands and extends more than 4,828 kilometers (3,000 miles) from west to east. Its pearl farms are in remote areas, on several islands both north and south of the equator. The Indonesian *Pinctada maxima* oyster resembles the Australian variety. The silver-lipped oyster is found more frequently south of the equator and the gold-lipped variety is found more frequently north of the equator. This means Indonesia is ideally situated to be a major producer of both white and gold South Sea pearls. Its water temperatures (26 to 31 degrees Celsius) are higher than those of Australia, so the growth periods can be shorter—about 18 to 24 months.

Before 1995, wild mollusks were used for culturing pearls in Indonesia. However, overfishing of wild stock made oyster hatcheries necessary. Pearl farms usually have their own hatcheries, which raise pearl oysters from larvae to the point where they can be used to produce cultured pearls.

The Autore team at one of their Indonesian pearl farms. The Autore Group focuses on hatchery-grown *Pinctada maxima* shells to minimize the need to use its quota for wild oyster fishing. The additional benefit of hatchery-produced oysters is that they help increase the quantities of wild oysters because of subsequent spawning. *Photo courtesy of Autore Pearls.*

Pearl farming in the Mergui Archipelago of Myanmar. *Photo courtesy of Rio Pearl.*

Myanmar (formerly Burma)

Rich banks of *Pinctada maxima* oysters are found in the Mergui Archipelago, on the western coast of Myanmar. *The Book of the Pearl* by Kunz and Stevenson reports that after the diving suit was introduced in the late 1800s, huge profits were made from pearl diving in the area, with prices reaching $10,000 per pearl. In order to derive revenue from the industry, the Burmese government divided its pearl territory into defined areas and leased the diving rights.

In 1954 Kikiro Takashima established a pearl farm on Sir Malcolm Island in the Mergui Archipelago as a joint venture with the Burmese government. The high quality of its cultured pearls earned Myanmar a reputation as a source of the finest South Sea pearls. Unfortunately, the farm was nationalized in 1963 and the Japanese pearl farmers were forced to leave. As a result, Burma's pearl cultivation dwindled, and by the 1980s both the quality and quantity of pearls produced were low.

Thanks to the reestablishment of foreign pearl companies in Myanmar since the 1990s, Myanmar cultured pearls have regained their high-quality status. As the gold-lipped oyster is predominant in this region, most Myanmar pearls have a cream to golden color, but that is changing. The Hong Kong–based firm Rio Pearl experimented with different breeding techniques to make the shells whiter and the oysters strong and healthy. By 2021 Rio Pearl was able to produce white Burmese South Sea cultured pearls.

A top-quality Australian South Sea cultured pearl necklace (17–18.5 mm) from A & Z Pearls. *Photo by Diamond Graphics.*

Australia

Australia has played a major role in the development of cultured saltwater pearls. As described in chapter 1, William Saville-Kent succeeded in producing *Pinctada maxima* blisters, which were called "half-pearls" and exhibited in London, two years before Mikimoto's first akoya cultured blisters. Following that, Saville-Kent became the first person to culture loose pearls, influencing the development of pearl cultivation in Japan. He is also credited as a pioneer of the concept of sustainable fisheries, to help replenish marine life diminished by overfishing.

According to Strack, in 1906 Saville-Kent founded the first pearl farm in the South Pacific, the Natural Pearl Shell Cultivation Company, which produced blisters used to make mabe pearls that sold at high prices. However, the Australian government believed culturing pearls would be detrimental to the local natural pearl and mother-of-pearl industries, so it enacted the Pearling Act of 1912, outlawing all pearl-culturing attempts. This law remained in place until 1949; during that time only farming of the shells was allowed. This likely resulted in Indonesia's becoming the first country to commercially produce whole round cultured pearls, in 1928. Burma (Myanmar) became the second commercial producer of South Sea cultured whole pearls in 1954.

The first commercial harvest of Australian South Sea round cultured pearls took place in 1958 at Kuri Bay, named after Tokuichi Kuribayashi, president of the Pearl Shell Fishing Company, which had been actively fishing for shells and natural pearls along Australia's northern coast before World War II, according to Müller. Kuribayashi had trading partners in Australia, the United States and Japan during the development of the South Sea cultured pearl industry in Australia. Strack notes that the 1958 harvest of round South Sea pearls was considered a sensational event on the world market, resulting in huge prices for the pearls.

In 1990 the Paspaley Pearling Company acquired Pearls Pty. Ltd., the company that had established the original Kuri Bay pearl farm. By 1991 Paspaley controlled more than 60 percent of all the pearl farms in Australia. In October 1992 the company made history when Salvador Assael of New York sold a Paspaley necklace with 23 cultured pearls (16–20.1 millimeters) for a record price of US$2.32 million.

Instead of building and operating on land like other pearl farms, Paspaley takes its team of expert divers to the pearling grounds to dive for wild shells and does its pearl culturing on board a fleet of ships. Despite the development of hatchery technology over the past 30 years, Australia continues to rely on wild mollusks for culturing most of its pearls. This allows cultivators to avoid waiting the four to eight years needed for oysters to grow and produce large pearls. A quota system enacted in 1990 limits the number of wild mollusks that can be taken each year and divides that number among licensed pearl farmers. The limitations enforced by the quota system help protect the wild stock and prevent overproduction, forcing the farmers to seek quality in production over quantity.

After a bead nucleus is inserted into an Australian *Pinctada maxima* oyster, it takes a minimum of two years for a pearl to form, but the growth period may be as long as four years. Shells that produce the finest pearls are renucleated, while the rest are harvested for their adductor muscle meat and mother-of-pearl.

About 90 percent of silver-lipped oyster pearls are white, with the remaining gems falling in the creamy and golden range. Their average size range is 11 to 14 millimeters, but they can grow up to 20 millimeters or more in rare cases.

The pearling fleet of Paspaley Pearls Pty. Ltd. *Photo courtesy of Paspaley Pearls.*

The Paspaley Pearling Company

Paspaley was founded in 1935 by Nicholas Paspaley (1913–84) as a business that collected and sold mother-of-pearl shells for the button trade. After pearl buttons were replaced by more affordable plastic substitutes, the cultivation of Australian South Sea pearls became the company's primary focus. It has also diversified into other areas, such as aviation, retail and commercial properties. The Paspaley board of directors consists wholly of family members, including the children and grandchildren of the original founder. Its executive chair, Nicholas Paspaley Jr., is largely responsible for pioneering and revolutionizing the Australian South Sea pearl industry.

Golden South Sea cultured pearls from the Philippines, with diamonds. *Bollicine Collection necklace and photo by Jewelmer Joaillerie.*

Philippines

Pearl-farming projects to harvest round South Sea pearls began in the Philippines in the 1960s, but none of the farms showed much success until the end of the 1970s, and blister pearls were the main product, according to Strack. It was not until the 1980s that the Philippines established itself as a serious producer of cultured South Sea pearls.

The largest Philippine producer of pearls today, Jewelmer, was founded in 1979 by Filipino entrepreneur Manuel Cojuangco and Jacques Branellec, a Frenchman who had cultivated pearls in Tahiti. Their first pearl farm was established in the island province of Palawan. Not long afterward, the first experimental laboratory in the Philippines, where oysters were raised in a hatchery, was created. There Jewelmer worked with Japanese grafters to culture South Sea pearls. By 1989 the company had become a successful producer of golden South Sea pearls, displaying them in Monaco alongside other jewelry brands such as Cartier and Mikimoto.

Jewelmer's development of hatcheries in the Philippines allowed the gold-lipped oyster to become more prevalent. Now, instead of their shells being collected in the wild, they are grown in a protected environment on Palawan. Even though pearl farms operate in different places throughout the Philippines, Palawan is and will probably remain the dominant pearl-producing area.

Aerial view of one of Jewelmer's pearl farms and the unpolluted waters of the province of Palawan, the Philippines. *Photo by Romain Rivierre.*

The gold-lipped oyster has been cultivated in several countries over the years, but only the Philippines has focused primarily on cultivating its shell. In 1996, President Fidel V. Ramos declared the South Sea Pearl the national jewel of the Philippines. In honor of this recognition, the country's 1,000-peso note, its currency's largest denomination, features an image of the South Sea pearl.

Golden South Sea cultured pearls are rarer than those that are white; as a result, strongly gold-colored pearls generally cost more, all other factors being equal. According to the Cultured Pearl Association's "Pearls as One" course, the gold-lipped pearl oyster is native to warm tropical waters ranging from the northern and western tips of Australia to the Philippines in the north, Malaysia in the east and Papua New Guinea in the west. The shell is found at depths of 3 to 60 meters (nearly 10 feet to nearly 197 feet) and grows up to 30 centimeters (nearly 12 inches) in length. By contrast, the akoya shell does not normally exceed 8 centimeters (just over 3 inches).

A Jewelmer golden South Sea pearl at harvest. *Photo by Romain Rivierre.*

The harvest from the gold-lipped mollusk can yield up to 30 to 40 percent golden pearls, while the remainder range in color from light brown or yellow to cream, with about 10 percent of the pearls being white. The oyster produces golden nacre only when it is in peak health and cultivated properly in ideal environmental conditions. Its pearls range from 9 to 16 millimeters, with an average size of 10 to 12 millimeters, according to "Pearls as One."

Color is considered the most important value factor in gold South Sea pearls. The deeper the shade of gold, the more valuable the pearl; those that exhibit a 24-karat-gold coloration are the most expensive.

South Sea and Tahitian keshi pearl and diamond bracelet by Yoko London. *Photo courtesy of Yoko London.*

SOUTH SEA CULTURED KESHI

South Sea cultured keshi pearls do not contain a bead nucleus, and as a result they generally have a baroque (irregular) shape. When saltwater pearls are cultured, a bead nucleus is inserted into the gonad (sex organ) of the mollusk, along with a piece of mantle tissue from a donor oyster. Mantle cells from this insertion process sometimes become displaced and form an additional pearl sac in which a keshi pearl forms. A beadless keshi pearl can form too, if the nucleus is rejected by the oyster or if the mantle tissue is not in close contact with the bead.

Most beadless freshwater pearls are produced by inserting a piece of donor mantle tissue into the connective tissue of a mussel's mantle. However, mantle-grown beadless pearls are a new type of baroque saltwater pearl. Pearl researcher and professor Dr. Henry Hänni has summarized the formation of beaded and beadless cultured saltwater pearls with the following chart. "Beaded" means containing a solid bead nucleus, usually made of shell, but the bead can also be an inexpensive cultured freshwater pearl.

LIMITED COMBINATIONS FOR CULTURING SALTWATER WHOLE OYSTER PEARLS

Gonad-grown	beaded	akoya, Tahiti, South Sea, etc.
	beadless	"keshi" bead rejected
Mantle-grown	beadless	new-type baroque
	beaded	—

Chart by Prof. Dr. H.A. Hänni © GemExpert.

PRICE FACTORS

South Sea pearls are priced according to their luster, surface quality, shape, color, size and nacre thickness. Autore Pearls identifies the first five factors as the "Autore Five S's": shine, surface, shape, shade and size. A low price does not necessarily mean low quality when it comes to shape, color and size. The low price results from a greater supply and lower demand for certain colors, shapes and sizes. Luster, surface quality and nacre thickness, on the other hand, do affect the actual quality of pearls. Luster and nacre thickness are usually the most important price factors. Since the nacre thickness of all Autore pearls is adequate, the company does not include it as a value factor when grading its pearls. Luster is also an indication of nacre thickness, because pearls with thin nacre usually have low luster.

Luster

The higher the luster, the more valuable the pearl. White South Sea pearls have lower luster potential than akoya and Tahitian black pearls. Take this into consideration when evaluating South Sea pearls. Pearls with excellent luster show mirror-like reflections, whereas pearls with poor luster produce very little reflection. For tips on how to judge luster, see chapter 3, pages 49–50.

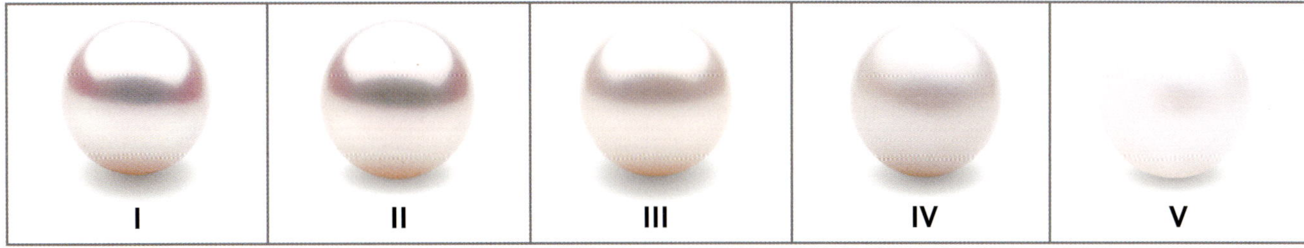

Luster qualities ranging from excellent (I) to poor (V). *Images © Autore Pearls Pty. Ltd.*

Surface Quality

Surface quality is determined by the size, number, nature, location, visibility and types of surface characteristics (also known as blemishes) that are on a pearl. Cracks, chips and missing nacre are the most serious flaws,

Surface qualities of South Sea pearls ranging from clean to heavily blemished to the unaided eye. *Photo © Renée Newman.*

while a tiny pit or spot is considered insignificant, especially when the pearls are in a strand.

Blemish grade will depend on whether the pearls are examined with the unaided eye or under 10-times magnification. The top grade for surface quality issued by the Gemological Institute of America (GIA) is "clean," because it is based on the visibility of blemishes to the unaided eye. The Pearl Science Laboratory of Japan never describes pearls as flawless or blemish-free, because it grades surface quality using 10-times magnification, and all pearls will display some sort of surface feature under magnification, even when they are clean to the naked eye. Unlike faceted diamonds, whose surfaces are cut and shaped by humans, the nacreous surface of pearls is built up over time and determined by nature.

Under the category of surface quality, Autore Pearls includes pearl *grain*, which refers to the composition of the pearl's skin and its structure. The tighter the structure of the pearl, the less evident its grain. Instead of listing nacre thickness as a separate category like GIA, Autore includes it in the surface classification; pearls with thin nacre would get a low surface grade. In other words, Autore's surface classification for pearls refers to the blemishes, the pearl grain and the nacre thickness.

Shape

The rounder the pearl, the more valuable it is. But round South Sea pearls are rare, and far more rare than round akoya pearls, which are smaller and have thinner nacre. The thicker nacre and longer growth periods of South Sea pearls lead to their having a wide variety of shapes. These cannot be described adequately using just the four akoya shape categories of round, near round, semi-baroque and baroque.

The basic classifications of South Sea pearl shapes include round, near round, oval, button, drop, semi-baroque, baroque and circled. However, when Autore grades and sorts its South Sea pearls, the descriptions are more detailed. These detailed descriptions are included in this chapter to increase awareness of the wide variety of shapes that South Sea pearls can have. Occasionally, in fact, South Sea pearls are incorrectly appraised as freshwater pearls because of their similar shapes.

Round and Near Round

Some pearl sellers determine whether a pearl is round by rolling it on a smooth surface. If the pearl rolls in a straight line, they identify it as round. If it looks roundish but moves off course, they call it near round. Autore classifies its pearls as round when the variation in diameter is less than 2.5 percent. Thus a pearl measuring 10 millimeters can have up to 0.25 millimeter of variance, and a pearl measuring 20 millimeters can have up to 0.5 millimeter of variance.

On the left is what Autore would classify as a round pearl. The pearl on the right is considered near round because the difference between diameter A and diameter B is more than 2.5 percent. *Images © Autore Pearls Pty. Ltd.*

Drop Shapes

Drop pearls are always longer than their horizontal axis. They include teardrop, oval and egg shapes, as well as the more unusual semi-drop and cone shapes.

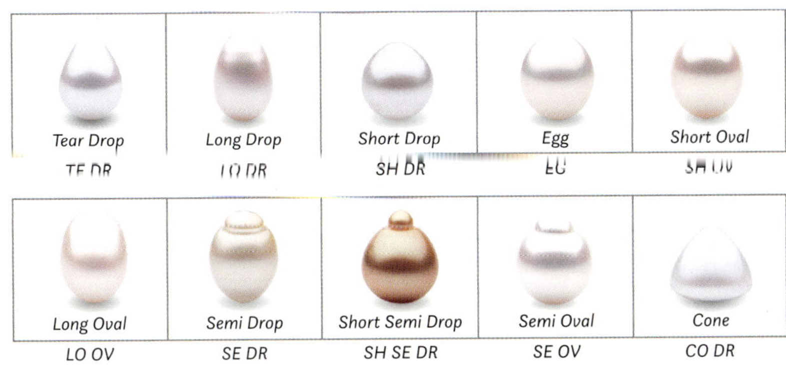

Examples of drop shapes.
Images © Autore Pearls Pty. Ltd.

Button Shapes

The vertical axis of a button pearl is always shorter than its horizontal axis. As with the drop-shape category, buttons can vary dramatically in appearance. High-button pearls can be similar to near-round pearls in appearance.

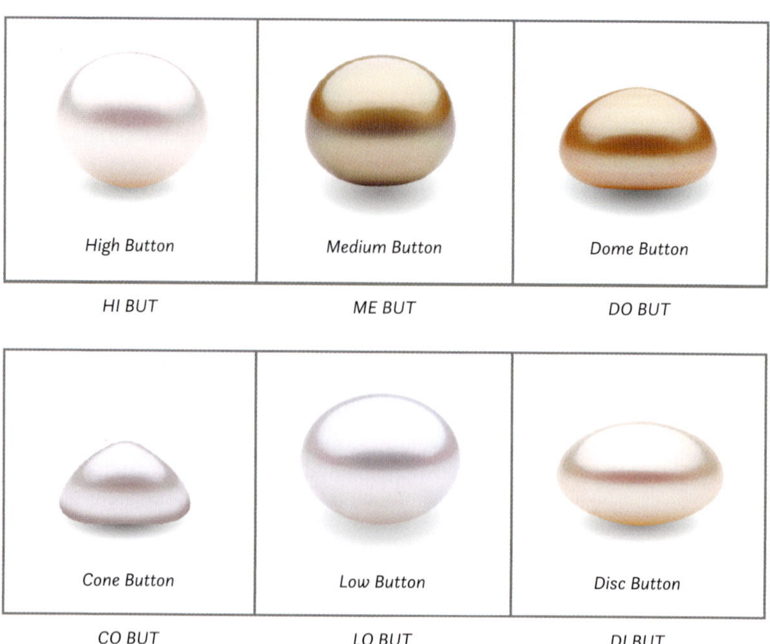

Examples of button shapes.
Images © Autore Pearls Pty. Ltd.

Baroque Shapes

Baroque pearls are the most unusual South Sea pearls produced by the *Pinctada maxima* oyster. They are irregular or free-form in shape, and occasionally they have what are called "fish tails." If one side of a baroque pearl is symmetrical or round, the pearl is classified as semi-baroque.

Examples of baroque shapes.
Images © Autore Pearls Pty. Ltd.

Circle Pearls

Pearls with one or more parallel grooves around the circumference are called circle or circled pearls. Any shape can be classified as a circle if rings or grooves are present. The only exception is when a drop pearl has a ring around its apex, in which case it is classified as a semi-drop. Autore identifies three categories of circle pearls: (1) one or two grooves; (2) three or more grooves but still good reflection; and (3) multiple grooves, distorting reflection.

Examples of circle pearls of different categories. *Images © Autore Pearls Pty. Ltd.*

Other Shapes

Shapes that are different from the preceding ones can be created by using a bead nucleus with a different, non-round shape. For example, heart-shaped beads can create heart-shaped pearls.

Heart-shaped cultured pearls in a necklace by the Japanese company Shinyu Inc., which was displayed at the 2024 Hong Kong International Diamond, Gem, and Pearl Show. *Photo © Renée Newman.*

As previously mentioned, round is the highest-priced shape if all other factors are similar, followed by near round, drop, button, baroque and circle. However, luster, color, size and surface quality may impact the price more than the pearl's shape.

No matter what their shape, South Sea pearls are generally sold undrilled if they are not on a strand. This allows the buyer to determine how the pearls will be used or mounted. Be willing to compromise on shape; this may be necessary because of the high price and limited availability of round South Sea pearls.

Color

As is the case with akoya pearls, color choice should be based on what looks best on the person who will be wearing the pearls. Color varies depending on which variety of *Pinctada maxima* oyster the pearl comes from—silver-lipped or gold-lipped. The silver-lipped oyster, the principal variety found in Australia, tends to produce silvery white pearls,

The ranges of South Sea pearl colors.
Images © Autore Pearls Pty. Ltd.

WHITE RANGE

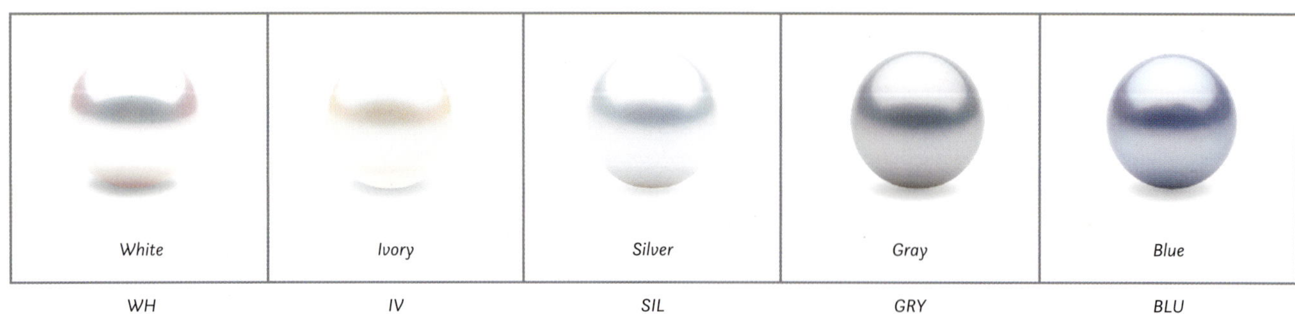

YELLOW RANGE

which Autore classifies as white, ivory, silver or blue. The gold-lipped variety, which is more commonly found in countries such as Indonesia, Thailand and the Philippines, is more likely to produce gold, yellow or cream-colored pearls.

The body color of South Sea pearls is judged similarly to that of akoya pearls. Usually white pearls are more valued than yellowish and cream-colored ones, but there is one major exception. Pearls with a strong natural golden color can sell for as much and even more than white pearls of the same size and quality. The more saturated the color, the more valuable the pearl—provided the color is natural. Overtones and iridescence are also very desirable in South Sea pearls. For white pearls, pink and silver overtones are more highly valued than bluish-gray and greenish overtones. Bluish overtones, however, are appreciated if they are combined with pink.

When buying golden South Sea pearls, be sure to ask if the color is natural. Many of them are artificially colored, especially those that exhibit a strong gold or grayish gold. If the color is natural, have it written on the sales receipt. It is also advisable to have expensive pearls checked by a gem laboratory. Chapter 11 has a more detailed discussion of pearl treatments.

Size

South Sea pearls generally range in size from 9 to 20 millimeters. The size of semi-round pearls is determined by their average diameter or by the smallest measurement of diameter. The size of baroque pearls is most accurately represented by stating the length, width and height; however, sometimes only the two largest measurements are given. Baroque pearls can have greater length measurements than round ones. As would be expected, the larger the pearl, the greater its value, all other factors being equal.

The size of a cultured pearl is determined primarily by the size of its bead nucleus. The bigger the oyster, the bigger the bead it can accept and the bigger the pearl it can grow. Consequently, small Japanese oysters, which measure 8 centimeters (3.15 inches) across, produce smaller pearls than the South Sea silver-lipped and gold-lipped oysters, which can measure 30 centimeters (12 inches) across. Black-lipped *Pinctada margaritifera* oysters, which also produce white pearls, grow up to about 20 centimeters (8 inches) across and usually produce a pearl between the size of those from silver-lipped and akoya oysters.

South Sea pearl strands are not normally sold in half-millimeter increments the way akoya pearls are. They are usually graduated, with larger pearls in the center and smaller ones on the ends, because it is very difficult to find matched South Sea pearls of just one size. (Also, it is not practical to place large pearls at the back of the neck, where they will not necessarily be seen.) When shopping for strands of South Sea pearls, it is best to specify a size range. The most typical Australian South Sea strand is probably 11 to 13 or 14 millimeters in length. Dealers can create special strand layouts, such as 12 to 13 millimeters or 14 to 15 millimeters, on request. But these are costly, and a deposit may be required before the dealer will make up the strand.

Nacre Thickness

Big pearls do not necessarily have thick nacre. As with akoya pearls, the nacre thickness of cultured South Sea pearls has decreased from what it was in the 1970s. Judging from the standards published by producers of black pearls, South Sea pearls today should have a nacre thickness of at least 1 millimeter of the radius. One millimeter may sound thick compared to the minimum standard suggested for akoya pearls—0.4 millimeter per side—but keep in mind that akoya pearls have a finer-grained nacre than South Sea pearls, and they are smaller. A 0.5 millimeter thickness on a 6 millimeter akoya pearl is one-sixth of its radius, but so is a 1 millimeter thickness on a 12 millimeter South Sea pearl. Therefore it is reasonable for buyers to expect nacre at least 1 millimeter thick on South Sea pearls, especially considering their high cost.

Thin nacre is not as easily detected in South Sea pearls as it is in akoya pearls. Because of the thicker nacre, the shell layers of the bead do not show up as well with transmitted light, and it is harder to see the bead nucleus through the drill hole. In addition, these pearls are often already mounted in jewelry, so the drill holes may not be visible. Experienced dealers can often detect thin nacre by evaluating the quality of the luster. South Sea pearls with thin nacre may have a shiny surface, but they will not have a deep, lustrous glow. To avoid buying South Sea pearls with nacre that is too thin, you should select pearls with a good luster and deal with jewelers who consider nacre thickness important.

≈

Like all other pearls, those from the South Seas come in a wide range of qualities and prices. Some sell for more than $2,000 each and others may sell for just $20. The price factors discussed above are what determine the value. For example, if you take a $2,000 South Sea pearl, make it smaller, add lots of flaws, give it a baroque shape, color it yellow and give it a dull, drab luster, what is the result? A $20 South Sea pearl!

6

Black Pearls

Black pearls are not necessarily black. They often have a light to very dark gray body color, and they may also look green, pink, lavender, blue or brown. It is the oyster source, not the pearl color, that determines whether pearls are called black pearls. *Black pearl* is simply a generic term used in the trade that refers to pearls from these mollusks:

- black-lipped pearl oysters (*Pinctada margaritifera*), found in the western to central Pacific Ocean and the Indian Ocean
- Panamic black-lipped pearl oysters (*Pinctada mazatlanica*), also called Mexican black-lipped oysters, found in the eastern Pacific Ocean between Baja California and Peru
- rainbow-lipped pearl oysters (*Pteria sterna*), found in the eastern Pacific Ocean between Baja California and Peru
- pen shell clams (*Atrina rigida* or *Atrina vexillum*). The pearls from these mollusks may be either nacreous or non-nacreous. *Atrina* mollusks are found in various areas, including the Indo-Pacific, the Gulf of California, the Mediterranean and the Atlantic coast.

SOURCES OF BLACK PEARLS

Some people mistakenly identify all black pearls as Tahitian pearls. However, Tahitian pearls are found only in French Polynesia and are marketed in Tahiti. Pearls from the Cook Islands are Cook Island pearls, not Tahitian pearls. Black pearls from Fiji are called Fijian pearls. Black pearls from the Gulf of California can be called La Paz, Mexican, Baja

Tahitian cultured pearls from the black-lipped *Pinctada margaritifera* oyster, in necklaces from Robert Wan. *Photo courtesy of Robert Wan.*

California or Sea of Cortez pearls, or simply black pearls. Some sellers call black pearls from the rainbow-lipped *Pteria sterna* oyster "rainbow pearls" because of their natural rainbow-like colors. Baja California pearls from the *Atrina rigida* clam are called pen pearls.

French Polynesia

French Polynesia comprises 118 islands and atolls spread over an area of open ocean about the size of Western Europe. Tahiti is its commercial and political hub, so Polynesian pearls are referred to as Tahitian pearls.

The first European to land on Tahiti was the English explorer Samuel Wallis (1728–95) in 1767, followed by the French captain Louis Antoine de Bougainville (1729–1811) in 1768. Soon afterward, the trade in natural pearls and especially mother-of-pearl from the black-lipped *Pinctada margaritifera* oyster developed quickly. According to *Black Pearls of Tahiti*, by Jean-Pierre Lintilhac, initially a person had only to stand waist-deep in the water to pick up pearl oysters, but they gradually became scarce. Even though the government started regulating oyster and pearl fishing in 1860, natural black pearls had almost disappeared a century later; only four or five natural pearls were found in all of French Polynesia in 1960.

An overhead view of Marutea Sud, an atoll in French Polynesia. The biodiversity of its pure lagoon makes it an ideal place to cultivate high-quality Tahitian pearls. *Photo courtesy of Robert Wan.*

Robert Wan selecting pearls for one of his Tahitian cultured pearl necklaces. *Photo courtesy of Robert Wan.*

In 1962 Jean-Marie Domard, a veterinarian in charge of the Ranching and Fisheries Service of Polynesia, brought in a Japanese technician to graft 5,000 black-lipped oysters. Four years later, more than 1,000 cultured pearls were harvested. Nobody would have predicted then that in only a few decades Tahitian cultured pearls would become French Polynesia's most important export.

Several additional farms began appearing in the late 1960s and early 1970s. Early pearling pioneers included Robert Wan, Jean-Claude Brouillet, Jacques Branellec and Jacques and Hubert Rosenthal. Robert Wan was able to sell his entire first harvest of black pearls to the grandson of Kokichi Mikimoto. Thereafter, Wan continued to supply the Japanese market with Tahitian cultured black pearls.

In 1973 Jean-Claude Brouillet met the American pearl dealer Salvador Assael in Saint-Tropez, France. After learning about Assael's expertise in South Sea pearls, Brouillet asked Assael to show some of his Tahitian cultured pearls to his high-end clientele. Eventually Assael partnered with Brouillet to buy several pearl farms and shells. In 1978 he showed a strand of newly cultivated Tahitian pearls to Harry Winston in New York and challenged him to sell it. Winston sold that strand within a week, and later quickly sold the rest of the fine pearls of that harvest. That inspired Assael to launch a successful media blitz, announcing "A new gem is

Tahitian cultured pearls of various body colors from the black-lipped oyster. *Pearls and photo courtesy of Robert Wan.*

born" and describing the pearls as the ultimate luxury product. Soon the finest jewelry houses in the world, including Cartier, Bulgari, Tiffany & Co. and Van Cleef & Arpels, carried Tahitian pearl jewelry. The pearls were elevated to the status of the most valuable cultured pearls, with one strand selling for $500,000.

In 1984 Brouillet sold the Marutea Sud atoll, which held his pearl-farming operation, to Robert Wan, his main competitor. This allowed Wan to expand his business and become French Polynesia's largest producer of Tahitian cultured pearls. It also meant that he was able to add to his base of Japanese customers through access to Assael and the American market. Wan's success with pearls inspired him to establish in Tahiti the world's only museum dedicated to pearls.

The average size range for Tahitian cultured pearls is about 8 to 13 millimeters, but some have been as small as 6 millimeters. The largest one, measuring 26 millimeters, is in the Robert Wan Pearl Museum in Papeete, Tahiti.

Before 2000, Tahitian pearls generally had body colors of light gray to black, greenish black and brownish black with varying overtones, such as pink, green and blue. However, over the years techniques were developed to cultivate Tahitian pearls in black-lipped oysters with other natural body colors, including yellow and white. The choice of the mantle tissue graft plays an important role in determining pearl color.

A technician inserting a shell-bead nucleus into a black-lipped oyster during the grafting process. *Photo courtesy of Robert Wan.*

Multicolored Tahitian strands have become quite popular. Designers like to use them for one-of-a-kind jewelry, and pearl collectors buy them to increase the variety and size of their collections. Another benefit is that multicolored strands are usually more affordable than matched strands, because finding well-matched pearls of high quality is more

Divers check on the grafted oysters after they have been placed in panel nets in the lagoon to secure them as they grow and develop pearls. These nets allow for easy inspection and provide a safe environment, keeping the oysters separated and preventing them from being eaten by fish. *Photo courtesy of Robert Wan.*

time-consuming. The most expensive Tahitian pearls have a dark gray to green body color with strong pink and green overtones. Finding matches for them is a challenge, especially when they are larger than average, so high-quality large pearls are used most often for pendants, earrings and brooches.

Fiji

The Fijian black-lipped pearl oyster, *Pinctada margaritifera typica*, is a subspecies of the oyster used in French Polynesia; it has a wider spectrum of mother-of-pearl hues on the lip of the interior shell. As a result, Fijian cultured pearls tend to be more colorful than Tahitian pearls and are considered a separate category. The colors are natural and not the result of any treatments.

The first Fijian cultured pearls were produced in the 1960s by Japanese pearl technicians Yasuharo Tokito and Dr. Koji Wada, in Namarai Bay on the large island of Viti Levu. Wada moved on to French Polynesia, but Tokito remained and became known as the father of the Fijian pearl industry. He shared his knowledge with other pearl farmers, including Justin Hunter, who founded Fiji's largest pearl farm, J. Hunter Pearls Fiji, in 1999.

Hunter relies primarily on his hatchery-produced spats, which is the name given to pearl mollusk larvae after they permanently attach to a surface. Wild spat collection is less reliable, as some seasons yield only a handful while others may provide an abundance. To ensure a consistent supply, J. Hunter uses both hatchery-produced and wild spats. When

A colorful J. Hunter Pearls Fiji cultured pearl necklace by Assael. *Photo courtesy of Assael.*

A cultured Fijian pearl shell blister in a ring by Assael. *Photo courtesy of Assael.*

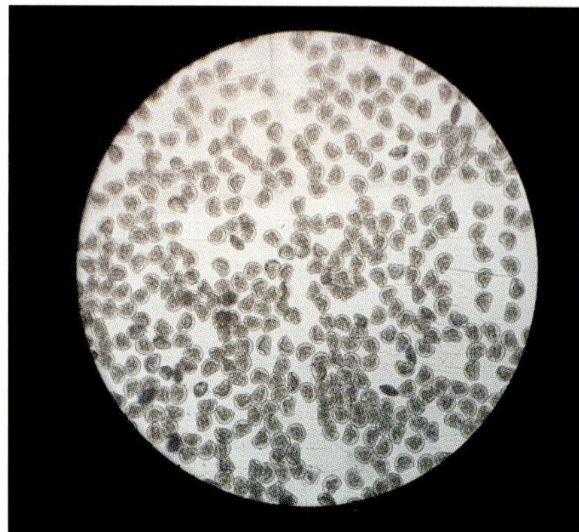

Fijian black-lipped pearl oyster larvae that are several days old, viewed through a microscope in the J. Hunter Pearls hatchery. *Photo courtesy of J. Hunter Pearls Fiji.*

The J. Hunter Pearls crew moving panel nets with oysters from their farm site to their land-based seeding shed in Savusavu, Vanua Levu. There the oysters will be implanted by the company's technicians before being returned to the pearl farm. *Photo courtesy of J. Hunter Pearls Fiji.*

the oysters are around 24 to 30 months old, they are implanted with a shell-bead nucleus. After about 15 to 18 months the pearl is extracted; then the same oyster is reseeded to grow a bigger pearl.

Cook Island cultured pearls. *Necklaces, earrings and photo courtesy of Paka's Pearls.*

Cook Islands

Natural pearls from the black-lipped *Pinctada margaritifera* oyster have been harvested in the Cook Islands since the 1890s, in the lagoons of Manihiki and Penrhyn (Tongareva). After trials during the 1970s, the first commercial pearl farms were established in the northern atoll of Manihiki in the 1980s. Today most Cook Islands black pearls are produced there by about 30 pearl farms.

Cook Islands pearls are generally cultured to develop to between 9 and 14 millimeters, but occasionally sizes will reach 21 millimeters. None of the pearls is artificially enhanced, nor are the oysters genetically engineered in any way. Their pearls pass through human hands rather than machines on every step of their journey from the shell into jewelry.

Mexico

Black pearls were first spotted by Europeans in present-day Mexico in 1533, when Spanish captain Fortún Jiménez (d. 1533) landed in Baja California and saw local Indigenous people wearing dark pearls. Two years later, in 1535, Hernán Cortés landed north of La Paz and noticed individuals wearing necklaces with pearls of different colors. For the next 400 years, natural black pearls from the *Pinctada mazatlanica* and rainbow-lipped *Pteria*

Left: Natural Baja California pearls and diamonds in a butterfly brooch designed by Collector Fine Jewelry/Pala International. *Photo by Mia Dixon.*

Right: Natural *Pinctada mazatlanica* pearls from the Gulf of California. *Photo by Douglas McLaurin.*

sterna oysters were an important export. In the late 1700s and early 1800s, La Paz became the black pearl center of the world. Empress Eugénie of France helped increase the popularity of the pearls in Europe when she wore a necklace of black pearls from Mexico.

Unfortunately, overfishing in the Gulf of California (also known as the Sea of Cortez) diminished natural pearl production in the area. To protect the oysters, the Mexican government banned the harvesting of natural oyster beds in 1939.

Pearl culturing in the Sea of Cortez began as a university research program in 1993, using the rainbow-lipped *Pteria sterna* oyster. It is found off the eastern Pacific coast, from Baja California to Peru. In warm El Niño years, it may also be present in California, but its presence there is not permanent. The pearls from this oyster have high luster and rainbow-like colors, so they are called "rainbow pearls," even though they are classified as black pearls. Their colors may be lavender, pink, red, blue, green, purple, silver, gold, black or brown, in varying shades and combinations; it is not unusual to see multiple colors on a single pearl.

Natural *Pteria sterna* rainbow pearls. *Photo by Douglas McLaurin.*

The first experimental round pearls were produced in 1996 at the Monterrey Institute of Technology in Guaymas, Mexico. Eventually the research program became a commercial operation, Perlas del Mar de Cortez. The company trademarked its products as Cortez Pearls, which now include whole and mabe saltwater cultured pearls from the rainbow-lipped *Pteria sterna* oyster that are cultured by Perlas del Mar de Cortez. The company is based in Bacochibampo Bay in the Sea of Cortez,

A strand of Cortez cultured whole pearls and loose mabe pearls from Kojima Pearls. *Photo by Sarah Canizzaro.*

near the city of Guaymas. Because of their rarity, Cortez Pearls are usually featured as individual items in jewelry. Fewer than 10 necklaces are produced each year, but they can be custom made.

Cortez round and baroque pearls range from 8 to 12 millimeters in diameter and have a good nacre thickness, since they are in the oyster for 20 to 24 months. Their natural counterparts are found in sizes from seed to 30 carats, but in Mexico they are traditionally counted as pearls only if they are bigger than 5 millimeters and of good quality. The rest are called *morralla*, which in Mexico means "spare change."

Although they may look similar, most cultured Cortez Pearls can be distinguished from cultured Tahitian pearls by their distinctive red to pink fluorescence under long-wave ultraviolet light, according to an article in the spring 2004 issue of *Gems & Gemology*. Cortez Pearls also show a greater range of natural iridescent colors, including some shades that are not exhibited by black pearls from other areas of the world. All pearls produced and sold by Perlas del Mar de Cortez are untreated and of natural color.

Under long-wave ultraviolet light, you can see the distinctive red fluorescence of the cultured *Pteria sterna* Cortez Pearl at the far right. Douglas McLaurin, the photographer, says that both natural and cultured *P. sterna* pearls react with the same red/pink fluorescence, but natural pearls seem to fluoresce more strongly. Also, the lighter the color of the pearl, the weaker the fluorescence (a light pink); darker pearls display a blood-red fluorescence. *Pearls courtesy Columbia Gem House; photo by Douglas McLaurin.*

The same pearls viewed under normal lighting. From left to right: a dyed black Chinese freshwater pearl; a white South Sea pearl; a Japanese akoya pearl; an artificially black akoya (dyed with silver nitrate); a Tahitian black pearl; a Mexican black pearl from a *Pinctada mazatlanica* oyster; and finally a Cortez Pearl from a *Pteria sterna* oyster. *Pearls courtesy Columbia Gem House; photo by Douglas McLaurin.*

Pen Pearls

Natural pen pearls from the Pinnidae family of mollusks are found worldwide and can be nacreous or non-nacreous. The nacreous pen pearls from the Gulf of California—from the *Atrina rigida* clam—are predominately black or gray with varying overtones such as green, magenta, blue, purple, lavender and so on. Non-nacreous pen pearls from the Gulf of California can be green, brown, yellow, orange or black, but they are not used much in jewelry because they tend to crack, since they are mostly protein. Natural pearls of any color and from any mollusk are rare.

Nacreous pen pearls set in earrings from Pacific Coast Pearls. *Photo by Gwendolyn Rankin.*

PRICE FACTORS

Black pearls are priced according to their luster, surface quality, shape, color, size and nacre thickness, as follows:

Luster

The higher the luster, the more valuable the pearl. Expect a higher luster from dark pearls than you would from white South Sea pearls. The best pearls are highly reflective. (See chapter 3 for tips on how to judge luster.)

Surface Quality

Surface blemishes can decrease the price of black pearls considerably, which is an advantage for consumers. A black pearl can often be mounted in a way that hides its imperfections when worn. It can also be faceted to remove blemishes.

If you select pearls that are mostly blemish free, you can enjoy one or more clean-looking pearls for a lower price. Remember that blemishes on single pearls tend to be more obvious than those in strands; it is normal for pearl strands to have some flaws.

A 13.5 mm faceted Tahitian cultured pearl ring with opal inlay, garnets and diamonds, by Mark Schneider. *Photo courtesy of Mark Schneider Design.*

Above: Drop, near-round and round Tahitian cultured pearls from King Plutarco Inc. Drops come in a wide range of shapes and sizes. The drops with the smoothest tops and most symmetrical form are usually priced the highest, all other factors being equal. Designers, however, often prefer unique, asymmetrical shapes. *Photo © Renée Newman.*

Below: A necklace featuring cultured Fijian circle pearls. *Necklace and photo from J. Hunter Pearls Fiji.*

Shape

Round and near-round shapes are the most expensive. Drop shapes are the next most expensive, followed by button shapes, which are shorter vertically, with a wider horizontal axis. The more symmetrical these shapes are, the higher their value. Baroque and circled pearls, with ring-like formations around them, are the least expensive. See chapter 5 for a more detailed description and images of these pearl shapes.

When you need to cut down on the price of a black pearl, shape is a good category on which to compromise. In fact, many designers and buyers would argue that baroque and circled pearls often make more interesting jewelry pieces than round pearls.

A peacock-colored Tahitian cultured pearl and emerald pendant by Matt Harris Designs. *Photo courtesy of Matt Harris Designs.*

Color

Most pearls from the black-lipped oyster have a black to light gray body color, but the color can also be brown, green, blue, pink, purple or, in extremely rare cases, white. The overtones, when present, tend to be green, pink, purple or blue. Yellowish-green overtones are described as pistachio-colored.

The way in which black pearl color is judged and described can vary depending on the dealer or lab describing it. Nevertheless, usually the darker and more intense the color of black pearls, the more valuable they are. The finest pearls display iridescent body colors and overtones.

Black pearls with a green body color and pink overtones—described as peacock-colored—are much prized. As a result, in May 2023 the Gemological Institute of America announced that it would add a comment to its reports using the trade color term "Peacock" for cultured pearls from the black-lipped oyster. A Peacock comment would be added free

Above: The natural color diversity of Tahitian cultured pearls. *Pearls and photo courtesy of Robert Wan.*

Below: Exceptionally rare Tahitian natural-color white pearls cultured in the black-lipped oyster by Kamoka Pearls. *Photo by Josh Humbert.*

of charge if the pearl had "a body color with a hue that contains green, of mid-to-strong saturation and mid-to-dark tone, and with moderate or stronger overtone (usually pink, but may be other hues) or orient."

The Pearl Science Lab of Japan uses different terminology for peacock pearls in its lab reports. The Lab's highest-quality designation for black-lipped oyster pearls is "Aurora Lagoon," which is used for pearls with a green outer ring and a pink-to-red inner hue. The name comes from the pearl's green color, like that of a Tahitian lagoon.

If you visit Asia or search the Internet, you may see strands labeled "Tahitian pearls" selling for $100 or even less. They are probably artificially colored akoya or freshwater pearls whose natural color was undesirable. Sellers are supposed to disclose that pearls have been dyed or otherwise treated, but not all do.

In French Polynesia pearl treatments are illegal. Tahitian pearls are attractive in their natural state and are only washed before being exported or set in jewelry. However, after Tahitian pearls have been exported, they may undergo luster and color treatments outside the country to make them appear more valuable than in their natural state. In other words, if you buy Tahitian pearls in French Polynesia, you are buying untreated pearls. Elsewhere, you should ask if the pearls are of natural color and luster and request that it be indicated on the receipt.

Size

Naturally, the bigger the black pearl, the more expensive it is. The average size range for Tahitian pearls is about 8 to 13 millimeters, but some are as small as 6 millimeters or as large as 20 millimeters. Some baroque black pearls may reach 25 to 30 millimeters in length. Size has a great impact on price. For example, a 1 millimeter increase in the size of a medium-quality pearl can raise its price by 100 to 200 percent.

At the retail level, cultured pearls tend to be described and priced according to their size in millimeters. However, weight may be used as an additional means of identifying them. This is the opposite of the case with natural pearls and round diamonds, where the price is based on their weight and measurements may also be used to help identify them.

On the wholesale level, large lots of pearls are sold according to their weight, which is usually measured in momme (1 momme = 3.75 grams = 18.75 carats). The pearls are graded into various categories and each category is assigned a per momme price.

Nacre Thickness

The thicker the nacre, the more valuable the pearl. Dr. Jean-Paul Lintilhac, the developer of two pearl farms in Tahiti, has recommended that black pearl nacre comprise at least 1 millimeter of the radius. The Tahitian government used to impose a minimum nacre thickness for all exported pearls of 0.8 millimeter, the depth expected from at least 18 months of growth. However, that requirement was dropped in 2017, so the only way to make sure your pearls have a thick layer of nacre is to have them X-rayed or to deal with reliable sellers.

It can be hard to understand why one pearl may cost $50, for example, and another may cost $500. But consider how the preceding factors can work together to lower the price. If a pearl costing $500 decreased a little in size, its price might drop 50 percent, to $250. Going from a very high to very low luster could make its price drop another 50 percent, to $125. If that pearl then acquired lots of flaws, its price would drop even further—down to $50 or less.

Pearl pricing is not as mathematically precise as portrayed in the preceding example. Nevertheless, the quality factors discussed can have a similar effect on any given pearl's price. It therefore pays to consider those factors as you are shopping and comparing prices.

7 Freshwater Pearls

Pearls that grow in mollusks living in lakes, ponds, rivers or streams are called freshwater pearls. Natural freshwater pearls have been found worldwide, but almost all cultured freshwater pearls are from China. Two mussel families produce freshwater pearls: the Margaritiferidae and the Unionidae, the latter of which is the largest family, with more than 600 species.

SOURCES OF FRESHWATER PEARLS

Europe

According to Elisabeth Strack, in the August 2023 issue of *Jewellery Business*, the only pearl-producing mussel of importance in Europe is *Margaritifera margaritifera*, also known as the European pearl mussel. This mollusk is listed as endangered, so pearl fishing in Europe today is prohibited. Overfishing and pollution from industry and agriculture contributed to the decline of European mussels. However, for centuries they were abundant in rivers and streams, and the pearls found in them became part of European culture and history.

Natural pearls have been found throughout Europe, but the major sources were Great Britain, Germany and Russia. According to the Roman historian Suetonius, pearls were one of the reasons for Julius Caesar's invasion of Britain in 55 BCE. Most of Great Britain's pearls were actually found in Scotland; the largest is said to be the Kellie pearl, which is set in the crown of Scotland, although its exact size is not known.

The second largest Scottish pearl is the 10.5 to 10.6 millimeter lustrous white Abernethy pearl, found in 1967 by Scotland's last pearl fisherman,

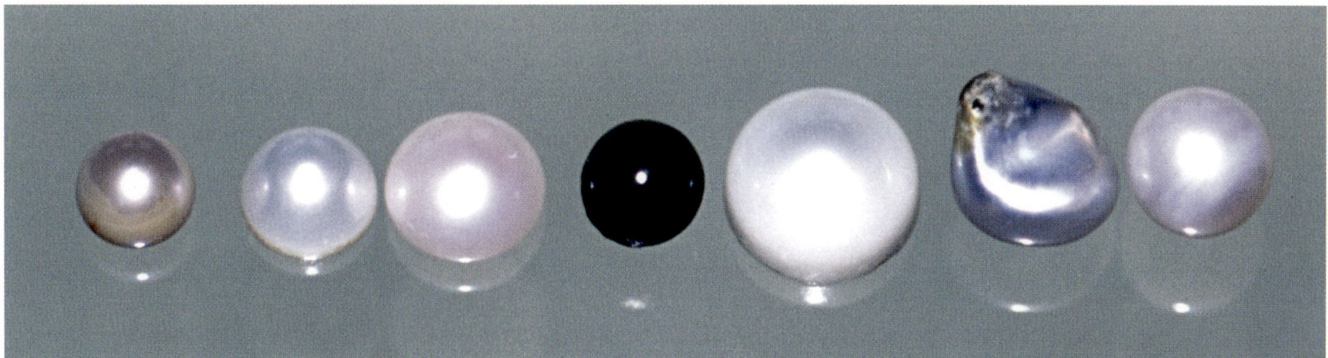

Scottish natural river pearls from *Margaritifera margaritifera* mussels. *Pearls and photo from Alan Hodgkinson.*

William (Bill) Abernethy. Considering that the average size of Scottish river pearls is between 3 and 4 millimeters, it is not surprising that the Abernethy pearl made headline news, then and in August 2024, when it was sold at a Lyon & Turnbull auction in Edinburgh for £93,951 (US$123,000), a record price for a Scottish freshwater pearl. Its beauty and the present-day rarity of natural Scottish pearls were key factors in the record price. In 1998 pearl fishing became illegal in Scotland.

The most important pearl-fishing areas in Germany were the streams of Bavaria and Saxony. The pearls occurred in a variety of colors, including white, gray, brown and black. In her 2006 book *Pearls*, Elisabeth Strack states that examples from Bavaria were still significant in the natural pearl market in 2006, but they were only old stock from Saxony. Strack notes that "it takes 20 to 25 years for a pearl of 4 mm to grow and 40 to 50 years for a pearl of 6 to 7 mm. The growth rate is 0.05 mm per year." Pearl fishing is no longer allowed in Germany.

A European freshwater *Margaritifera margaritifera* shell and the Abernethy pearl, which sold for £93,951 (US$123,000) at auction in August 2024. *Photo by Stewart Attwood, courtesy of Lyon & Turnbull Auctioneers.*

Almost every Russian church contains crosses, book covers and religious paintings decorated with river pearls from northern Russia. As early as the 10th century, Russian royalty wore dresses and head ornaments embroidered with them. Natural river pearls were an important part of the culture, especially from the 18th and 19th centuries until the Russian Revolution in 1917, when they started losing popularity. Pearl fishing in Russia was prohibited after the European pearl mussel was listed in 1996 as endangered on the International Union for Conservation of Nature (IUCN) Red List.

Natural pearls have also been found in Sweden, but that country is better known for being the home of the Swedish botanist and zoologist Carl Linnaeus (1707–78), who cultured the world's first round pearls in the mid-1700s, using the local freshwater mussel *Unio pictorum*. Some members of the trade would label his pearls cultured round blisters, because they grew between the shell and the mantle instead of within a

Examples of the round freshwater pearls Carl Linnaeus produced in the mid-1700s, by drilling a hole in a freshwater mussel and inserting a piece of limestone attached to a silver wire between the shell and the mantle tissue. The mussels were returned to the riverbed for five years to grow round cultured pearls. *Photo © Linnean Society of London.*

Carl Linnaeus, also known as Carl von Linné, was the "father of modern taxonomy," creating a uniform binomial system for classifying organisms. He is also the first person on record to culture round pearls, by modifying the Chinese method of creating blisters. *FineArt/Alamy Stock Photo.*

pearl sac and were attached to the shell at one spot. Nevertheless, Linnaeus's pearls were an important achievement.

Linnaeus is also noted for being the "father of modern taxonomy"; he formalized the binomial nomenclature system for organisms that is still widely used in the biological sciences. All the scientific names we've encountered in this book—such as *Pinctada fucata* for the akoya pearl oyster and *Pinctada maxima* for South Sea pearl oysters—are examples. He was also the first naturalist to place humans (*Homo sapiens*) in the animal kingdom. Because of his achievements, Linnaeus was ennobled by the King of Sweden and took the name Carl von Linné.

United States

All American pearl mussels belong to the freshwater Unionidae family, and most have been found in the northeastern states, Texas and the Mississippi River Valley and its tributaries. Unlike in Europe, pearl fishing still exists in America, but not nearly to the extent of the latter half of the 1800s. A pearl rush began in 1857 after Jacob Quackenbush found a 15 millimeter pink pearl in a New Jersey mussel and sold it to Tiffany & Co. for $1,500. Later that pearl was bought by Empress Eugénie, the wife of the French emperor, Napoleon III.

After the depletion of mussels in New Jersey, interest in pearling extended to Pennsylvania, Ohio, Texas and, in 1889, to the Mississippi River Valley in southwestern Wisconsin. Kunz and Stevenson describe the river pearls of Wisconsin as "remarkable for their beauty, luster, and diversified coloring and some lovely shades of pink, purple and especially metallic green."

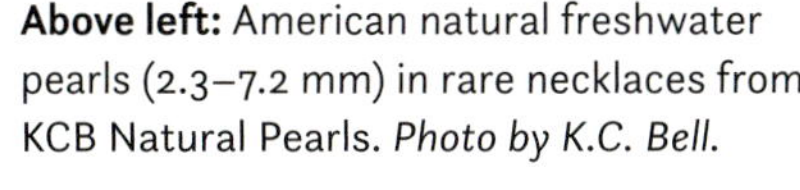

Above left: American natural freshwater pearls (2.3–7.2 mm) in rare necklaces from KCB Natural Pearls. *Photo by K.C. Bell.*

Above right: Natural Mississippi River pearls from the private collection of John Latendresse, in earrings by Paula Crevoshay. *Photo by Crevoshay Studio.*

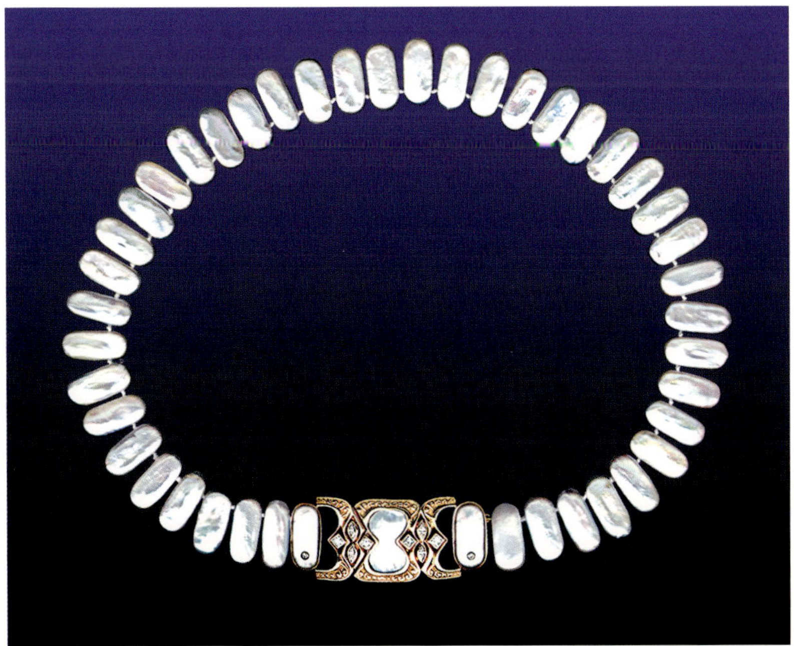

Necklace of American freshwater pearls cultured before 2001, accented with a diamond and mother-of-pearl 18-karat gold clasp. *Jewelry design © by Eve J. Alfillé; photo by Matthew Arden.*

Left: An American Arts and Crafts pin from the Pearl Society Collection, with natural Mississippi River pearls in various shades of pink to purple. *Photo by Matthew Arden.*

Right: Natural American freshwater pearl feathers and a gem-studded cultured American freshwater pearl in a brooch by A & Z Pearls. *Photo by John Parrish.*

During the late 1800s, American natural freshwater pearls were the main source of income for many U.S. jewelers, and they were the second most important pearls on the world market after those from the Persian Gulf. The introduction of cultured pearls eventually caused their value to plummet, as with other natural pearls, and American mussels became more sought after for their shell value and mother-of-pearl. Most cultured pearls contain a shell bead nucleus from an American mussel, and the mother-of-pearl was used to make buttons.

As described in chapter 1, in 1983 John Latendresse and his wife, Chessy, succeeded in harvesting their first bead-nucleated American freshwater pearl. By 1985 their American Pearl Company had become the first and only commercial producer of American freshwater cultured pearls. Their Tennessee pearl farm produced cultured pearls for retailers until 2000, when John passed away. Today the pearl farm is a tourist attraction called Birdsong Resort.

Japan

The Japanese are credited with being the first to successfully cultivate whole freshwater pearls on a commercial scale, at Lake Biwa, Japan's largest lake. The technical roots of cultivating whole freshwater pearls are attributed to Dr. Masayo Fujita, the "father of freshwater pearl cultivation," who worked for Mikimoto after 1916.

Biwa pearls initially had a mother-of-pearl bead nucleus and were first harvested in August 1925, according to Strack in *Pearls*. By the 1930s they

Japanese Lake Biwa cultured pearl clown brooch by A & Z Pearls. *Photo by John Parrish.*

were being sold overseas. Some merchants from India would buy Lake Biwa pearls from Fujita and then resell them for huge sums of money in the Middle East as highly valuable Persian Gulf pearls.

After World War II, Lake Biwa became known for its cultured baroque beadless freshwater pearls, which were produced by simply inserting a small graft of living mantle tissue from a donor mussel into a mollusk. Cultured Biwa beadless pearls were first sold to American GIs and Indian dealers, who assumed that they were natural.

Lake Biwa pearls were cultured in the *Hyriopsis schlegelii* mussel. In 1931 Dr. Fujita transported some of these mussels to Lake Kasumigaura, north of Tokyo—Japan's second-largest lake. By the early 1950s

The only remaining freshwater pearl farm in Japan: the Lake Kasumigaura pearl farm owned by Kiyoshi Yoneguchi. *Photo by Sarah Canizzaro.*

Japan Kasumi freshwater cultured pearls. The mussel is a crossbreed of *Hyriopsis cumingii* and *H. schlegelii*. *Necklace and shell from Kojima Pearl Company; photo by Sarah Canizzaro.*

the mussels were thriving and Japanese cultured freshwater pearls were being produced at Kasumigaura and marketed as cultured Biwa pearls.

The Biwa mussels had a high mortality rate because of water pollution caused by fertilizers and pesticides from agriculture. The need for stronger pearl-producing mussels prompted Lake Kasumigaura pearl farmers in the 1960s to crossbreed *Hyriopsis schlegelii* and *H. cumingii* to produce a *Hyriopsis* hybrid, according to a summer 2018 article in *Gems & Gemology*. This hybrid can grow larger and more lustrous cultured pearls in colors such as pink, purple, gold, orange and white, with a rainbow iridescence. A few of the farmers used the hybrid to produce round beaded pearls.

During the 1970s and early 1980s, freshwater pearl production in Japan employed thousands of people. However, according to Fuji Voll of Pacific Pearls, production ceased in 1985 because of water pollution, which killed the traditional Japanese mussels. Of the five operators active in the production of the pearls, only three resumed business in the 1990s. As of 2025, Kiyoshi Yoneguchi, of Lake Kasumigaura, was the only person still producing freshwater cultured pearls in Japan.

Pearls cultivated at Kasumigaura average in size from 11 to 16 millimeters and are called Japan Kasumi pearls. They command premium prices because of their rarity, strong iridescence, high luster and unusual provenance. More information about these and other freshwater pearls can be found at http://shop.pacificpearls.us.

Triangle sail mussel (*Hyriopsis cumingii*) shells. *Photo © Renée Newman.*

China

Very little has been published about natural freshwater pearls in China, but we know they were used for religious statues and reserved for people in power. In April 2010 a Qing Dynasty emperor's court necklace, consisting of a strand of 108 natural freshwater pearls and colored gem beads, sold for 67,860,000 HKD (US$8.66 million) at a Sotheby's Hong Kong auction.

China was the first country to culture blisters and assemble them into mabe pearls. Evidence of Buddha images overgrown with nacre dates to the Han Dynasty, around 100 BCE. Regular production of cultured freshwater Buddha blisters probably began as early as the 12th century.

The Chinese began to culture non-beaded whole freshwater pearls in 1962, when Professor Xiong Daren of the Fisheries Institute of Zhanjiang conducted experiments with tissue-grafting triangle sail pearl mussels (*Hyriopsis cumingii*), writes Strack in *Pearls*. His method was applied at freshwater farms near Suzhou, where scientists from Shanghai University supervised him. Three years later, the entire harvest was sold to the Japanese. Chinese freshwater pearls were marketed by Japan until the 1980s.

In the late 1970s and 1980s, cockscomb mussels (*Cristaria plicata*) became the preferred mollusks for cultivating Chinese freshwater pearls, because they were more abundant and cost less than triangle sail pearl

Changes in Chinese Freshwater Cultured Pearls from 1978 until the Early 2000s

Left: One of the first strands of natural-color pink freshwater pearls cultured in China (1978) with a neckpiece set with a tourmaline carved by Doug Klein. *Design © Fred & Kate Pearce; photo by Tommy Elder.*

Right: Rice-shaped freshwater pearls cultivated in China in the 1980s. *Necklace and earrings design © Fred & Kate Pearce; photo by Tommy Elder.*

Left: Necklace and earrings by Fred and Kate Pearce, with Chinese freshwater pearls cultured in the early 1990s. *Photo by Tommy Elder.*

Right: Natural-color 8–9 mm Chinese freshwater cultured pearls from the early 2000s with a neckpiece of drusy quartz carved by Dieter Lorenz. *Design © 2003 Fred & Kate Pearce; photo by Ralph Gabriner.*

Left: A Chinese freshwater pearl farm in Zhuji in 2008. The capped empty green soda bottles were used as indicators for where the mussels were located. *Photo © Renée Newman.*

Below left: Three mussels per net pouch during the three-to-seven-year growth period. *Photo © by Renée Newman.*

A pearl farmer holding a mussel from the Zhuji pearl farm. *Photo © Renée Newman.*

mussels. However, the pearls they produced were usually wrinkled and often looked like Rice Krispies cereal.

In the 1990s, Chinese pearl farmers switched back to triangle sail mussels (*Hyriopsis cumingii*), which produced fewer but smoother and rounder pearls. The use of younger, thinner pieces of mantle tissue for grafts that could be rolled into a ball also helped produce more round and near-round freshwater cultured pearls, according to a summer 2001 article in *Gems & Gemology*. Size as well as quality improved during the 1990s. Longer cultivation periods—four to six years instead of two to three—helped increase the size of beadless freshwater cultured pearls to more than 8 millimeters instead of the average 4 to 7 millimeters. As

A sorting room at the Grace Pearl Factory in Zhuji in 2008. New machines can sort three pearls per second, based on their color, shape and surface quality. *Photo © Renée Newman.*

Workers at the Grace Pearl Factory select quality pearls and string them. *Photo © Renée Newman.*

noted in the summer 2007 issue of *Gems & Gemology,* improvements in quality continued into the late 1990s as Chinese researchers imported Japanese pearl mussels (*Hyriopsis schlegelii*) and crossbred them with native triangle sail mussels (*H. cumingii*).

Today almost all freshwater pearls are cultured in China. Even though they are beginning to be cultured in India, freshwater pearls sold at gem shows and in jewelry stores are assumed to be Chinese cultured freshwater pearls unless otherwise stated. Even those identified as Biwa or Kasumi pearls have usually been cultured in China, which is why freshwater pearls cultured in Japan are identified by their sellers as "Japanese Biwa" or "Japan Kasumi" cultured pearls.

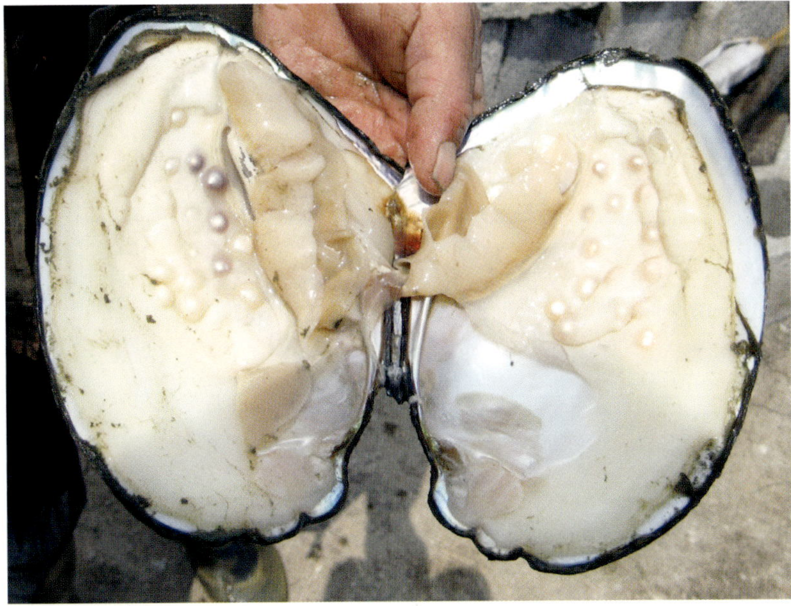

Beadless freshwater pearls embedded in the mantle tissue of a newly opened mussel in the first harvest. *Photo © Renée Newman.*

The same mantle-grown pearls after they have been removed from the mussel and rinsed in water. *Photo © Renée Newman.*

Types of Chinese Freshwater Cultured Pearls

Mantle-Grown Beadless Pearls

A beadless mantle-grown pearl is produced by simply inserting a piece of mantle tissue from a donor mussel into a small incision in the mantle of a live mussel. The mantle is a membranous tissue that secretes nacre and lines the inner surface of mollusk shells. Mantle cells can form a small pocket—a pearl sac—within which they continue to secrete nacre. The pearl sac grows over time through cell division; in this way, the pearl also grows. More than 30 pearls of various colors and sizes can form in the same mussel when it is implanted with multiple pieces of mantle tissue. Prior to 2000, almost all Chinese freshwater pearls were cultivated by this method.

Left: Mantle-grown coin pearls of various shapes with a flat shell nucleus in the first harvest, produced between 2000 and 2004. *Pearls and photo from Shogun Pearls.*

Right: Lightweight coin pearls from Fuji Voll of Pacific Pearls. The broken pearl in the bottom right corner grew around a textured piece of imitation leather. *Photo by Marcia Fentress.*

Mantle-grown beadless second-harvest pearls, also known as petal pearls, from Sea Hunt Pearls. *Photo by Lee Carraher.*

Mantle-Grown Beaded (Coin) Pearls

To create a "coin" pearl in the first harvest of a mussel, a flat bead nucleus is implanted along with a piece of donor tissue into the mantle of a live mussel and left for one to four years. The flat nuclei come in a variety of shapes, including round, square, oval, star, drop, rectangular and diamond. Usually the nuclei are made of shell, but plastic can be used to create lightweight pearls (because they are so light, some vendors misidentify them as non-nucleated coin pearls). Large quantities of coin pearls appeared at gem shows in the early 2000s.

Mantle-Grown Beadless Second-Harvest (Petal) Pearls

After a coin pearl is harvested, the live mussel can be returned to the water. Within the empty sac of the coin pearl, another pearl may grow without undergoing a grafting process. It is usually a thinner pearl, called a petal, second-harvest, second-generation, reborn or keshi-type pearl. These beadless second-harvest freshwater pearls became available in the early 2000s.

Since the pearl grows spontaneously, without the insertion of a piece of mantle tissue or bead nucleus, some freshwater pearl sellers called them keshis or keshi-type pearls, to differentiate them from other freshwater cultured pearls. However, in 2010 the World Jewellery Confederation (CIBJO) defined *keshi* as a trade term for a beadless cultured pearl formed accidentally or intentionally by human intervention in marine (saltwater) pearl oysters.

Cultured freshwater fireball pearl necklace from King's Ransom. *Photo by Betty Sue King.*

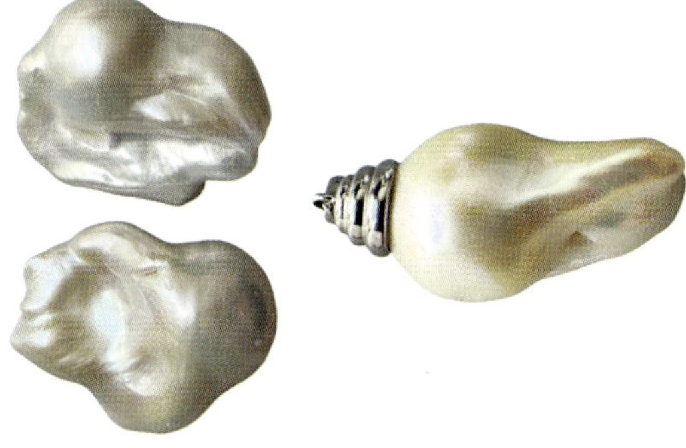

South Sea cultured pearls that resemble some freshwater cultured fireballs. *Photo by Sarah Senzer.*

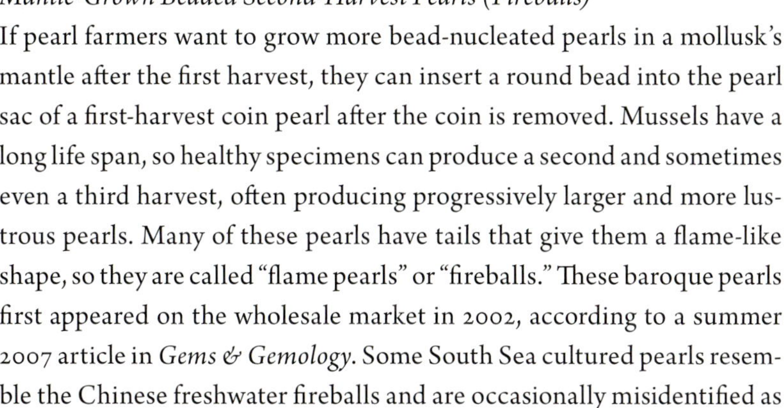

Mantle-Grown Beaded Second-Harvest Pearls (Fireballs)

If pearl farmers want to grow more bead-nucleated pearls in a mollusk's mantle after the first harvest, they can insert a round bead into the pearl sac of a first-harvest coin pearl after the coin is removed. Mussels have a long life span, so healthy specimens can produce a second and sometimes even a third harvest, often producing progressively larger and more lustrous pearls. Many of these pearls have tails that give them a flame-like shape, so they are called "flame pearls" or "fireballs." These baroque pearls first appeared on the wholesale market in 2002, according to a summer 2007 article in *Gems & Gemology*. Some South Sea cultured pearls resemble the Chinese freshwater fireballs and are occasionally misidentified as freshwater pearls.

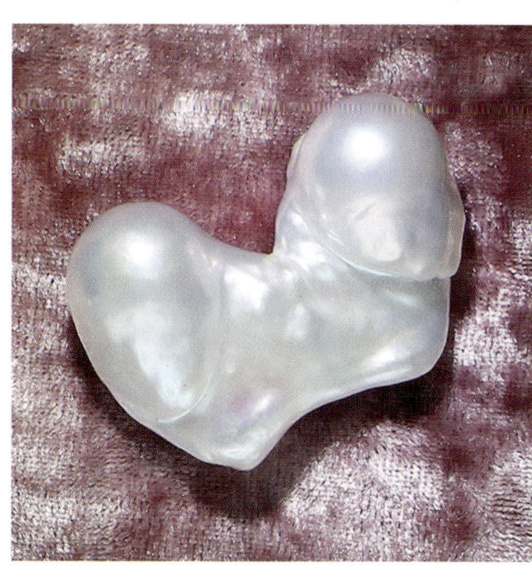

"Dolly Parton bustier" double fireball cultured pearl from King's Ransom, measuring 40 by 15 by 15 mm. *Photo by Betty Sue King.*

Left: Gonad-grown beaded (Edison) pearls measuring 11 to 14 mm, from King's Ransom. *Photo by John Parrish.*

Right: Cultured baby Edison pearls measuring 3 to 3.5 mm, from King's Ransom. *Photo by Betty Sue King.*

Gonad-Grown Beaded (Edison, Ming, AK Freshwater) Pearls

Pearl technicians can produce round pearls without tails by implanting a piece of mantle tissue and a bead nucleus directly into the gonad (sex organ) of the mussel instead of into the connective tissue of its mantle. This is the method used to cultivate saltwater and Japanese Biwa nucleated pearls, and it is surgically more demanding than the method used for cultivating flame pearls. Fuji Voll of Pacific Pearls calls these gonad-grown beaded Chinese pearls "in-body bead-nucleated pearls." He introduced them to the trade in 2008 at the Tucson Gem Show. His pearls were large, lustrous, nearly round and without tails, and textured like Japanese Kasumi cultured pearls.

Gonad-grown beaded pearls were gradually improved and after 2010 began to look smoother. Grace Pearl introduced these new, smooth beaded freshwater pearls under the brand name Edison. The company said that being able to produce such large, round, flawless and lustrous freshwater pearls was as miraculous as the inventions of Thomas Edison, so they decided to name them after him. Gonad-grown beaded pearls have also been sold under the brand name Ming. These pearls are larger than beadless pearls, usually at least 10 millimeters, like South Sea pearls. Some are more than 20 millimeters in size.

Small beaded freshwater pearls grown like akoya pearls became available in 2022. Since the white strands look like akoya cultured pearls and are grown in the same way, some sellers call them "AK" freshwater pearls. King's Ransom calls them "baby Edison" pearls. They range in size from 2 to 10 millimeters. According to the pearl wholesaler Eusharon, it normally takes around one or two years to cultivate AK freshwater beaded pearls, and each mussel can produce about 8 to 12 pearls. The nucleus of the pearl is small

Chinese beaded freshwater pearls combined with cultured Australian South Sea, Tahitian and Indonesian golden pearls and diamonds create this Aurora Collection necklace by Yoko London. *Photo courtesy of Yoko London.*

Left: Hollow soufflé cultured freshwater pearls from Pearl Paradise. *Photo by Jeremy Shepherd.*

Below: Soufflé cultured pearls carved out and lined with reclaimed emeralds in Pearl Geode earrings by Hisano Shepherd. *Photo by Hisano Shepherd.*

and the nacre is said to be very thick (more than 2 millimeters). During the COVID-19 shutdown, akoya cultured pearls were in short supply, so these new, small beaded pearls were a welcome addition to the pearl market.

After large, round pink and purple freshwater beaded pearls appeared on the market, designers started adding them to South Sea and Tahitian pearl pieces to create impressive and even more colorful pearl jewelry.

In January 2010 Jack Lynch of Sea Hunt Pearls announced a new type of Chinese freshwater pearl, which is nucleated with a hard piece of dried pond mud. As the pearl forms, water seeps into the area around the nucleus and dissolves the hardened mud. When the pearl is drilled, liquid drains out, leaving a hollow area and thus creating a lightweight pearl ideal for earrings. The walls of the pearl are very thick and stable. These hollow pearls are called soufflé or lost-nucleus pearls. They tend to be very large and often exhibit a metallic luster. The hollow nature of soufflé cultured pearls has led to new possibilities for jewelry design. One designer in Los Angeles, Hisano Shepherd, slices and carves the pearls to create a line of jewelry called Pearl Geodes.

The chart below summarizes the various types of cultured freshwater pearls.

LIMITED COMBINATIONS FOR CULTURING FRESHWATER WHOLE PEARLS		
Mantle-grown	beadless	Biwa, U.S., Chinese freshwater pearls
Mantle-grown	beaded*	Chinese freshwater coin, round pearls
Mantle-grown second-harvest	beadless	"petal pearls," "freshwater keshi," "reborn pearls," "second-harvest pearls"
Mantle-grown second-harvest	beaded	"flame pearls," "fireballs"
Gonad-grown	beadless	probably sold together with second-harvest beadless pearls and/or first-harvest mantle-grown beadless pearls
Gonad-grown	beaded	Edison and Ming cultured pearls; the first Biwa pearls and Japan Kasumi cultured pearls

**"Beaded" means containing a solid bead nucleus, usually made of shell, but it can also be an inexpensive cultured freshwater pearl. Adapted from a chart by Prof. Dr. H.A. Hänni © GemExpert.*

PRICE FACTORS

The grading of freshwater pearls is more variable than that of saltwater pearls. Nevertheless, there is agreement about certain price factors. Freshwater pearls are generally valued according to the following criteria: luster, shape, smoothness, surface quality, color, size and nacre thickness.

Luster

The higher and more even the luster, the greater the value of the pearl. Low-quality freshwater pearls may seem lustrous to a layperson because often part of their surface is very shiny. However, if some areas of the pearls look milky, chalky or dull, they are considered to have a low luster. In high-quality freshwater pearls, there is an evenly distributed luster and high contrast between the light and dark areas.

When judging freshwater pearls for luster, examine them on a white background and be sure to roll them so you can see their entire surface area. If possible, compare strands of different qualities. It is important that your eye become sensitive to luster variations, because luster is one of the most important determinants of value in pearls of all types.

Shape

Usually, the rounder a pearl is, the greater its value. Good symmetry can also make a shape more valuable. Large, round gonad-grown beaded

One-of-a-kind free-form freshwater pearl brooch by Barbara Heinrich, with 18-karat gold hammered petals and bezel-set diamonds. *Photo by Tim Callahan.*

Chinese near-round beadless cultured freshwater pearls (top), which resemble the strand of round beaded saltwater akoya pearls (bottom). But the freshwater pearls cost much less. *Photo © Renée Newman.*

pearls are the most expensive type of freshwater pearl. High-quality baroque (free-form) shapes are in demand among designers who want to create distinctive, one-of-a-kind jewelry.

Smoothness

The smoother the pearl, the more valuable it is. However, even though bumpy, wrinkled, textured surfaces can lower the value of freshwater pearls, the bumps and wrinkles are not considered flaws. Consequently, here smoothness is treated as a separate category from surface quality. An advantage of Japan Kasumi pearls with bumpy, wrinkled surfaces is that they often have stronger colors than pearls with smooth surfaces.

Surface Quality

Cracks and obvious blemishes such as discoloration, pits and cavities can considerably decrease the value of a pearl, especially if it is otherwise of high quality. Flaws in baroque pearls tend to be less noticeable and therefore less consequential than those in smooth, symmetrical pearls.

Color

Body color does not affect the price of freshwater pearls as much as it does that of saltwater pearls. When freshwater-pearl dealers are asked to specify the most valued body colors, they give various answers, but they generally agree that deep, intense colors such as dark purple can command premium prices and that natural color is more valued than treated colors. Freshwater pearls of all types come in a variety of natural body colors, including white, pink, purple, lavender, orange and yellow. Some

Various colors of gonad-grown beaded Edison pearls measuring 10–11.3 mm, from King's Ransom. *Photo by Betty Sue King.*

pearls are even bicolored. Since the color grading of freshwater pearls is so variable, the best way to learn how an individual pearl dealer prices color is to ask.

Size

Luster, surface quality and shape are more important factors than size and weight for beadless freshwater pearls. When these factors are equal, a gonad-grown beaded pearl's value increases with size. Beadless pearls generally range in size from 2 to 12 millimeters and are measured in both 1 millimeter and half-millimeter increments. Beaded freshwater pearls can be as small as 2 millimeters and as large as 20 millimeters.

Nacre Thickness

Nacre thickness is not much of an issue for cultured freshwater pearls because beadless pearls are all nacre, and the nacre of beaded freshwater pearls is generally thicker than that of akoya pearls. One of the biggest selling points of freshwater pearls is that they usually have a higher percentage of pearl nacre than their saltwater counterparts.

≈

The quality of Chinese freshwater cultured pearls has greatly improved since they entered the market in the 1970s. Wrinkled and rice-shaped pearls have been mostly replaced with smoother pearls, and beaded freshwater ones are becoming both larger and smaller. Large beaded freshwater pearls have entered the luxury market and are now strung with South Sea and Tahitian pearls to create impressive, colorful necklaces. However, affordably priced beadless freshwater pearls are still widely available in a variety of colors, shapes and sizes. No matter what your budget is, you will be able to find cultured freshwater pearls that fit your needs.

The legal fishing of natural freshwater pearls has ceased in Europe because the mussels have been listed as endangered. In America, however, pearl fishing is permitted, and pearls are still found in the Mississippi region, although natural saltwater pearls are more abundant and found in many regions of the world. Oysters and mussels are not the only sources of natural pearls. They are also found in snails, clams, scallops and other mussels. The next two chapters will discuss pearls from these mollusks.

8

Pearls Produced by Sea Snails

The core definition of a *pearl* is an organic gem composed of calcium carbonate ($CaCO_3$), protein material and water that forms within a mollusk. Therefore it is not only oysters and mussels that can produce pearls, but also many other types of mollusks, including sea snails. Four types of sea snails are known to produce pearls: abalone (*Haliotis* spp.), conch (multiple species), bailer shell (*Melo melo*) and horned helmet (*Cassis cornuta*). These organisms are classified as univalve mollusks, which are gastropods. The snails use a muscular foot for movement and attachment to surfaces and have a single spiral shell made of calcium carbonate that is used as a protective covering. This chapter discusses where these snails are found and the types of pearls sometimes found in them.

ABALONE PEARLS

Abalones are found off the coasts of Pacific North America, South America, Japan, China, South Korea, South Africa, the British Channel Islands, France, Spain, Australia and New Zealand. Technically the abalone is classified as a large snail of the family Haliotidae and the genus *Haliotis*, which means "sea ear," referring to the flattened shape of the shell. The name abalone is probably derived from the American Spanish word *abulón*.

The richest source of natural abalone pearls has been Baja California and the U.S. California coast, especially Morro Bay and the Channel Islands. Eight species of abalone are found in California alone. *Haliotis rufescens*, or red abalone, is the largest of the approximately hundred

Baja California natural abalone pearls from Pala International. *Photo by Mia Dixon.*

species found worldwide and produces the largest gem-quality natural abalone pearls. Even though commercial abalone fishing began in California in the mid-1800s, abalone pearls did not gain general popularity until the beginning of the 1990s. This was partly thanks to their promotion by natural-pearl dealer Wes Rankin.

Abalones are unique because they can create pearls with colorful concentric layers of nacre, unlike other pearl-producing snails, whose pearls are non-nacreous. The primary sources of abalone pearls and mother-of-pearl for jewelry and decorative ornaments have been off the coast of New Zealand and the North American Pacific Coast, especially the coasts of California and Baja California.

Natural abalone pearls usually have unique baroque shapes that are sought after by designers. Their most common shape resembles a horn or a shark's tooth. Their iridescent colors may include any combination or shade of green, blue, pink, purple, silver or, on rare occasions, creamy white. Blue and green are the most common colors.

Fine-quality natural abalone pearls have an almost metallic luster and may vary in price from $100 to $2,000 and higher per carat, depending on size and quality. They can be as small as a tiny seed, but the largest abalone pearl on record weighs 810 carats. It was found near Cedros Island, off the coast of Baja California, and sold to the late pearl dealer James Peach, who named it "Le Perle Venetia" after his wife.

A horn-shaped natural pearl weighing 112.08 carats, found in a California abalone in 1990. It inspired Wes Rankin, the diver who found it, to start a natural pearl company. *Pearl and photo courtesy of Pacific Coast Pearls.*

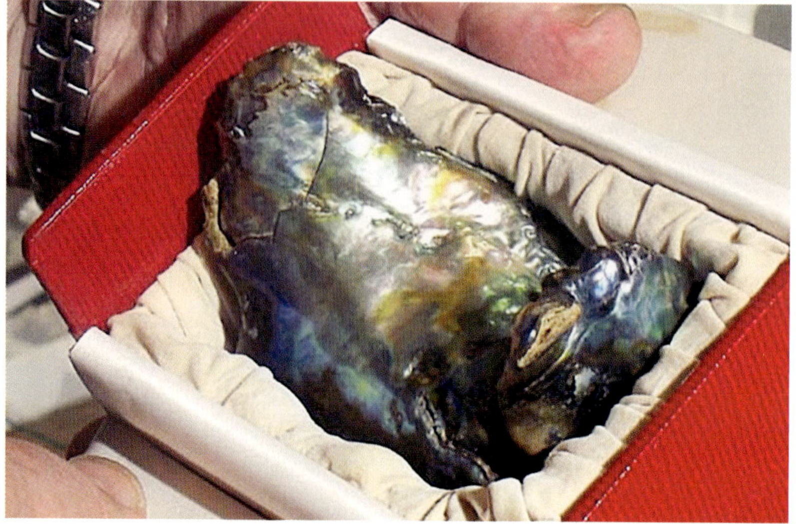

The world's largest abalone pearl (810 carats) as displayed by its owner, the late James Peach. *Photo by Robyn Hawk.*

Abalone mabe pearls from Blue River Gems and Jewelry. The shell backing can be seen on the underside of the drop-shape mabe at top left. *Photo © Renée Newman.*

New Zealand *pāua* mabe pearls. *Earrings design © Eve Alfillé; photo by Matthew Arden.*

Abalone Blisters and Mabe Pearls

Natural blisters can form in abalones when marine invaders penetrate the shell and are covered by nacre. Cultured blisters form when a half-bead nucleus (often plastic or soapstone) is cemented to the inside of the shell or inserted between the mantle and the shell. After the abalone secretes nacre over the bead, the blister is cut from the shell and the bead is removed so the pearl can be cleaned, to prevent deterioration. The hole is then filled with a paste or wax (and sometimes also a bead) and covered with a mother-of-pearl backing. In essence, mabe pearls are assembled cultured blisters.

Abalone mabe pearls have been cultured in California, Baja California, British Columbia, South Korea and Chile, but New Zealand produces the most cultured abalone mabe pearls. *Haliotis iris* is the species found off its rocky coast. It is commonly called *pāua*, the name given to it by the Indigenous Maoris. New Zealand's pāua fishery is managed by strict quotas that allow only a set amount can be caught each year. Even then, the only permitted method of harvesting is by freediving—without the use of underwater breathing apparatus.

Unlike California abalone pearls, pāua pearls are not normally sold at gem shows, because divers very rarely find a pearl in a pāua. However, since the 1990s, New Zealanders have been successful at producing pāua mabe pearls and creating jewelry with them. A wide variety of pāua shell jewelry is also made in New Zealand and sold locally and abroad.

Cultured Abalone Whole Pearls

Abalone are hemophiliacs, meaning their blood does not clot properly. This is one reason why attempts to culture abalone pearls have often failed. Abalones can bleed to death after a bead nucleus is surgically implanted into their body, but no cutting is required to produce cultured blister pearls.

Chilean abalone pearls cultured by Atacama Pearls and harvested from 2022 to 2024. The smallest pearl, top right, is 10 by 7 mm. The largest is 42 by 17 mm. *Photo by Alejandra Santos.*

Left: A Chilean cultured abalone pearl ring by Atacama Pearls, shown on a red abalone (*Haliotis rufescens*) shell. *Photo by Alejandra Santos.*

Right: A 48-month-old Chilean abalone at the Abalone Pearls Technology Facility. *Photo courtesy of atacamapearls.com.*

Another problem is that, unlike oysters, abalones are continually moving over rocks looking for food. As a result, their large central foot exerts constant pressure on the area where a bead and accompanying mantle tissue piece would be inserted. This can cause separation of the bead-and-tissue implant, and a pearl may not form.

In 2012 Dr. Rubén Araya Valencia, Jaime Maturana Zúñiga and their team at the University of Antofagasta, Chile, began a research project on producing whole abalone cultured pearls, an attempt to develop a new source of income for Chilean abalone farmers. By August 2018 they had produced whole cultured pearls with a nacreous outer layer 0.5 to 0.6 millimeter thick after a growth period of 16 months, using 6 millimeter round beads. About 50 percent of the pearls were of acceptable gem quality and showed a variety of colors, often combining gold, blue, silver and green hues. They had been created using a patented method for producing free pearls in abalone.

The Antofagasta University scientists sent samples of their cultured pearls to the Gemological Institute of America in 2022. The Chilean pearls GIA examined had been cultured using traditional freshwater shell-bead nuclei of 5 to 8 millimeters inserted into grafting channels in the visceral mass of red abalones (*Haliotis rufescens*), which had been imported into Chile from Mexico in the 1990s for abalone farming. By 2024 Chilean whole cultured abalone pearls were being offered for sale in jewelry on the Atacama Pearls website.

Nacreous Versus Non-Nacreous Pearls

Both nacreous and non-nacreous pearls consist of two carbonate minerals—aragonite and calcite—plus an organic protein-binding agent and water. However, the structure of the aragonite is different for each type of pearl, and so is the resulting appearance. Non-nacreous (also known as porcelaneous) pearls lack both the soft iridescence of mother-of-pearl and the brighter iridescence of abalone pearls. Instead, non-nacreous pearls such as conch, bailer shell and horned helmet pearls often have a silky or porcelain-like surface, which can also have a flame-like pattern.

Scanning electron microscopes (SEMs) have helped scientists discover that these two pearl types look different because the shape and arrangement of their aragonite are different. According to Dr. H.A. Hänni, former director of the Swiss Gemmological Institute Laboratory, nacre consists of submicroscopic layers of aragonite tablets stacked on top of each other, whereas non-nacreous pearls consist of bundles of fiber-like and slat-shaped aragonite crystals stacked crosswise. This unusual structure creates a pattern of brighter and darker areas, with a flame-like appearance not seen in nacreous pearls. Light striking the sides of the aragonite bundles is reflected, whereas light falling on the profile of the bundles is absorbed.

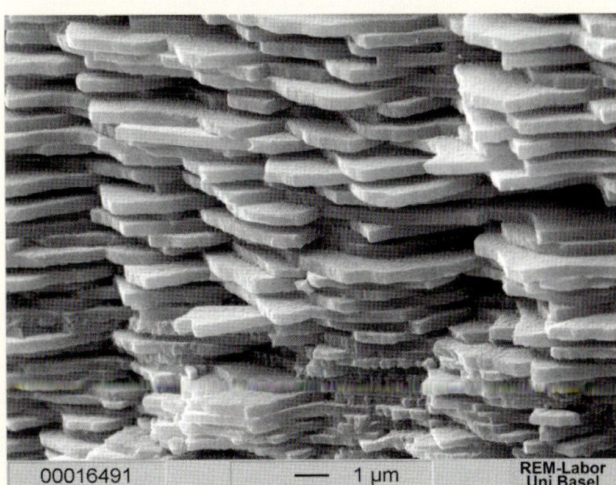

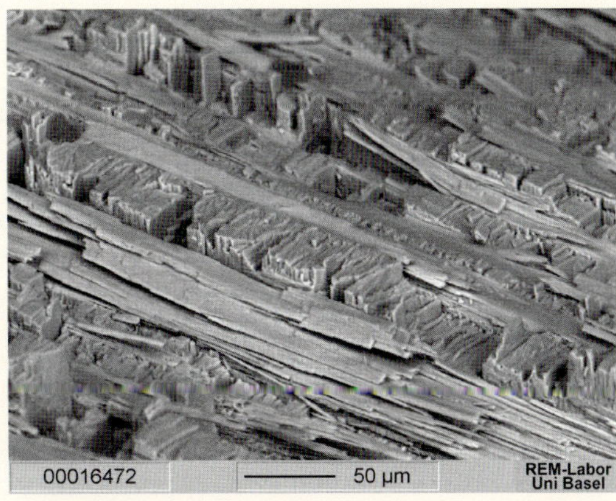

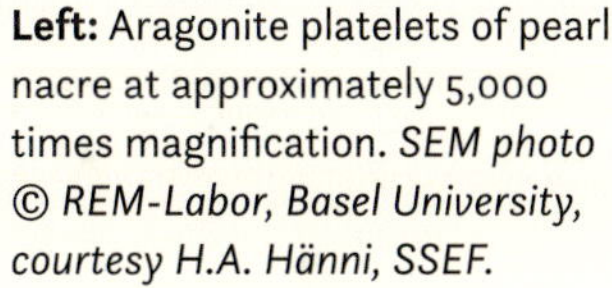
Left: Aragonite platelets of pearl nacre at approximately 5,000 times magnification. *SEM photo © REM-Labor, Basel University, courtesy H.A. Hänni, SSEF.*

Right: Scanning electron microscope image of the broken surface of a pink conch pearl, showing its almost perpendicular orientation of slats and fibers of aragonite, which form in layers. *SEM photo © H.A. Hänni, SSEF.*

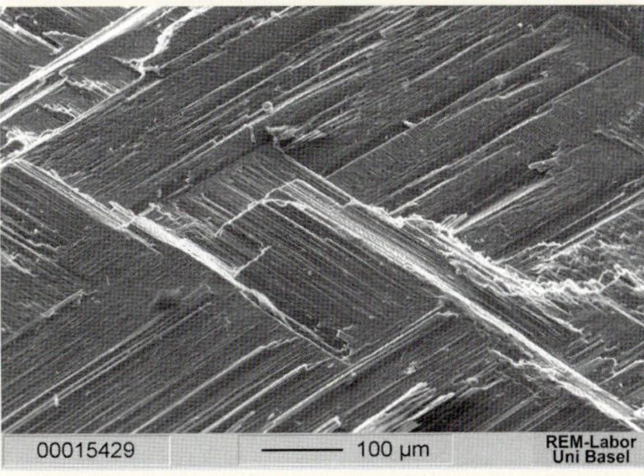

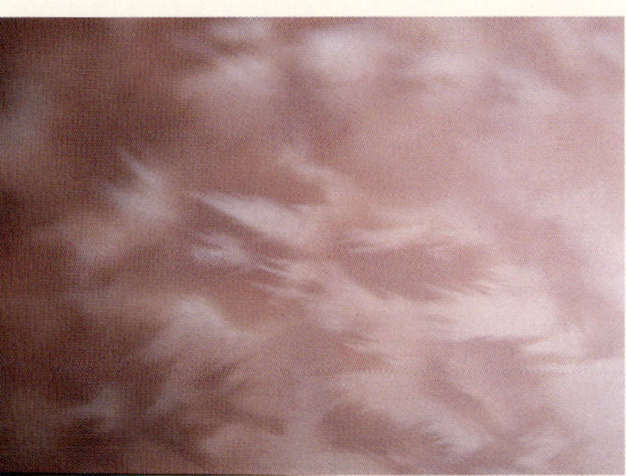

Left: Bundles of conch aragonite fibers in a crosswise orientation. *SEM photo © H.A. Hänni, SSEF.*

Right: Close-up view of the flame structure of a pink conch pearl, showing brighter and darker areas. This is caused by small domains of aragonite bundles with different orientations. *Photo © H.A. Hänni, SSEF.*

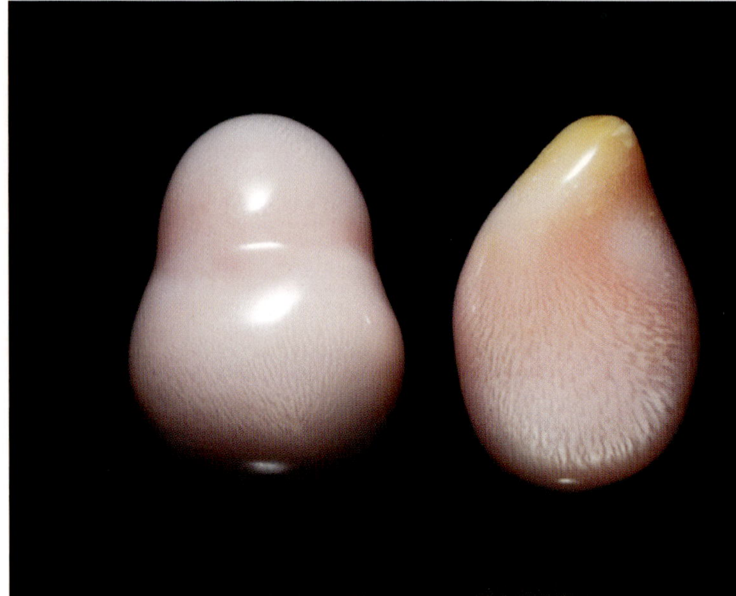

Left: Conch pearl and diamond bracelet created by Busatti. *Photo from Luca Busatti.*

Right: Conch pearls with flame patterns from Pala International. *Photo by Mia Dixon.*

CONCH PEARLS

Conch pearls are also called pink pearls, though some are orange, brown, white, yellow or purplish. They are formed in the queen conch (*Aliger gigas,* originally known as *Strombus gigas*), a large sea snail found in tropical waters from southeastern Florida to the West Indies and the Caribbean Sea. It can grow up to 33 centimeters (13 inches) and purifies its water habitat by feeding off algae and seagrass. This conch is not yet an endangered species, but it is subject to quotas and to fishing bans in some places, such as Florida, in order to prevent its disappearance.

Most conch pearls range in size from 3 to 14 millimeters and have oval, drop or baroque shapes, although they are occasionally round or button shaped. Like other porcelaneous pearls, conch pearls have a Mohs hardness ranging from 5 to 6 (on a scale from 1 to 10), making them more resistant to scratching than nacreous pearls, which have a 2.5 to 4 Mohs hardness (see chapter 13, pages 222–23, to learn more about the Mohs hardness scale).

Conch pearls are generally priced by carat weight. The most valuable ones are symmetrical and have a distinct flame pattern and a strong pink to peach color. Because of the rarity of conch pearls, even small, pale, irregular ones can retail for more than $500 per carat. Better-quality conch pearls may sell for more than $2,000 per carat. In November 2012 a Cartier conch pearl, enamel and diamond bracelet sold at Sotheby's Geneva for about US$3.5 million.

Conch-shell cabochons and beads cost a fraction of the price of conch

Left: A queen conch shell. *Photo and shell from Mikimoto (America) Ltd.*

Right: A multistrand conch-shell bead necklace that was sold for $2,250 at a Heritage Fine Jewelry auction in September 2017. *Photo © Heritage Auctions, HA.com.*

pearls. Some unethical vendors have sold conch-shell beads as conch pearls, but conch-shell bead jewelry can be an attractive and affordable jewelry choice. Reputable sellers will identify the material as conch shell.

The queen conch is valued for both its meat and its pearls, and its shell is used for decoration, as a musical instrument, and for jewelry, carvings, tools, art objects and calcium carbonate fertilizer. Queen conchs can reach 30 years of age; the older the shell, the thicker and stronger it is.

In November 2009 GIA announced that attempts to culture conch pearls had finally been successful. Scientists from Florida Atlantic University's Harbor Branch Oceanographic Institute developed novel seeding techniques that enabled them to produce more than 200 beaded and non-beaded cultured pearls from the queen conch. Fortunately, the culturing technique does not require sacrificing the conch in the process. According to GIA's *Science Daily*, "The 100 percent survival rate of a queen conch after seeding and the fact that it will produce another pearl after the first pearl is harvested will make this culturing process more efficient and environmentally sustainable for commercial application."

Left: The conch-pearl culturing facility at Florida Atlantic University's Harbor Branch Oceanographic Institute. *Photo © Renée Newman.*

Right: Live queen conchs at the Institute. In addition to helping the conch move and attach itself to rocks, its foot acts as a defense against predators and contains tasty white meat. *Photo © Renée Newman.*

Horse-conch pearls from Kojima Pearl. This pair weighs 4.15 carats and the pearls measure 7.2 and 6 mm. *Photo by Sarah Canizzaro.*

X-radiography clearly shows the beads or the tissue-related cavities in the beaded and non-beaded samples. GIA worked with the co-inventors, Dr. Héctor Acosta-Salmón and Dr. Megan Davis, to develop other identification criteria to distinguish cultured conch pearls from their natural counterparts. Scientists in Honduras have also successfully cultured conch pearls, but as of the publication of this book, cultured conch pearls are not being commercially produced. It appears that it is easier to culture such pearls than to make a profit from their production.

In the pearl trade, "conch pearl" normally refers to a pearl from the queen conch (*Alger gigas*). However, the horse conch (*Triplofusus giganteus*, formerly *Pleuroploca gigantea*) is another sea snail species from the Caribbean that can produce porcelaneous pearls. The horse conch is the Florida state shell, and its pearls are so rare that they are seldom mentioned in pearl literature or discussed in the trade.

According to Bari and Lam in *Pearls*, only about 30 horse conch pearls were known in 2009, but more have been found since then. The authors describe them as dazzling, similar to those of the queen conch. One of the largest horse-conch pearls is white with beautiful flame effects, while the others are orangey brown and reddish brown.

Bari and Lam also identify the trapezium horse conch (*Pleuroploca trapezium*), describing it as a beautiful sea snail widely used in interior decoration in the Philippines. It has yielded a few pearls that resemble its shell.

The shell of a trapezium horse conch (*Pleuroploca trapezium*). *Tamara Kulikova/Alamy Stock Photo.*

MELO PEARLS

Melo pearls are porcelaneous pearls that form inside sea snails called bailer shells, melon shells or boat shells (their scientific name is *Melo melo*). These mollusks are found in Southeast Asia off the coasts of Vietnam, Malaysia, Thailand and Myanmar. Their pearls are by-products of harvesting the mollusk for food and are so rare that they are considered collector's items. When large, they can fetch unusually high prices. In October 2010 an orange 224.3-carat melo pearl sold for US$722,500 at a Christie's auction in Dubai.

Considered "fireballs of nature," melo pearls have a spiritual significance for Buddhists in Southeast Asia, where they are a symbol of heavenly perfection. In Vietnam melo pearls used to be so sacred that they were not allowed to be drilled or worn; they were simply preserved and treated as objects of devotion.

Unlike conch pearls, melo pearls are usually round or near round, but they can also be oval or have a baroque shape. They are usually orange, tan or brown in various saturations, but intense orange is the most prized color. Because of the large size of the mollusk—which can grow to 12.5 to 36.5 centimeters (nearly 5 to 14 3/8 inches) in length—melo pearls can reach up to 20 to 30 millimeters in size and weigh more than 200 carats. They are believed to grow over several decades.

A flame pattern is a key price factor. The stronger and broader the pattern, the more value it adds to the pearl. Weight, surface quality, color and shape are also important price factors.

Melo pearls and other rare natural pearls can sometimes be found at auctions for extremely low prices if sellers and bidders are unaware of their usual value. A buyer at a Heritage Auction in December 2018 paid only $6,000 for a brooch set with five small melo pearls (6.8 to 11.5 millimeters), diamonds and freshwater cultured pearls.

Above: The distinctive flame pattern of a top-quality melo pearl weighing 190 carats, from Wolf Bialonczyk.

Below: A 43-carat translucent melo pearl from Wolf Bialonczyk.

Photos © bialonczyk.at.

Above: A 33-carat melo pearl ring by Wolf Bialonczyk. *Photo © bialonczyk.at.*

Right: A melo pearl, diamond and cultured freshwater pearl clip brooch that was sold at a Heritage Auction in December 2018. *Photo © Heritage Auctions, HA.com.*

A melo pearl bailer shell from Pala International. *Photo by Mia Dixon.*

Another bailer shell from Pala International. *Photo by Mia Dixon.*

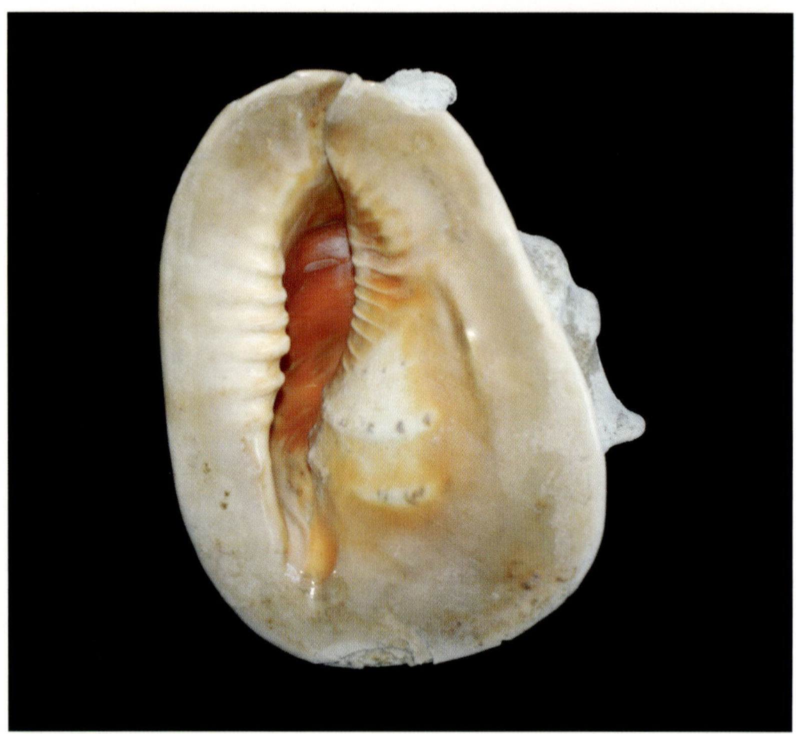

A horned helmet (*Cassis cornuta*) shell from Pacific Coast Pearls. *Photo by David Rankin.*

A queen helmet (*Cassis madagascariensis*) shell cameo carved by Wounaan artist Lider Peña for Rainforest Design. *Photo by Roslyn Zelenka.*

HELMET PEARLS

The best-known helmet pearl is produced by the horned helmet (*Cassis cornuta*), a large sea snail found around coral reefs in many places, including the Red Sea, the Pacific Ocean and the Indian Ocean. Its pearl, often referred to as a *Cassis cornuta* or a Cassis pearl, has a porcelain-like surface that can display a flame pattern. The snail is protected in Queensland, Australia, because it hunts the crown-of-thorns starfish, which feeds on corals.

Considering the rarity of *Cassis cornuta* pearls, it was surprising to see them in a ring and necklace at the booth of Somewhere in the Rainbow, a modern gem and jewelry collection, at the 2024 American Gem Trade Association's GemFair in Tucson, Arizona. In an article in that year's spring issue of *Gems & Gemology*, Eric Fritz says the necklace was designed by Jim Grahl of Balboa Island, California, and the pearls were sourced from Europe by Carlos Chanu over the course of one year.

Another helmet mollusk is the emperor or queen helmet (*Cassis madagascariensis*), which is found in waters throughout the Caribbean, from Florida to Cuba, the Bahamas and Panama (but not Madagascar, as its scientific name implies). Its shell is used to make cameos in Italy, as well as in Panama by the Indigenous Wounaan people. According to Bari and Lam, as of 2009 only one pearl from the emperor helmet was known to exist, and it was in the collection of the Qatar Museums Authority. However, the summer 2022 issue of *Gems & Gemology* discusses an oval pinkish-orange porcelaneous pearl that was reportedly found in a queen helmet from Key West, Florida.

A *Cassis cornuta* pearl necklace designed by Jim Grahl, which is now part of the Somewhere in the Rainbow Collection. *Photo © Renée Newman.*

9

Pearls from Scallops, Clams, Saltwater Mussels and Nautiluses

The bodies of clams, scallops and saltwater mussels are enclosed by a shell consisting of two hinged parts, like oysters and river mussels, and they are therefore classified as bivalves. However, pearls from clams, scallops and saltwater mussels are usually non-nacreous and natural, as is the pearl of the chambered nautilus (*Nautilus pompilius*), a species of cephalopod. In this chapter we will discuss these other pearl-producing mollusks and show examples of their rare and interesting creations.

SCALLOP PEARLS

Scallops are saltwater mollusks from the Pectinoidea superfamily. The two main types are the giant lion's paw (*Nodipecten subnodosus*) and the spiny oyster scallop (*Spondylus* spp.).

Giant Lion's Paw Scallop Pearls

The best-known lion's paw pearls are from the *N. subnodosus* scallop, whose shell resembles a lion's paw, hence the name (and *mano de león* in Spanish). This is the shell that the Shell Oil Company uses in its logo.

Giant lion's paw scallops are found off the coast of Baja California, Mexico. According to Pacific Coast Pearls, nobody in the gem trade had ever seen a natural pearl from this scallop before 2000. These rare pearls are by-products of scallop harvesting and come in various shapes—rounds, drops, buttons, ovals and baroque—and in sizes from seed to 40 carats.

The colors of lion's paw pearls range from white to deep royal purple, with varying shades of orange, pink and purple in between. The

surface of the pearls has a shimmering sheen, particularly when viewed under a bright light, according to an October 2004 article in the *Journal of Gemmology*.

The August 2012 issue of *Aquaculture* reported that scallops can be relaxed in 20 to 40 minutes by using magnesium chloride or 2-phenoxyethanol. This process helps them survive the excision of a section of mantle tissue for the successful production of cultured pearls.

Left: Lion's paw scallop pearls in a *Nodipecten subnodosus* shell. These were found off the coast of Baja California, Mexico. *Pearls and shell from Pacific Coast Pearls. Photo © Renée Newman.*

Right: Lion's paw scallop pearls from Baja California, Mexico, collected over a period of several years and sorted by Sarah Canizzaro of the Kojima Pearl Company. She also drilled and strung the pearls, which range in size from 4.7 to 9 mm and form a 47 cm (18.5 in.) necklace. *Photo by Sarah Canizzaro.*

Spiny Oyster Pearls

"Spiny oyster" is a misnomer for scallops of the *Spondylus* genus. The two most important species that produce pearls are *Spondylus calcifer* and *S. princeps*. The latter is found on the gulf side of Baja California, down the Pacific coast of Mexico and through Panama to northwestern Peru. *S. calcifer* is found in the Sea of Cortez (Mexico) and Ecuador, as described in the "Lab Notes" section of the fall 2016 issue of *Gems & Gemology*.

Spondylus princeps pearls usually have a body color that is white to cream, with various saturations of pink, orange and brown, whereas *S. calcifer* pearls display purple and white, with or without some yellowish brown. The pearls of both species have a porcelaneous surface.

Spiny oyster (*Spondylus princeps*) pearls on display at the Pacific Coast Pearls booth, at the 2024 Tucson Gem & Jewelry Exchange (GJX) gem show, Tucson, Arizona. *Photo © Renée Newman.*

Below left: Spiny oyster pearl and spinel ring by Assael. *Photo courtesy of Assael.*

Below right: An unusual *Spondylus calcifer* pearl from the Kojima Pearl Company. *Photo by Sarah Canizzaro.*

Archaeological research in the Salango region of Ecuador indicates that the shell of the spiny oyster was used for beads and pendants as early as 1500 BCE. The oysters were revered by the ancient Andean peoples, who also used their shells in rituals and for architectural decoration. Shell artifacts were traded to the Ecuadoran interior until the Spanish conquest. More can be learned about these ancient uses from the 2019 article "Spondylus: The Pre-Columbian Use of the Thorny Oyster" by K. Kris Hirst, at https://www.thoughtco.com/precolumbian-use-of-the-thorny-oyster-170123.

CLAM PEARLS

Clams generally have a thicker and more dome-shaped shell than scallops. They are mainly burrowing animals, using their foot to dig into the sand, whereas scallops can swim through the water by rapidly opening and closing their shells, which propels them forward.

Natural-pearl sellers are not able to identify the species of a clam pearl if they are unsure of its origin, so many pearls from clams are simply identified as "clam pearls." Most of them are white or cream colored, but they may also have tints of yellow, orange or purple. Their shape is often near round or oval, but they may also be baroque. Three types of clam pearls that are often identified in the pearl trade are quahog pearls, giant clam pearls and pen pearls.

Clam pearls from Pacific Coast Pearls. *Photo © Renée Newman.*

Quahog Pearls

Clam pearls from the bivalve clam *Mercenaria mercenaria* are called quahog pearls, after the Algonquian word for the mollusk (pronounced *koh-hog* or *kwa-hog*). This common hard clam is found along the North Atlantic coast and has a purple stain on the back of its shell. In 1987 it was officially designated the state mollusk of Rhode Island.

Quahog pearls occur in various colors. White is the least rare and often the most affordable color, while purple to lavender are the rarest and most valuable. Other colors include beige, brown and black. Usually the more uniform the color, the higher the price, except for some pearls with attractive bicolor and tricolor patterns. Most quahog pearls are below 7 millimeters in size, but exceptionally large pearls can range from 14 to 20 millimeters.

On June 3, 2015, *Kovels Antique Trader* reported that a quahog pearl discovered in a policeman's seafood soup sold for $16,500, including the buyer's premium. The pearl was accompanied by a Gemological Institute of America (GIA) report describing it as a "Natural undrilled Quahog saltwater pearl, 11.43 mm × 8.36 mm, 6.22 carats, from a Northern Quahog clam with GIA report, 'no indications of treatment,' 'natural light purple.'" A Japanese collector bought the gem through a U.S. pearl broker.

Necklace and earring layout of quahog (*Mercenaria mercenaria*) pearls from Pacific Coast Pearls, showing their various colors. *Photo by Tish Rankin.*

The Golash quahog pearl brooch (circa 1835), named after Alan Golash, the Rhode Island jeweler who bought it at an antique store in 2000 for a mere $14—it had been misidentified by the store as costume jewelry. The 14 mm round button pearl is one of the largest and finest quahog pearls ever found. It was on display at the Somewhere in the Rainbow booth during the 2024 American Gem Trade Association Tucson GemFair. *Photo © Renée Newman.*

A 12 mm quahog pearl shown in a clamshell from Pala International. *Photo by Mia Dixon.*

A *Tridacna gigas* giant clam shell at the Sea Things shop in Ventura, California. This specimen is 80 to 100 years old and weighs more than 318 kg (700 lb.). *Photo © Renée Newman.*

Above: A *Tridacna gigas* giant clam pearl from the T. Stern Collection, courtesy of Société des Perles Fines. *Photo by J. Grahl.*

Below: An *Atrina vexillum* pen pearl from the T. Stern Collection, courtesy of Société des Perles Fines. *Photo by J. Grahl.*

Giant Clam Pearls

Tridacna gigas, found in the Indo-Pacific region, is the best-known pearl-producing giant clam. Pearls from it are porcelaneous and usually white, but they may also have a brownish patch. In August 2016, a 34 kilogram (75 pounds) "pearl" made headlines worldwide via the Associated Press as the world's largest pearl. It was said to have been discovered 10 years earlier by a fisherman in the Philippines, who had found it in a giant clam and then kept it under his bed as a good-luck charm.

Because of the media blitz, the Swiss Gemmological Institute Laboratory (SSEF) received numerous requests to analyze similar "giant pearls." The results of the lab's examinations of five pearls were published in the *Journal of Gemmology.* The article, by Michael Krzemnicki and Laurent Cartier, was titled "Fake Pearls Made from *Tridacna gigas* Shells." As the title suggests, the pearls that were tested were fakes. The gemological brief stated: "Although the authors have not personally studied the 'giant pearls' claimed to originate from *Tridacna* clams that have recently appeared in the media, we are convinced that most—if not all—of them are in fact fakes that were manufactured from the shell of *Tridacna* clams. This opinion is based on their apparent similarity in shape, layered structure and surface polish to the study samples we described above."

An *Atrina* pen pearl necklace and earring set from Pacific Coast Pearls. *Photo by Gwendolyn Rankin.*

Pen Pearls

Pinnidae mollusks are a family of large saltwater clams sometimes known as pen (or pin) shells. They have the elongated shape of many clams and do not look much like scallops, but some sources say they can move in the water like scallops and have a similar flavor. A fall 2014 *Gems & Gemology* article notes that the Pinnidae family is widely distributed among the oceans of the world, from the Mediterranean to the Red Sea, the Arabian Gulf and the Indo-Pacific, as well as the waters around Florida, Texas, Mexico and the Caribbean.

The pen pearls illustrated in the fall 2014 *Gems & Gemology* article are mostly black to dark gray or dark brown, like the pearls from Pacific Coast Pearls shown in the photograph above. However, the pearls pictured in the Pinnidae section of Elisabeth Strack's *Pearls* are mostly orange and yellow—typical colors for Mediterranean pen pearls from the *Pinna nobilis* mollusk. The color depends on the species and the region where the pen shell is found. *Atrina vexillum* pen pearls from the Philippines are usually black to dark purple, and *Atrina* pearls from Mexico are generally black or blackish brown.

Unlike scallop and other clam pearls, pen pearls can be either nacreous or non-nacreous. The non-nacreous pen pearls are susceptible to cracking, whereas those that are nacreous are more durable, resulting in a much higher value.

An extremely rare strand of natural wild-found *Modiolus philippinarum* pearls from the Kojima Pearl Company. These were collected over decades from mussels found on Indo-Pacific shorelines. This strand is a shining example of both patience and expert drilling. *Photo by Sarah Canizzaro.*

Saltwater mussel pearls from Pacific Coast Pearls. *Photo © Renée Newman.*

SALTWATER MUSSEL PEARLS

Modiolus americanus saltwater mussels are also called tulip mussels or American horse mussels; they are part of the Mytilidae family. These mollusks are found in moderately shallow waters in Mexico's Sea of Cortez and along the Atlantic coast of North America, ranging from North Carolina to the West Indies. Most pearls from *M. americanus* are purple, gray or black. Even though Pacific Coast Pearls (based in Petaluma, California) has a good supply of mussel pearls, very little has been published about them.

As its name indicates, *Modiolus philippinarum*, commonly called the Philippine horse mussel, is found in the Philippines, where it is fished as seafood. Its pearls resemble those of the American horse mussel. A natural deep purple color is the most sought after from this species.

A *Nautilus pompilius* shell sliced in half to reveal its intricate chambers. *Diego Grandi/ Shutterstock*.

NAUTILUS PEARLS

The chambered nautilus (*Nautilus pompilius*) is a cephalopod, which is a class of mollusk that includes the squid and the octopus. In addition to a foot divided into tentacles, cephalopods have a head with a mouth and eyes and a skull made of cartilage that contains a complex brain. Unlike snails, which have a single coiled shell, the chambered nautilus has an elaborate shell with multiple chambers lined with nacre. The southwestern Pacific Ocean and coastal areas of the Indian Ocean are the main places where this animal is found.

Curiously, even though the inside of its shell is nacreous, the few pearls the nautilus has produced have been non-nacreous and white. As for their rarity, Bari and Lam write in *Pearls* that, as of its 2009 publication date, only five nautilus pearls were known. On the other hand, the nautilus shell is historically renowned, not only in Asia but also in Europe. Bari and Lam write: "Its shell mesmerized the whole of Europe to the point where it was sometimes made the principal exhibit of a natural history collection or a cabinet of curiosities."

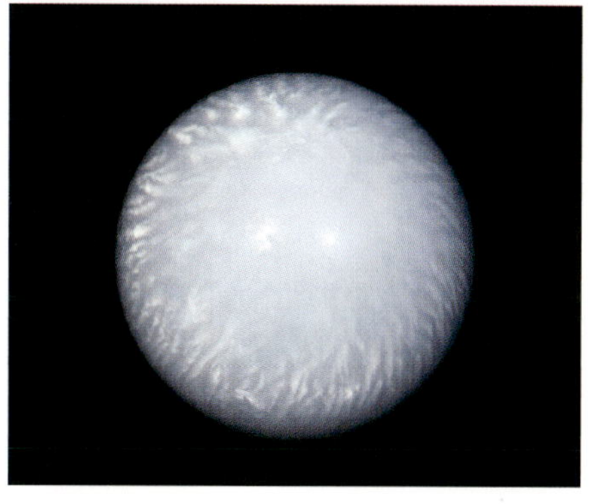

Right, above: A *Nautilus pompilius* blister pearl weighing 4.4 carats and measuring 8.8 by 7 mm, from Stephen Metzler. *Photo by Stephen Metzler.*

Right, below: An *N. pompilius* pearl with a beautiful flame pattern, from the T. Stern Collection. *Photo by Harold & Erica Van Pelt.*

10 Imitation Pearls

Imagine a rosary-bead maker watching a fish being scaled in a basin of water. The water shows colorful pearly reflections that seem to form as the fish scales dissolve. The bead maker then gets the idea to filter the water, recover the pearly substance from it and mix it with varnish. Later he coats the inside surface of a hollow glass bead with the pearly mixture and then fills the bead with wax. The result? The birth of the modern-day imitation pearl.

This occurred in France in the 17th century, and Jacquin was the name of the rosary-bead maker. "Essence of orient"—pearl essence—is the name of the mixture he discovered. Today the finest imitation pearls usually have several coats of pearl essence.

TYPES OF IMITATION PEARLS

Even though pearl essence is used to make many of the best imitation pearls, such as Majorica (or Mallorca) pearls, imitations come in a variety of types. The main ones are:

- **Hollow glass beads containing wax:** These pearls, made by the same process as Jacquin's, are most likely to be found in antique jewelry.
- **Solid glass beads:** Majorica brand imitation pearls are an example of this type. They may be covered with as many as 40 coats of pearl essence, hand-polished between each coat. Glass imitation pearls can also be coated with other substances, such as synthetic pearl essence, plastic, cellulose and lacquer.

- **Plastic beads:** These may have the same types of coatings as the glass variety. Plastic imitation pearl necklaces sometimes hang poorly because of their light weight.
- **Mother-of-pearl shell beads:** These are coated with the same substances as plastic and glass imitations. Coatings made from powdered mother-of-pearl and synthetic resin may also be used. One company calls such beads "semi-cultured," but that is just a misleading term for imitation pearls. Powdered mother-of-pearl coatings are not a new concept. Centuries ago, Native Americans produced imitation pearls by applying such coatings to clay beads and then baking them.

  Mother-of-pearl shell beads are often called "shell pearls." You can find "shell pearl" necklaces on the Internet for less than $10, although the better ones will cost more. Sometimes they are misrepresented as real pearls. "Simulated" and "faux" pearls (the French word for "fake") are two other terms used to designate imitation pearls.

Imitation pearls can be distinguished from natural and cultured pearls by using the tests described in the following sections.

OBSERVATION TESTS THAT REQUIRE NO SPECIAL EQUIPMENT

Heaviness (Heft) Test

Bounce the pearls in your hand. If they feel unusually light, they are most likely made of plastic or filled with wax. Cultured and natural pearls are about two and a half times heavier than plastic pearls. This test is useful only for detecting beads made of plastic or wax. Solid glass beads and pearls with glass or shell bead nuclei will feel about as heavy as cultured or natural pearls.

Overtone Test

Look for overtone colors in the pearls. These are colors that overlie the body color. On white pearls it is easiest to see them in the darker areas

The top two strands are cultured pearls and the bottom strand is good-quality imitation pearls. Genuine pearls of good quality typically have pink, green, silver or blue overtones, whereas imitations tend to lack overtones and be more uniform in color. A good way of distinguishing imitation from genuine pearls is to examine them with a 10-power magnifier. *Photo © Renée Newman.*

of the pearls, whereas on black pearls they are easier to see in the lighter areas. Imitations frequently have no overtones, and when they do, they all tend to look the same. It is normal for cultured and natural pearls to have green, pink, blue and/or silver overtones, and these overtones often vary in color within a strand. They are easiest to see in strong artificial light or sunlight. Note, however, that low-quality pearls with thin nacre may lack overtones.

Surface Magnification

Examine the surface of the pearl with a 10-power magnifier, such as a loupe. If it looks grainy and speckled, there is a good chance it is an imitation. Real pearls normally look fine-grained and smooth, but sometimes dirt or pits may make them appear a bit grainy. Occasionally, too, freshwater and South Sea pearls may look a little grainy, but other surface characteristics—such as random blemishes, overtone color and drill-hole appearance—can prove that they are not imitation.

If you have access to a microscope, use it to examine the surface at the highest possible magnification. At 50 power and above, a rough, pitted surface definitely indicates an imitation. Gas bubbles may also be present.

A surface with tiny, crooked lines that give it a scaly, fingerprint or maze-like appearance at high magnification is characteristic of cultured and natural pearls. These scaly lines are not always evident at first; the surface may look smooth except for possible blemishes and dirt. Try using a strong direct light source, such as a fiber-optic light, and shine it on the pearl from various angles to find the scaly lines.

It is curious that pearls, which feel gritty to the teeth, can look so smooth under 10-times magnification, whereas imitations, which feel smooth, tend to appear grainy and speckled. The less smooth an imitation is, the rougher it looks under magnification. On real pearls, it is those "scaly line" ridges that cause their gritty feel.

The top pearl is an imitation pearl under 10-times magnification. Note the glittery, grainy, speckled surface and lack of overtone color. The bottom pearl is a cultured pearl with a pink overtone and smoother-looking surface. *Photo © Renée Newman.*

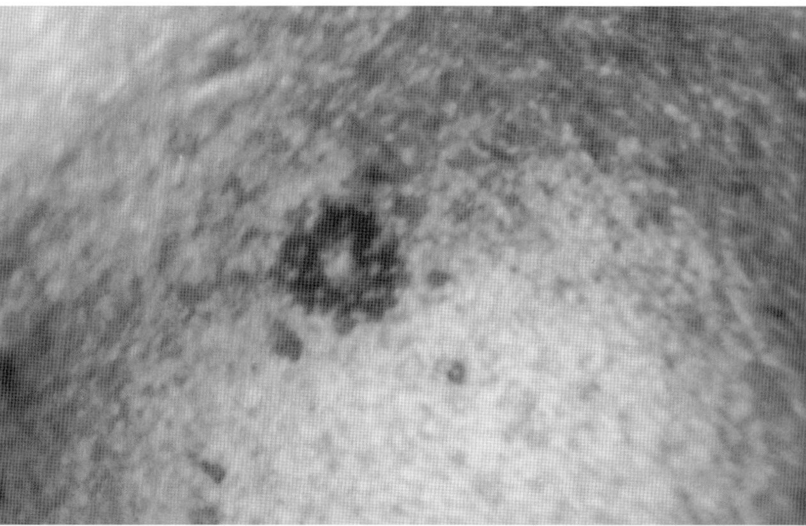

Left: The grainy surface texture of an imitation pearl viewed at 10-times magnification.

Right: The same imitation pearl at 64-times magnification. Note the rough surface. *Photos © Renée Newman.*

The surface of a Tahitian cultured pearl seen at 64-times magnification. The maze-like patterns prove that the pearl has real nacre and is not an imitation. *Photo © Renée Newman.*

The best way to learn what the surfaces of pearls and imitations look like under magnification is to examine many examples of each. Once you can recognize how distinctive their surface textures are, you will not need to perform any of the other tests to identify an imitation pearl.

Drill-Hole Test

Examine the drill-hole area of the pearl with a 10-power or stronger magnifier. On some pearls it may be hard to see into the drill hole. Cultured pearls tend to show the following characteristics:

- A clear dividing line often exists between the nacre and the nucleus.
- The edges of the drill holes are often sharp and well defined, but when the nacre wears away, it can leave the holes looking jagged and rough at the edges.
- The drill holes tend to be straight and cylindrical.
- The pearl nacre coating is normally thicker than the coating of imitations.

Drill Holes of Cultured and Imitation Pearls

Cultured Pearls

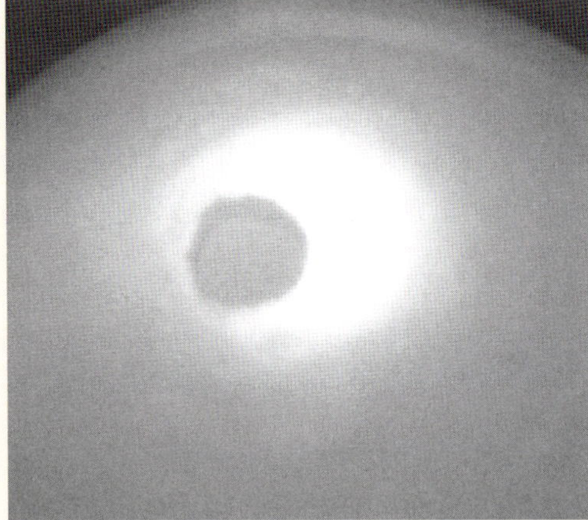

Left: Note the well-defined edges of this cultured pearl's drill hole.

Right: A straight drill hole and the separation line between the core and thin nacre indicate that this is a cultured pearl. *Photos © Renée Newman.*

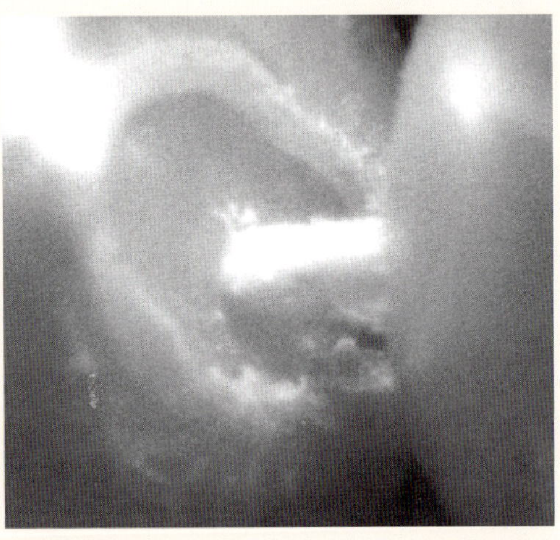

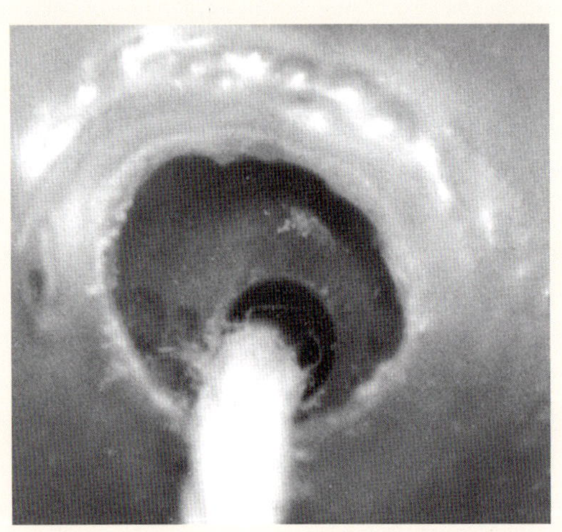

Left: This cultured pearl's coating has worn away at the drill hole. Imitation pearls do not have coatings this thick.

Right: The nacre has separated from the core in this pearl. Such a separation would not be characteristic of an imitation pearl. *Photos © Renée Newman.*

Imitation Pearls

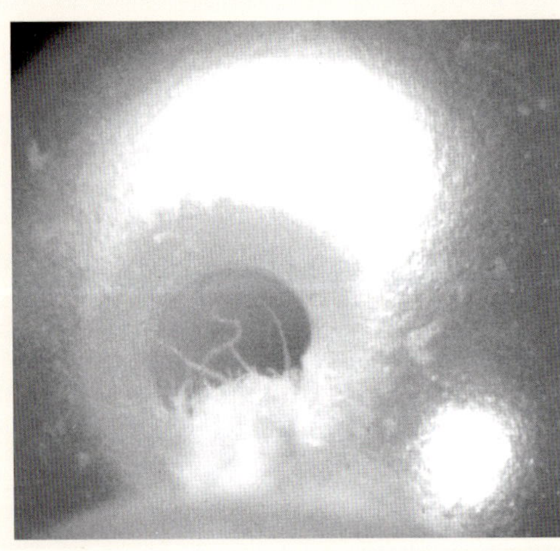

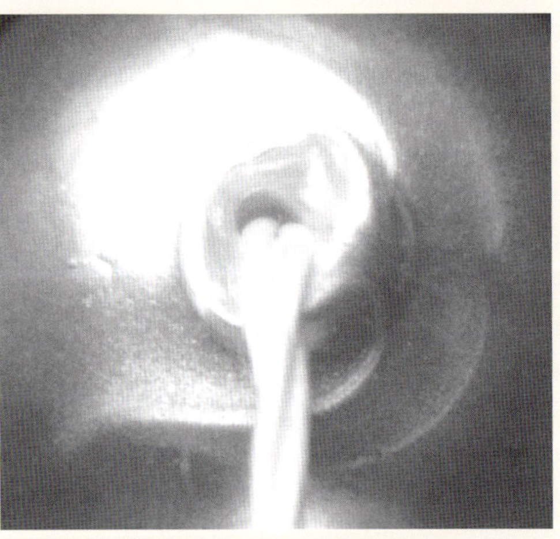

Left: The very thin, ragged coating, the angled drill hole and the lack of a dividing line between core and coating indicate that this is an imitation.

Right: The swirly formation around the drill hole and the very thin, glossy coating are clues that this shell bead pearl is an imitation. *Photos © Renée Newman.*

Imitation pearls tend to show these characteristics:

- Typically there is no clear dividing line between the coating and the rest of the pearl at the drill hole. Occasionally one may see a light line, but the other characteristics of the drill hole will look like those of imitations. If you are in doubt, look at the drill-hole opening on the opposite side of the pearl and on other pearls in the strand.
- The coating around the edges of the drill hole may have flaked off, making it look ragged or uneven.
- The drill hole may be angled outward at the surface of the pearl.
- The coating often looks like a thin layer of shiny paint. Its thinness can be seen at the edge of the drill hole or around bare areas that expose the inner bead.
- Rounded ridges may have formed around the drill hole.
- If the bead is made of glass, its glassy luster may be apparent.

Matching and Uniformity Test

Note the shape, luster, color and size of the pearls. Imitations often seem perfectly matched, whereas cultured or natural strands tend to have variations among the pearls.

Two strands of imitation pearls showing almost no variation in shape, luster, color or size, and no overtone colors or typical pearl blemishes. These shell pearl necklaces were sold on the Internet as a Tahitian black pearl necklace and a South Sea white pearl necklace. *Photo © Renée Newman.*

Tooth Test

If pearls feel gritty or sandy when rubbed very lightly along the biting edge of your upper front teeth, it is likely that they are cultured or natural pearls. If they feel smooth, they are probably imitations.

There are a few problems with this test. If it is not done properly, you risk scratching the pearls—and it is unsanitary. Considering the possibility of contagious diseases such as COVID-19 and RSV, it can be risky to put pearls in your mouth that have been touched by other people and possibly also tested against their teeth. Rubbing the pearls against a different surface than teeth can also potentially scratch them.

Another problem is that the test does not always work. Some imitation pearls feel gritty too, and according to the fall 1991 issue of *Gems & Gemology*, real pearls may also feel smooth. A cultured pearl sent to GIA's New York laboratory gave a smooth tooth-test reaction because the surface had been polished. Therefore, do not rely solely on this test. If you do use it, combine it with magnification tests.

Price Test

Consider the price of the pearls, especially when buying online. If it seems unbelievably low, the pearls could be imitation, defective or stolen merchandise. Jewelers cannot stay in business if they sell goods below their cost. However, in some cases it does not matter if bargain "pearls" turn out to be imitation, if they are attractive.

A high price does not necessarily indicate that the pearls are real cultured or natural pearls. In some cases fake pearls have been misrepresented as genuine in order to make more profit. In other instances, the provenance and emotional value of imitations have increased their price. The most famous example is the US$211,500 paid for Jackie Kennedy's triple-strand faux pearl necklace by the Franklin Mint, a collectibles company, at a 1996 Sotheby's auction. The company's co-owner, Lynda Resnick, explained why she was willing to pay such a high sum for fake pearls in her 2009 book *Rubies in the Orchard: How to Uncover the Hidden Gems in Your Business*.

An imitation pearl necklace that was sold on the Internet for $10 as a 14 mm South Sea pearl necklace. The price, the lack of overtone colors, the flaked coating, swirly formations around the drill holes and speckled surface texture under magnification are all clues that this strand is fake. *Photo © Renée Newman.*

Resnick had worshipped Jackie Kennedy all her life. For her, the First Lady was the epitome of class, managing to be beautiful, stylish and refined while still being refreshing. Resnick had seen photos of Jackie wearing those pearls at state dinners, on trips abroad and while looking after her children. So when she saw them in the Sotheby's auction catalog, she knew she had to buy the pearls at any cost. Her husband and company co-owner thought she was nuts. She finally convinced him the necklace would be a worthwhile purchase by spreading photos across his desk of Jackie wearing the necklace, including a photo of a young John F. Kennedy Jr. on Jackie's lap pulling at those same pearls.

After the auction, Resnick received Jackie's necklace in its original Bergdorf's department store silk-lined box. She and her company then analyzed the 139 European glass faux pearls and made exact reproductions from a mold, color-matching them to their creamy originals, with the same 17 coats of lacquer as the originals. Their work was rewarded. In her book, Resnick wrote: "At $211,000, the pearls turned out to be a phenomenal bargain. We sold more than 130,000 copies at $200 a strand—for

Young John F. Kennedy Jr. playing with the faux pearl necklace that fetched US$211,500 at a Sotheby's 1996 auction of Jackie Kennedy's estate. *Everett Collection Historical/Alamy Stock Photo.*

a gross of $26 million. Owning the original pearls gave us the credibility to sell the copies; it certified and rewarded our collectors' faith that they were getting as close to the real deal as anyone could. By wearing those iconic pearls, women everywhere could channel a bit of Jackie." A paragraph later she added: "Value is real even when the product is 100 percent fake."

In August 2010 the pearls were sold again, at a Bonham's auction in the United Kingdom for £30,000 (approximately US$46,500), including premium. The auction site listed the provenance as "Sotheby's New York, Jewelry from The Estate of Jacqueline Kennedy Onassis, 24th and 25th April 1996, lot 461."

Jackie was not the only famous person to wear imitation pearls. Coco Chanel combined real pearls with fake ones. The pearls worn by Audrey Hepburn in *Breakfast at Tiffany's* were all imitation. Many wealthy people during the 1950s wore fakes because it was an easy way to get pearls that were well-matched for color, luster and size.

≈

Distinguishing imitations from real oyster pearls is not difficult; even laypeople can learn how to detect imitations with a 10-times magnifier, but it takes practice. It is more challenging to distinguish cultured pearls from those that are natural. Chapter 2 discusses how gemologists can prove if a pearl is natural or not and describes the high-tech equipment required for that type of testing, as well as for the detection of treatments, which can have a large negative impact on price.

Special equipment and expertise are also required to prove if non-nacreous pearls, such as clam pearls, are genuine, although visual evidence can often indicate if they are fake. Pearl dealer Jeremy Shepherd said in a July 2, 2024, post on Pearl-Guide.com, "Over the past few years, we've been inundated with images of claims of supposed giant clam pearls, almost all of which come from the Philippines. This is likely due to a story about a supposed 75-pound (34 kilo) pearl a Filipino fisherman had kept under his bed for a decade." An SSEF article in the 2017 *Journal of Gemmology* agrees that its shape, layered structure and poor surface polish provided strong combined evidence that the 75-pound Filipino object had been manufactured from *Tridacna* shell.

When buying unusual natural pearls, deal with reputable experts, because their rarity means that the average jeweler does not have experience in identifying them. No matter what type of pearls you want to buy, if they are very expensive, it is advisable to get a lab report from a respected gem lab confirming their identity and treatment status.

11 Pearl Processing and Treatments

After pearls are removed from a mollusk, they must be cleaned and washed to get rid of residues and odors. They are typically tumbled with salt in rotating barrels during this process. The tumbling must be closely monitored; otherwise, some of the nacre may wear off. There are other treatments, however, that are not considered routine and should therefore be disclosed. Many of these are covered in this chapter, as well as tests that can be done to detect treatments.

Cultured freshwater pearls in a bleaching solution. The metal container keeps them warm at a specified temperature. *Photo © Renée Newman.*

PEARL TREATMENTS

Bleaching

Akoya pearls and Chinese freshwater pearls are commonly bleached with chemicals and intense light sources. This process whitens them and makes their color more uniform. However, improper bleaching can soften the nacre and make it more susceptible to wear, especially if the nacre is thin. Assume that white akoya and freshwater pearls have been bleached unless otherwise specified. Good-quality white South Sea cultured pearls do not need to be bleached, so they are sometimes described as "completely natural"—meaning that their color is natural, not that the pearls are of natural origin instead of cultured.

Optical Brightening or Fluorescence Whitening

The summer 2020 issue of *Gems & Gemology* contains an article comparing known samples of akoya cultured pearls brightened with chemical agents with their non-brightened counterparts. These brighteners are

Further bleaching under and over fluorescent lighting helps whiten the cultured pearls, but bleaching solution is also required. *Photo © by Renée Newman.*

A typical buffing machine in China in 2008. *Photo © Renée Newman.*

A Japanese polishing machine used for large quantities of pearls. *Photo © Renée Newman.*

different from bleaches, generating a blue fluorescence that masks yellow tones and brightens the pearls. The GIA lab is able to detect optical brightening agents by using fluorescence spectroscopy in combination with visual fluorescence observations under long-wave UV radiation.

A study in the summer 2021 issue of *Gems & Gemology* indicates that some naturally colored freshwater pearls undergo the optical brightening process as well. Although a pearl's color is not affected by it, its luster could benefit from the process because it can increase the pearl's reflection in the visible spectrum.

Buffing

Buffing is done to improve luster and remove superficial scratches. Beeswax or chemical polishes are sometimes used during the process to add luster; however, wax wears off quickly and the chemicals may eat away the nacre. Buffing without chemical intervention is considered acceptable if it is done to clean off oil and dirt and remove minor scratches.

Coating

In her book *Pearls,* Elisabeth Strack states that akoya and South Sea white and black cultured pearls have been treated with silicone polymers in Japan. The coating is mainly applied to Tahitian cultured pearls of lower quality.

Close-up view of cultured freshwater fireball pearls with a colored metallic coating. Note the bald spots on the bottom left and top center examples where the coating has rubbed off. The $35 price tag for this strand is another indication that the pearls are not a natural color. *Photo © Renée Newman.*

Coated cultured pearls found on display. When viewed with 10-times magnification, their speckled surface resembles that of imitation pearls. However, the blemishes and irregularities of these pearls indicate that they are not fakes. *Photo © Renée Newman.*

Large dyed Chinese freshwater cultured pearls are also sometimes coated with a transparent polymer film to improve their luster. This coating can be detected by its strangely smooth feel compared to uncoated pearls, and occasionally by bald spots where the coating may have worn away. Some thick coatings may show bubbles and pockets of dirt under magnification. Polymer coating is not a well-accepted trade practice because it is not permanent; it eventually wears off. Good-quality pearls do not need to be coated to look lustrous. When viewed under 10-times magnification, the coating may have the same speckled appearance as the coating on imitation pearls.

Some cultured freshwater pearls have a natural metallic luster and a gold or bronze color when harvested, but sometimes low-grade pearls are coated to resemble naturally metallic-appearing pearls. Then they are sold at very low prices, allowing pearl cultivators to sell off products with undesirable colors. The disadvantage is that this coating can wear off, unlike a dye, which is more permanent.

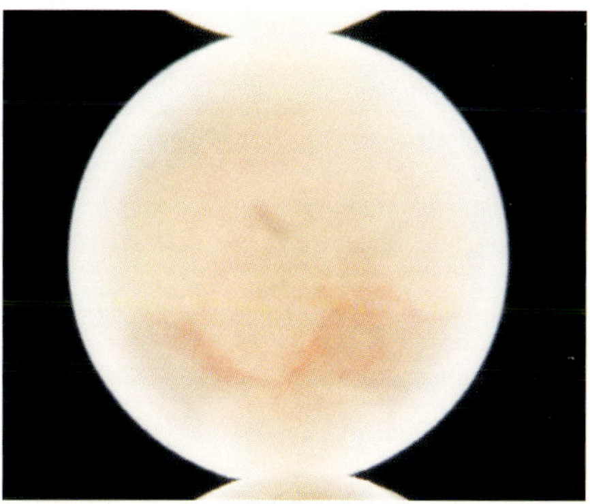

Pink dye in pearl cracks.
Photo © Renée Newman.

Filling

Low-quality cultured baroque pearls are occasionally filled with an epoxy substance if they are partially hollow or have a loose nucleus. This helps the bead nucleus stay in position when the pearls are restrung, and it makes the pearls more solid and improves their durability.

According to Stephen J. Kennedy in the January–March 1998 issue of *Australian Gemmologist*, hollow natural pearls are often filled with foreign materials to bring them to somewhere near the weight one would expect for a pearl of that size. Natural pearls are often sold by weight, which can lead to this practice. Such fillings can be detected by X-radiography.

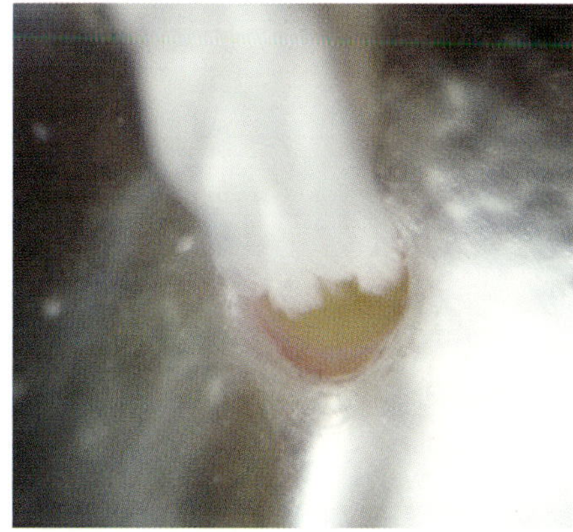

Pink dye in a pearl drill hole.
Photo © Renée Newman.

Dyeing

Akoya pearls are often soaked in pink dye to give them a desirable tint. This process is called "pinking." The dye can usually be detected in the drill holes or in cracks.

Yellow South Sea pearls may also be dyed to make them seem more valuable. Shane Elen of the GIA Research Department has written some excellent articles on identifying treated and untreated South Sea yellow pearls in *Gems & Gemology*'s summer 2001, spring 2002 and summer 2002

High-quality akoya cultured strands from Pearl Paradise. The top strand features natural-color unbleached cultured pearls; the bottom strand is pinked pearls. *Photo by Jeremy Shepherd.*

Pearls with visible dye concentrations. *Photo © Renée Newman.*

issues. An update published in the winter 2012 issue states: "While most dyed yellow or 'golden' cultured pearls can still be detected with relative ease using magnification, some show very clean surfaces lacking any evidence of dye. We have demonstrated that these can be identified by non-destructive, advanced instrumental techniques such as UV-Vis reflectance and PL spectroscopy." In other words, one must rely on labs with high-tech equipment to confirm that the color of golden pearls is natural.

Off-color freshwater pearls are often dyed, sometimes with colors that are obviously not natural. Consumers like these dyed pearls because they are attractive and low-priced, and designers buy them because they can use them to create unique, affordable jewelry.

If pearls are not properly dyed, the color will not be stable. Therefore, it is important to buy dyed pearls from reputable jewelers. It is more likely that the color will be stable, and if there is a problem, you will be able to return the pearls and get a refund.

Akoya and freshwater cultured pearls are sometimes dyed gray or black to either create a color not available naturally or to imitate Tahitian

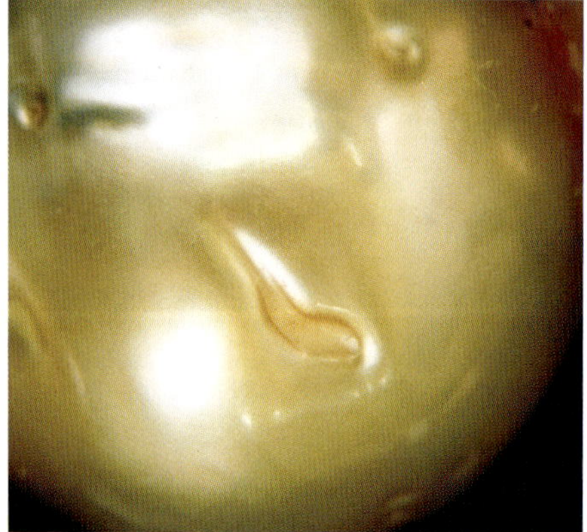

Magnified view of a blemish with dye concentrations on a dyed golden South Sea cultured pearl.

Dye concentrations and black nucleus visible in blemishes on two dyed cultured pearls. *Photos © Renée Newman.*

A colorful array of dyed freshwater cultured pearl strands from Pearl Concepts, Inc. *Photo © Renée Newman.*

Unique dyed freshwater cultured pearls from King's Ransom. *Photo by Betty Sue King.*

pearls. This is acceptable if the color treatment is disclosed, but not if the treatment was done intentionally to deceive people into thinking they are buying Tahitian pearls.

Irradiation

Irradiation involves bombarding pearls with gamma rays. This blackens the shell-bead nucleus of akoya and South Sea pearls and can make their nacre appear dark if it is thin. This method works best on freshwater pearls. Sometimes pearls are both dyed and irradiated, according to the spring 2024 issue of *Gems & Gemology*. Irradiation can give them an iridescent bluish or greenish gray color, and the dye will further darken their appearance.

Silver Salt Treatment

Silver salt treatment is the most common way of blackening akoya pearls. The pearls are soaked in a weak solution of silver nitrate and diluted ammonia and then exposed to light or hydrogen sulfide gas. Unfortunately, the silver nitrate tends to weaken the pearls and make them more susceptible to wear. This treatment can usually be detected by X-radiography.

Dyed Bead Nucleus

Occasionally shell-bead nuclei are dyed before they are inserted into the oyster. Afterward the dark bead may show through the nacre and make the pearl nacre look darker.

Metal Injections

Metal fluids may be injected into the pearl sacs of mollusks during the culturing process. This treatment is meant to induce various colors in the pearls, depending on the metal used.

Heat Treatment

Golden South Sea pearls are occasionally heated to intensify their color. High-tech lab equipment is required to detect whether a heating process has been used.

Proprietary Color Treatments

The Ballerina Pearl Company developed a proprietary chemical and physical process to give Tahitian pearls a pistachio color (yellowish green to greenish yellow), according to the spring 2016 issue of *Gems & Gemology*. The company also developed a similar process to make Tahitian cultured pearls look brown; around 2005, brown Tahitian cultured pearls, known as chocolate pearls, were becoming increasingly available. Cultured pearls treated by the Ballerina process can be identified by their unusual coloration, characteristic fluorescence, UV-Vis-NIR reflectance and Raman spectra, and trace element composition, as detailed in the winter 2006 issue of *Gems & Gemology*.

Treated Tahitian cultured chocolate pearls. *Jewelry and photo from King Plutarco, Inc.*

An article in the fall 2008 issue of *Gems & Gemology* discusses the durability of these treated pearls. The pearls GIA studied did not change color when exposed to daylight, cosmetics and some chemicals; subtle changes were noticed after exposure to heat; and more significant changes were observed when the samples were exposed to chemically reactive household cleaning solutions.

Maeshori

Maeshori is a Japanese term meaning "before treatment" (*mae* is "before" and *shori* is "treatment"). It can refer to a variety of treatments done to freshwater, akoya and some South Sea cultured pearls that may vary from one pearl factory to another. Today *maeshori* usually refers to a proprietary nacre-tightening and luster-improvement process involving heating and cooling and sometimes chemicals. The effects of the process are not always permanent; the resulting luster may diminish over time.

SIMPLE TESTS FOR DETECTING TREATMENTS

Color-treated pearls are not fakes, but they are normally considered less valuable than those of natural color. There is an especially large price difference between true black and golden South Sea pearls and those that have been treated, so you should know how to protect yourself from being charged a natural-color pearl price for a treated pearl. Even if the price is fair, you may just prefer pearls of natural color. You can reduce your chances of being misled by using the tests and recommendations discussed in this section.

Price Test

If the price is very low compared to natural-color pearls of the same size, shape and overall quality, that is a sign the pearls might be treated. For example, natural-color Tahitian pearls are typically expensive, so if the price is low and you are not in Tahiti, assume that the pearl is dyed unless otherwise told. (It is illegal to import or sell dyed black pearls in Tahiti.) Some websites have been known to sell dyed freshwater pearls as natural-color Tahitian pearls for prices as low as $25 per strand.

Dyed golden pearls can be sold anywhere, so always ask if the color is natural. If the store claims the color is natural, ask them to write that on the receipt. Reports from respected gem laboratories are used to help confirm whether expensive pearls are of natural color.

Blackened freshwater pearls sold on a website as a Tahitian pearl necklace for $25, including shipping. The low price, off-round shape and dye concentrations are clues that these are not Tahitian pearls. *Photo © Renée Newman.*

Drill-Hole Test

If possible, look into the drill hole with a 10-power magnifier, such as a loupe. If the nacre is white but the nucleus looks dark, that indicates the pearl has been colored by irradiation or the nucleus has been dyed. Also check to see if there is dye concentrated around the drill hole. Sometimes undrilled dyed golden pearls have pits or cracks that will allow you to detect a dark nucleus.

Natural golden South Sea cultured pearls with normal color variation. *Pendant & earrings from Divina pearls; photo by Christina Gregory.*

Color Test

Are the pearls so dark they are entirely black or so yellow they look fake? Are they non-typical colors, or do all the pearls in the piece have the exact same color? These are indications that the gems might be color treated. It is not easy to find several black or yellow pearls of exactly the same color.

If you are interested in black pearls, look at many examples of them. Next, look at dyed pearls and compare their color. Gradually you will get a sense of what the body colors and overtones of real black pearls look like. People who work with black or yellow pearls on a regular basis can usually spot color-treated pearls instantly, but even experts can be fooled. Therefore, when making a major purchase, have your pearls tested by an independent gem lab if they are not already accompanied by a report from a reputable lab.

Color-treated pearls from Pearl Concepts. *Photo © Renée Newman.*

Magnifier Test

Examine the surface of the pearl with a 10-power loupe. If the color in or around the blemishes is stronger and more intense than the rest of the pearl, this is a good sign that the pearl is dyed. The absence of visible dye is not proof of natural color, however; not all blemishes of dyed pearls will show dye.

SPECIALIZED TESTS FOR DETECTING TREATMENTS

The following testing methods require special equipment. They are used by gem laboratories and some appraisers and jewelers.

Fiber-Optic Test

If black pearls appear brownish under fiber-optic light but not under a tungsten light bulb, this suggests they have been dyed with silver nitrate. Good-quality natural-color Tahitian pearls usually retain their normal color under fiber-optic lights, although occasionally low-grade mottled Tahitian pearls will look brownish, according to Stephen Kennedy in the January–March 1998 issue of *Australian Gemmologist*.

Ultraviolet Fluorescence Test

When natural-color black pearls are examined under long-wave UV radiation, they generally exhibit fluorescence ranging from bright red (pearls from Baja California) to dull reddish brown (Tahitian pearls). Dyed pearls tend to show no reaction or fluoresce a dull green.

Fluorescence Spectroscopy

When excited by long-wave to mid-range UV light (200 to 300 nanometers), naturally colored pearls emit a fluorescence band between 320 and 400 nanometers, centered at 340 nanometers. The *Lab Notes* section of the spring 2020 issue of *Gems & Gemology* states: "Color treatments such as dyeing and irradiation tend to damage or mask the conchiolin in the nacre, significantly reducing the fluorescence intensity. By evaluating the intensity of a pearl's fluorescence in the UV region, it is possible to rapidly detect potential color treatments on pearls in a nondestructive manner."

Microscope Test

When pearls are viewed under a 100-plus-power microscope through crossed polarizing lenses, traces of chemical coloring can be seen if they exist, according to Yoshihiro Hisada and Hiroshi Komatsu in *Pearls of the World*.

X-Radiography

When an X-ray photo (X-radiograph) is taken, if pearls have been dyed with silver salts, a pale ring can often be seen between the nacre and the shell-bead nucleus. In addition, there is less contrast between the bead and the nacre than in an untreated pearl.

X-Ray Fluorescence Test

When pearls are exposed to X-rays, their emitted wavelengths can be measured with an instrument called a spectrometer to detect trace elements such as silver on their surfaces.

There is a wide variety of tests available for identifying color-treated pearls. Using a combination of the simpler tests will help you spot obvious cases of treatment, but when it comes to making a major purchase, it is wise to get help from professionals.

12 Creating Unique Pearl Jewelry with Colored Gems

Combining cultured pearls with colored gems is an ideal way to create one-of-a-kind pieces and expand one's inventory of pearl jewelry. The introduction of low-priced freshwater cultured pearls to the market in the 1970s made it possible for designers to create unique and affordable pearl jewelry with colored gems. Most pearl jewelry before then consisted of white pearl strands or pearl-and-diamond pieces. When colored gems were present, pearls were often used as accent stones in the piece. This chapter shows how the use of color in pearl jewelry has evolved since the Georgian period, beginning around 1714.

A Georgian amethyst and natural seed pearl brooch/pendant. *LangAntiques.com; photo by Cole Bybee.*

A Georgian natural pearl, green beryl and ruby floral bracelet. *LangAntiques.com; photo by Cole Bybee.*

PERIOD JEWELRY (EUROPEAN AND AMERICAN)

Jewelry historians and antique dealers often describe styles of jewelry (both European and American) with a period name, usually based on the reign of a particular monarch or on an art movement. Many of the periods overlap, and the beginning and ending dates can vary depending on the historical source. The dates in this section are based largely on Christie Romero's *Warman's Jewelry,* Gail Levine's *Auction Market Resource* and Anna M. Miller's *The Buyer's Guide to Affordable Antique Jewelry,* as well as information from dealers who sell antique and estate jewelry.

What follows is an outline of jewelry eras starting with the 18th century, followed by brief descriptions and examples of pieces from each period.

ERA	DATES
Georgian	1714–1837 (reigns of King George I to King George IV)
Victorian	1837–1901 (reign of Queen Victoria)
Art Nouveau	1890–1914
Belle Epoque	1890–1914
Edwardian	1901–15 (reign of King Edward VII and pre–World War I)
Art Deco	1915–40
Retro	1939–50
Mid-century	1950–70
Modern	1970–present

Period Jewelry Terminology

Antique jewelry: any piece that is 100 or more years old, as defined by the United States Customs Bureau. Webster's Dictionary defines the term *antique* more loosely as any work of art or the like from an early period.

Heirloom, estate or vintage jewelry: previously owned jewelry that is typically passed down from one generation to another. It can range from a few decades to 100 or more years old. "Vintage" and "estate" jewelry can also refer to pieces from an earlier era that have not previously been worn.

Collectibles: items from a specific designer, manufacturer or time period, collected according to the buyer's interests. Normally these pieces are no longer in production, but they do not have to be as old as antiques. For example, retro jewelry pieces are considered collectibles but are not true antiques, hence the phrase "antiques and collectibles."

Circa dating: establishing an approximate date of origin for a jewelry piece. The term *circa* covers a 10-year window on either side of the date. A circa date of 1900 means the piece was probably made sometime between 1890 and 1910.

An 1810 Georgian woven natural seed pearl parure, which is a set of jewelry pieces meant to be worn together. The seed pearls are sewn onto mother-of-pearl to form a wreath of lilies, meant to be worn as a necklace or tiara; a pendant of four triple-lobed frills; and two branches, each with three lilies, as part of a brooch or tiara. A close-up view is on the right of this caption. This parure is a fine example of delicate pearl handwork of the Georgian period. *Parure and photos from Adin Fine Antique Jewellery (AntiqueJewel.com).*

GEORGIAN (1714–1837)

Most pearl jewelry during the Georgian period was made by hand. If colored gems were included, they were usually rubies, sapphires, emeralds, garnets, amethysts, black onyx or lapis lazuli, often set with 18- or 22-karat gold. Enamel was also used to add color. Diamonds were commonly set in silver over gold to bring out their whiteness; in closed-back mountings their brilliance was intensified by foil backing. The backs of settings began to open up in the late Georgian period, after 1780. Brooches featuring eyes were popular during this era.

A Georgian "lover's eye" brooch set with natural half-seed pearls surrounded by rhodolite garnets. Foil backing is used with the closed-back mounts to enhance the stones' brilliance. The eye is hand-painted in watercolor, likely using brushes of a single hair or two. *Brooch from GeorgianJewelry.com; photo by Zachary Mial.*

A Georgian almandine garnet, diamond and natural pearl ring. This is a classic example of a cluster ring from the mid-18th century in terms of form, construction and materials. *Ring from GeorgianJewelry.com; photo by Zachary Mial.*

VICTORIAN (1837–1901)

A Victorian amethyst and natural pearl lavaliere. *LangAntiques.com; photo by Cole Bybee.*

Queen Victoria (1819–1901) loved pearls. According to royal experts, she gave each of her daughters and granddaughters a single pearl on their birthday as they were growing up, so that by the time they turned 18, they had enough pearls for a necklace. Most of Queen Victoria's pearl jewelry consisted of strands of pearls, which were natural because cultured pearls did not become available in commercial quantities until after 1901, the year she died.

Demantoid garnet, which was discovered in the Ural Mountains of Russia in the mid-1800s, was often used in late Victorian jewelry and was sometimes set with pearls. After the death of Queen Victoria's husband, Prince Albert (1819–61), mourning jewelry made with black onyx or jet became popular. Enamel continued to be used as a dramatic background for pearls and diamonds.

After the discovery of diamonds in South Africa in 1867, the gems became more plentiful. The introduction of electric lighting in the 1880s meant that diamonds and other faceted gems could sparkle more indoors and at night. Closed, foiled settings were gradually replaced by open-back mounts, and a greater variety of setting styles was used, including bezel, prong, "gypsy" and wirework settings.

Gold was readily available during the Victorian period, thanks to discoveries in California (1848), Australia (1851), the Black Hills of South Dakota (1874), South Africa (1886), Yukon (1895) and Alaska (1898). Most early Victorian diamond jewelry was handcrafted using 18- to 22-karat gold, some of it tricolor—yellow, white and rose. But in 1854 the British government legalized 9-, 12- and 15-karat gold in order to counter foreign competition. Jewelers in Britain were not required to mark their pieces during most of the 19th century, so it is not uncommon for jewelry from this period to be unmarked. By the end of the Victorian era, a high percentage of gold jewelry was being machine-made and mass-produced. Platinum jewelry had also been introduced to the market, but it was generally made by hand.

Victorian jewelry displays a wide variety of motifs: branches, shells, knots, buckles, flowers, vines, insects, birds, crosses, hearts, snakes, clasped hands and women with flowing hair. Many of the world's most famous jewelry firms were founded during the Victorian period, including Tiffany & Co. in 1837, Cartier in 1847 and Boucheron in 1858.

An English Victorian 15-karat gold necklace set with peridots and seed pearls. *LangAntiques.com; photo by Cole Bybee.*

A Victorian ruby, diamond and natural pearl lavaliere/brooch. *LangAntiques.com; photo by Cole Bybee.*

A Victorian Yogo sapphire, pearl and diamond 14-karat gold flower pendant/brooch, circa 1890. *LangAntiques.com; photo by Cole Bybee.*

A Victorian brooch/pendant of lapis lazuli, ruby, natural pearls, diamonds and silver over 18-karat gold. *LangAntiques.com; photo by Cole Bybee.*

A Victorian cultured pearl, pink sapphire, diamond, rose gold and silver bracelet. *Photo © Heritage Auctions (HA.com).*

A Victorian-era French star sapphire, diamond, synthetic ruby, natural pearl and 18-karat gold brooch. *Brooch and photo from Adin Fine Antique Jewellery (AntiqueJewel.com).*

A Victorian natural blister pearl, green enamel and diamond brooch, circa 1840. The pearl is almost 40 millimeters in length with lines and grooves that evoke the petals of a flower in bloom. *Brooch and photo from Adin Fine Antique Jewellery (AntiqueJewel.com).*

A Victorian sapphire, freshwater pearl and gold bracelet. *Photo © Heritage Auctions (HA.com).*

A Victorian amethyst, diamond and natural pearl tassel pendant/ brooch. *LangAntiques.com; photo by Cole Bybee.*

A Victorian garnet and seed pearl necklace/brooch. *LangAntiques.com; photo by Cole Bybee.*

A Victorian fly brooch set with a natural pearl, diamonds, emeralds and pink sapphires. *LangAntiques.com; photo by Cole Bybee.*

A Victorian convertible butterfly pendant/brooch set with rubies, sapphires, diamonds and natural pearls. *LangAntiques.com; photo by Cole Bybee.*

A Victorian mourning suite of black onyx and seed pearls with glass compartments containing locks of hair. *LangAntiques.com; photo by Cole Bybee.*

A Victorian gold turtle brooch by Riker Bros. set with a diamond, demantoid garnets, rubies and half seed pearls. *Photo © Heritage Auctions (HA.com).*

A Victorian seed pearl and green beryl pendant locket. *Photo © Heritage Auctions (HA.com).*

An Art Nouveau diamond, emerald, cultured pearl, plique-à-jour enamel, gold and silver brooch from Russia. *Photo © Heritage Auctions (HA.com).*

ART NOUVEAU (1890–1914)

The Art Nouveau ("new art") movement was created in France, and it sought to modernize jewelry design and move on from the classical and historical styles that had previously been popular. It was also a reaction to events in French society at the time, including women's battles to secure more rights for themselves outside the home through education and jobs. Women are common motifs in Art Nouveau jewelry.

The period is known for its flowing curved lines, botanical motifs and bright colors. This was the beginning of modern jewelry design. Many French jewelers adopted the style, but the one best known for his designs and artistry was René Lalique (1860–1945). He combined expensive gems with inexpensive materials such as ivory and horn and set them in 18-karat gold. One of the techniques Lalique is noted for and that became associated with Art Nouveau is plique-à-jour (French for "letting in day-light") enameling—translucent enamel with no metal backing, so that it resembles a stained-glass window.

In contrast to earlier periods, precious stones such as diamonds, rubies, emeralds and sapphires were used mainly as accents for larger, cabochon-cut semiprecious stones, including lapis lazuli, moonstone, malachite, carnelian and marcasite. Synthetic rubies and emerald triplets—two pieces of colorless beryl sandwiching a layer of green cement—also made their appearance in Art Nouveau jewelry. The motifs most frequently seen are women with flowing hair, human forms with insect wings, butterflies, peacocks, bees, swans, snakes and flowers. Silver, gold, copper and plated metals were all used in this type of jewelry. The Art Nouveau movement spread across Europe as well as to the United States.

An Art Nouveau enamel, natural pearl and 14-karat gold swan brooch by Krementz, circa 1900. *Brooch from GeorgianJewelry.com; photo by Zachary Mial.*

An Art Nouveau 14-karat rose-gold lizard brooch set with saltwater and freshwater half seed pearls, demantoid garnets and two ruby eyes. *Brooch from GeorgianJewelry.com; photo by Zachary Mial.*

A French belle-époque diamond, demantoid garnet, natural pearl and platinum pendant/brooch. *LangAntiques.com; photo by Cole Bybee.*

BELLE ÉPOQUE (1890–1914)

The French term *belle époque* means "beautiful era" in English. It can refer to the time between the end of the Franco-Prussian War in 1871 and the outbreak of World War I in 1914, or to the period during which Art Nouveau and Edwardian jewelry emerged. Belle-époque jewelry is sometimes described as the European counterpart of British Edwardian jewelry. But even though belle-époque pieces resembled Art Nouveau jewelry, they were generally bolder and more ornate in design and did not include plique-à-jour enameling. In the latter half of this period, jewelers began using cultured pearls in addition to natural pearls.

A French belle-époque sapphire, diamond, cultured pearl, platinum, gold and enamel brooch. *Photo © Heritage Auctions (HA.com).*

A belle-époque sapphire, diamond, natural pearl, platinum and gold pendant. *Pendant and photo from Adin Fine Antique Jewellery (AntiqueJewel.com).*

A belle-époque enamel, diamond, pearl, platinum and 18-karat gold necklace and brooch with an Austro-Hungarian hallmark. *Necklace and photo from Adin Fine Antique Jewellery (AntiqueJewel.com).*

Above: An Edwardian mother-of-pearl Madonna pendant with seed pearls, diamonds and synthetic sapphires.

Below: An Edwardian diamond, demantoid garnet and freshwater pearl necklace.

LangAntiques.com; photos by Cole Bybee.

EDWARDIAN (1901–15)

A heavy use of diamonds, platinum and pearls in delicate, lacelike mountings is the chief characteristic of Edwardian jewelry. Even though Edward VII's reign was only from 1901 to 1910, the lavish court style of the era influenced fashion in the decades before and after his ascent to the throne.

Edwardian jewelry was also inspired by the courts of the 18th-century French kings Louis XV and Louis XVI. In fact, it was a French jeweler, Louis Cartier (1875–1942), who was at the forefront of developing this style and who was the official jeweler for the English court. As a result, this style has also been identified as belle époque. Typical motifs are horseshoes, doves, ducks, fish, hearts, suns, stars, moons, wreaths of flowers, bow knots and arrows.

New gem cuts such as the marquise, the emerald and the baguette emerged during this period, thanks to improvements in diamond-cutting technology. Calibrated stones of standardized sizes and shapes became available for use in mass-produced jewelry.

With the development of a torch hot enough to work platinum, around 1890, platinum became the most common metal for fine pieces. For a while it was laminated with gold, much as silver had been, but gradually it became evident that the metal was strong enough to be used by itself for intricate mountings and secure diamond settings. Much of the metalwork was open, allowing underlying fabrics to show through. During World War I white gold came into common use because platinum was needed for the war effort, so its use in jewelry was temporarily banned.

Even though Edwardian jewelry was primarily white, pastel colors were also in fashion. Later pieces were set with darker colored gemstones, such as amethyst, alexandrite, chrysoprase and demantoid garnets.

The noted French houses that created Edwardian jewelry included Cartier, Boucheron, Chaumet and Georges Fouquet. In the United States, jewelry of this period was made by Tiffany & Co.; Black, Starr & Frost; Marcus & Co. and others. Most of the pieces by Russian imperial court jeweler Peter Carl Fabergé (1846–1920) can be classified as Edwardian, but many of his creations also display Art Nouveau lines and motifs.

An art deco ring set with rubies, diamonds and cultured pearls. *Ring and photo from Adin Fine Antique Jewellery (AntiqueJewel.com).*

Left: An art deco diamond, ruby, cultured pearl, platinum and gold brooch. *Photo © Heritage Auctions (HA.com).*

ART DECO (1915–40)

Geometric patterns, straight lines, symmetry and bold color contrasts characterize art deco jewelry designs. Platinum, diamonds and white gold continued to be used extensively, but there was a greater use of colored gemstones, some of which were synthetic. New shapes for side stones emerged in the form of bullets, half-moons and shields. Since cultured pearls were less expensive and more readily available during this period, they were used more frequently than natural pearls.

The motifs most often used were geometric, abstract or floral, often inspired by the aesthetics of ancient Egypt, China, Japan and India, among other cultures. Art deco Egyptian and Japanese motifs became popular following the celebrated discovery of King Tutankhamun's tomb in 1923 and new trade agreements between Japan and the United States.

Louis Cartier is the most famous art deco designer, but the works of Van Cleef & Arpels also had a strong influence on the period. Other leading designers and houses were Mauboussin, Jean Fouquet, Boucheron, Chaumet, LaLoche and the American firms Tiffany & Co.; Black, Starr & Frost; J.E. Caldwell & Co.; C.D. Peacock; Harry Winston; and Shreve, Crump & Low.

An art deco natural pearl, diamond and synthetic sapphire bar pin. *LangAntiques .com; photo by Cole Bybee.*

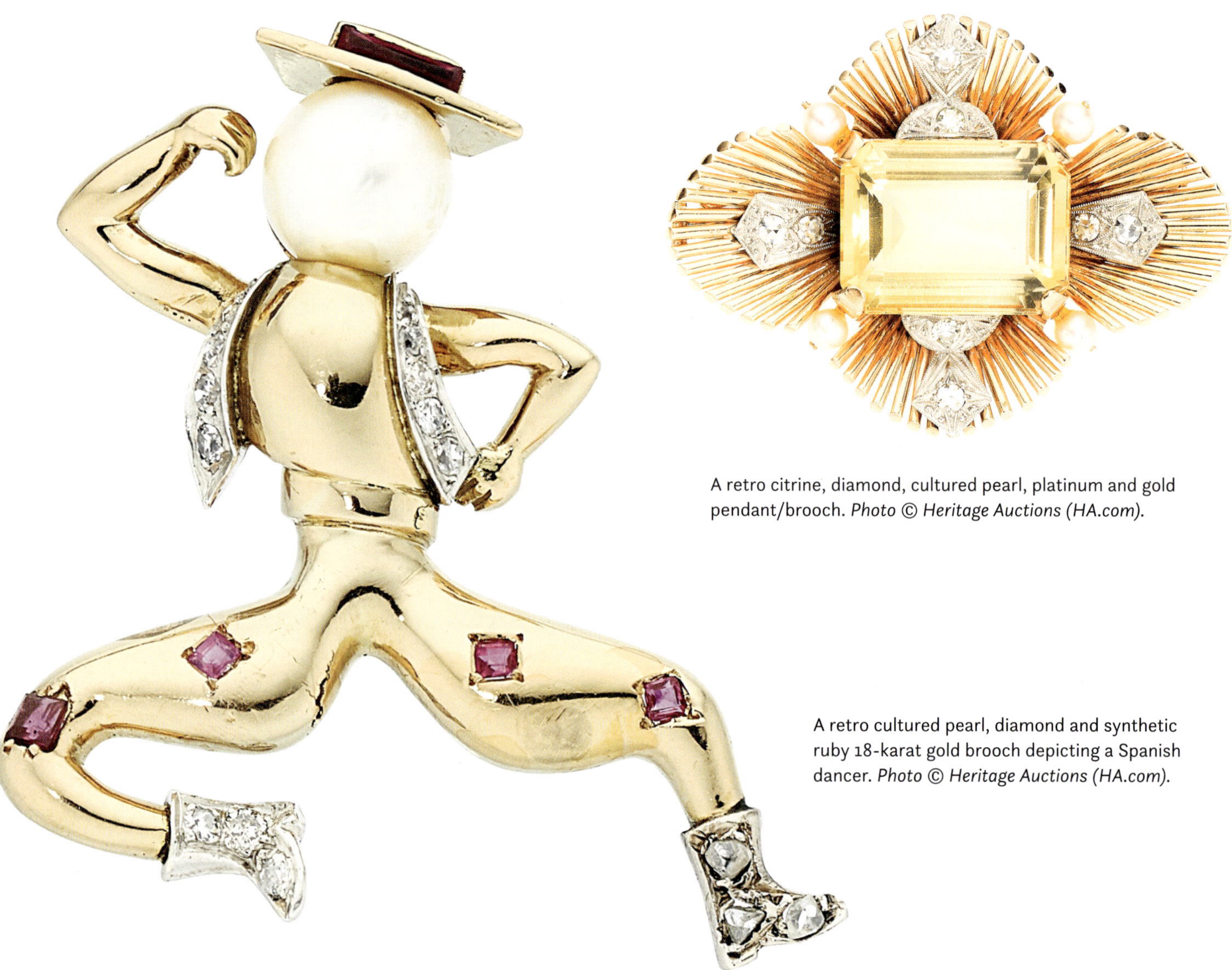

A retro citrine, diamond, cultured pearl, platinum and gold pendant/brooch. *Photo © Heritage Auctions (HA.com).*

A retro cultured pearl, diamond and synthetic ruby 18-karat gold brooch depicting a Spanish dancer. *Photo © Heritage Auctions (HA.com).*

RETRO (1939–50)

The all-white look of diamonds and platinum began to lose its appeal during the Great Depression of 1929–39. Then, when the U.S. government declared platinum a strategic metal during World War II, it was no longer used for jewelry in America. Platinum was replaced in fine jewelry by yellow gold and rose gold, and later by white gold. Colored gems such as citrine, aquamarine and tourmaline were often used in addition to rubies, sapphires and emeralds. Pearls were used primarily as accents.

Hollywood stars increasingly influenced fashion more than royalty, and France was no longer the jewelry design center of the world. Retro designs were bold, futuristic, colorful and three-dimensional. The main themes of the period were feminine, patriotic and industrial.

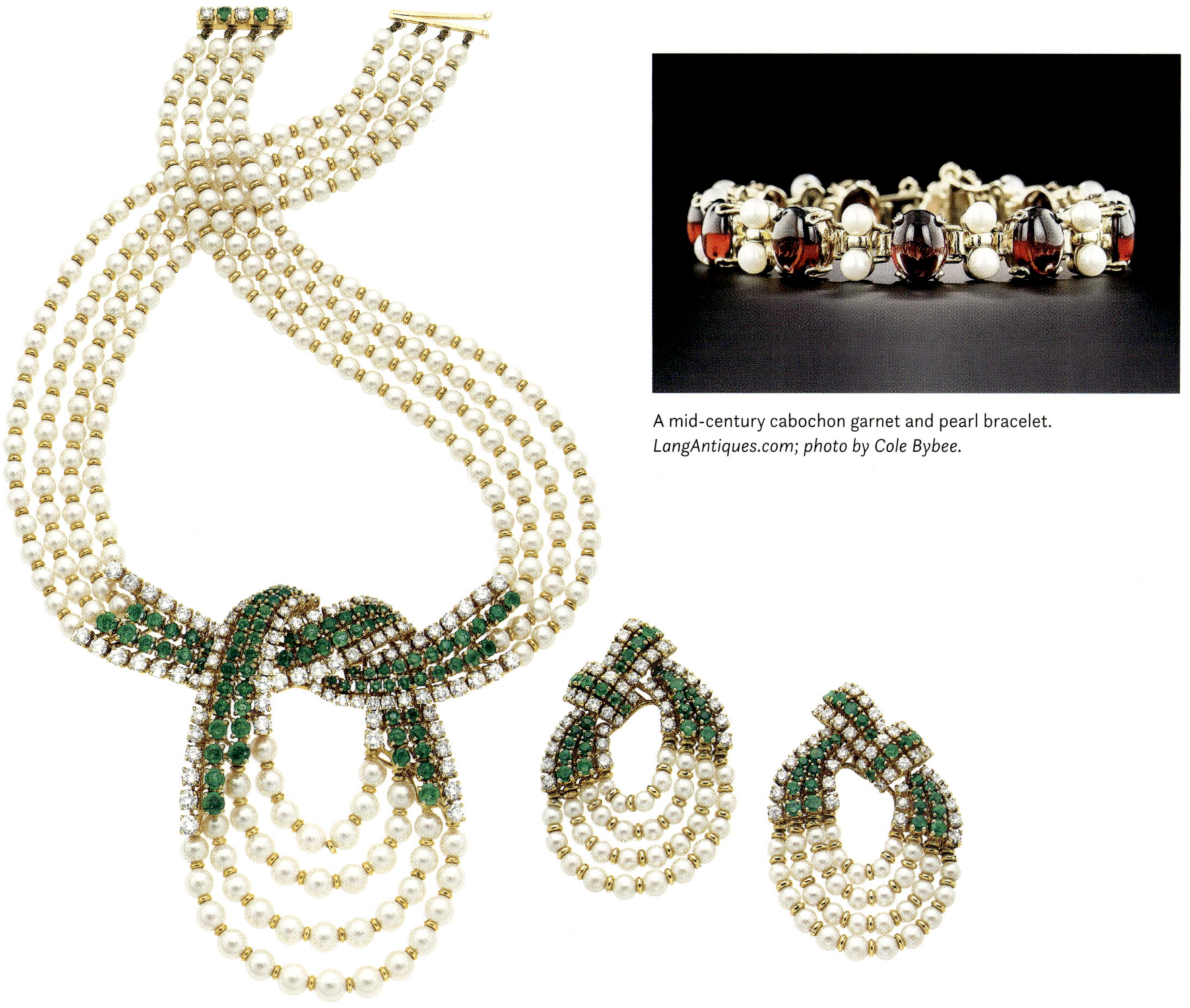

A mid-century cabochon garnet and pearl bracelet. *LangAntiques.com; photo by Cole Bybee.*

A Chaumet diamond, emerald, cultured pearl and 18-karat gold suite. *Photo © Heritage Auctions (HA.com).*

MID-CENTURY (1950–70)

Overall, mid-century jewelry tended to be more feminine and elegant than the bold styles of the retro period. After World War II the U.S. government lifted its embargo on platinum, so it could be used in high-end jewelry once again. However, the metal did not regain its previous popularity because white gold was less expensive and easier to work with, and the public had already accepted the change in metals.

Cultured akoya pearls were the main pearls used in European and North American jewelry, and usually they were worn as strands. Sometimes colored gem beads were added to the strands, and occasionally cultured akoyas were mounted in pieces with colored gems. In the Middle East, natural pearls remained the preferred choice for pearl jewelry.

Cultured freshwater pearls set with hand-carved prehnite, blue topaz, blue sapphire, pink sapphire, citrine and diamonds. *Ring and photo courtesy of Le Vian.*

MODERN (1970–PRESENT)

Fijian cultured pearl, jasper and spinel earrings by Assael. *Photo courtesy of Assael.*

The modern jewelry era represents a composite of many jewelry styles, including those that existed well before 1970. Pearl jewelry has become much more colorful because of the new types of cultured pearls that have become available and the wider use of colored gems in pearl pieces. It was only in the late 1960s that Tahitian cultured pearls appeared on the market. It was not until the 1980s that the Philippines established itself as a serious producer of golden South Sea cultured pearls. The biggest developments in Chinese freshwater cultured pearl production have occurred since 1980. During the past 30 years, designers have become more interested in natural abalone, conch, melo and clam pearls and are using them in jewelry. As a result, a high percentage of pearl jewelry today is very different from that which preceded 1970. Adding colored gems makes it even more unique.

"Treasures of the Sea" bracelet by Paula Crevoshay, set with Australian cultured South Sea pearls and moonstones, tsavorites, sapphires and diamonds depicting waves. *Photo by Crevoshay Studio.*

A natural conch pearl, sapphires, diamonds and tsavorites in a handmade ring by Paula Crevoshay. *Photo by Crevoshay Studio.*

A water-buffalo horn cuff by Alishan Halebian, featuring pink cultured pearls with bezel-set rubies. *Photo courtesy of Alishan.*

Toucan brooch by Rio Pearl, with a cultured Tahitian pearl body and head and beak set with fancy sapphires, green garnets and black diamonds, next to some ruby berries. *Photo courtesy of Rio Pearl.*

South Sea "keshi" cultured pearls, moonstones, pink tourmalines and diamonds in a Cynthia Renée custom brooch. *Photo by Brian Moghadam/Rockstone Photography.*

A natural abalone pearl, moonstone and diamond butterfly pin by Collector Fine Jewelry. *Photo courtesy of Pala International.*

A cultured freshwater pearl and mabe pearl pendant by Lydia Tutunjian, set with sapphires, amethysts and diamonds. *Photo courtesy of Alishan.*

A cultured freshwater pearl and lapis lazuli necklace by Sasha V. Flynn. *Photo courtesy of Adore Adorn.*

Earrings by Yoko London, with pink opals, pink sapphires, diamonds and cultured freshwater pearls. *Photo courtesy of Yoko London.*

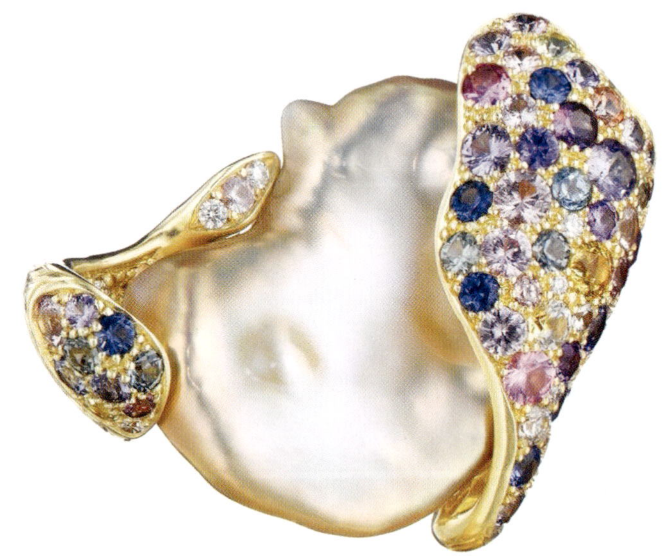

A Chinese cultured freshwater pearl embraced by a wave of sapphires, amethysts and diamonds in a brooch/pendant by Naomi Sarna. *Photo courtesy of Naomi Sarna.*

Freshwater cultured pearl earrings by Paula Crevoshay set with tsavorites, tourmalines and sapphires. *Photo by Crevoshay Studio.*

A melo pearl accented with mandarin garnets, Ural demantoids and diamonds in a ring by Wolf Bialonczyk. *Photo © bialonczyk.at.*

A necklace of rubies, sapphires, freshwater cultured pearls and South Sea cultured pearls by Eve J. Alfillé. *Photo by Matthew Arden.*

Boulder opal, cultured Fijian pearl and tanzanite earrings by Assael. *Photo courtesy of Assael.*

Cleopatra Collection earrings by Yoko London, featuring turquoise, mother-of-pearl, diamonds and cultured freshwater pearls. *Photo courtesy of Yoko London.*

Earrings by Le Vian set with cultured freshwater pearls, hand-carved prehnites, tourmalines, blue sapphires, pink sapphires and tsavorites. *Photo courtesy of Le Vian.*

Cultured Indonesian South Sea golden pearl and citrine with tourmaline accents in a pendant by Brenda Smith. *Photo by Drew Stauss.*

A Chinese freshwater cultured pearl skirt, accented with rubies, in a brooch by A & Z Pearls. *Photo by John Parrish.*

A carved Tahitian pearl pendant by Chi Huynh, inset with quartz druse and a cultured pearl. *Photo courtesy of Galatea.*

A Cynthia Renée custom-designed pendant made with a *maki-e* Tahitian cultured pearl and red spinel. *Maki-e* is a Japanese decorative technique for creating motifs on the surface of a piece. *Photo by Cynthia Renée, Inc.*

A flying lionfish brooch/pendant from the Autore Oceania Collection, set with South Sea cultured pearls, blue moonstones, black and white diamonds, and blue, orange and purple sapphires. The collection is inspired by Australian underwater creatures. *Photo courtesy of Autore Pearls.*

Tahitian cultured pearls, diamonds, tourmalines and amethysts in butterfly earrings by ASBA USA. *Photo courtesy of ASBA USA.*

A hand-carved Tahitian cultured pearl with a Kyocera opal center and ruby accent, in a pendant by Chi Huynh. *Photo courtesy of Galatea.*

A natural North American quahog clam pearl and spinel ring by Assael. *Photo courtesy of Assael.*

A cameo neckpiece hand-carved from a queen helmet (*Cassis madagascariensis*) shell by Wounaan artist Lider Peña for Rainforest Design, set in 950 silver with rubellite tourmaline and garnet. *Photo by Roslyn Zelenka.*

Tahitian cultured pearls, dendritic agate and brown diamonds in hand-fabricated earrings of granulated 22-karat gold by Zaffiro. *Photo courtesy of Zaffiro.*

Lapis lazuli, diamond and cultured pearl earrings by Mark Schneider. *Photo courtesy of Mark Schneider Design.*

A natural Chinese freshwater pearl crowned with white and black diamonds, moonstones, Ethiopian opals and multicolored sapphires. *Brooch by Naomi Sarna; photo courtesy of Naomi Sarna.*

Platinum bolo necktie by Mark Schneider, featuring a 13.1-carat trillion-cut tanzanite, a cultured black pearl, a cultured white pearl and yellow and white diamonds, with a citrine and black jade shield. *Photo courtesy of Mark Schneider Design.*

Tahitian cultured pearl, Sardinian coral and Maligano jasper earrings by Assael. *Photo courtesy of Assael.*

Willow Creek jasper, diamond and natural seed pearl tassel earrings by Assael. *Photo courtesy of Assael.*

Cultured mabe pearl, coral and diamond earrings by Matt Harris Designs. *Photo courtesy of Matt Harris Designs.*

Natural clam pearl, dendritic agate and Sardinian coral accented with diamonds and natural saltwater pearls, mounted atop mother-of-pearl. *Brooch by Assael; photo courtesy of Assael.*

“Aurora Borealis” pendant handcrafted by Daniel Moesker featuring natural abalone pearls from the Chatham Islands, New Zealand, and a 9.48-carat copper and manganese-bearing bicolor tourmaline, accented with diamonds, sapphires and Paraiba tourmalines. *Photo by Henk Van Mierlo.*

Dissimilar pearl ear cuffs by Brenda Smith Jewelry set with cultured freshwater pearls, cultured akoya keshi pearls and sapphires. *Photo by Drew Stauss.*

13 Style and Care Tips for Pearl Jewelry

The previous chapter showed how jewelers and designers have created unique pearl jewelry with colored gems. This chapter offers tips on creating stylish jewelry with single pearls and single strands of pearls. The second part gives advice on caring for pearl jewelry.

VERSATILE WAYS TO WEAR A STRAND OF PEARLS

No other gems offer more versatility than pearls. Queen Elizabeth I of England made the most of this feature. She wore yards of them as necklaces, hanging down as far as her knees. She had them threaded into her wigs, embroidered on her clothing and set in her crown and other royal jewelry. You, too, can enjoy the versatility of pearls.

One easy way to add style to a strand of pearls is to position an attractive clasp at the side or front of the necklace instead of at the back of the neck.

Button-shaped Tahitian cultured pearls with a strong magnetic clasp set with cubic zirconia. Magnetic clasps are ideal for people with dexterity problems such as arthritic hands, because they can easily be fastened or unfastened. In most cases they can be worn with pacemakers, but it is best to consult your doctor first if you have a pacemaker. *Necklace by Matt Harris Designs. Photo courtesy of Matt Harris Designs.*

Baroque cultured pearls from Myanmar, Australia, China and the Philippines, with an ammonite-shaped clasp. *Necklace design © Eve Alfillé; photo by Matthew Arden.*

Pin/clasp with carved black opal, freshwater cultured pearls and a South Sea pearl drop on a strand of South Sea cultured pearls. *Carving, design, fabrication and photo by Angela Conty.*

The following necklace styles can be created with just one opera-length strand (about 70 to 91 centimeters, or 28 to 36 inches) and a pair of hinged clasps, such as the Applaudere oyster clasp in the two photos directly below.

Hinged Applaudere clasps from A & Z pearls. *Photo © Renée Newman.*

A different configuration using the Applaudere clasps. *Photo by Richard Rubin.*

A single strand clasped in the front to form a single chain. *Cultured pearls and oyster clasps from A & Z Pearls; photo by Diamond Graphics.*

A single strand of adjustable length. *Cultured pearls and oyster clasps from A & Z Pearls; photo by Diamond Graphics.*

A single strand knotted in the front. *Cultured pearls and oyster clasps from A & Z Pearls; photo by Diamond Graphics.*

A double strand in front and a single strand at the back. *Cultured pearls and oyster clasps from A & Z Pearls; photo by Diamond Graphics.*

A single strand with a loop hanging in the front. *Cultured pearls and oyster clasps from A & Z Pearls; photo by Diamond Graphics.*

A triple strand in front and a double strand at the back. *Cultured pearls and oyster clasps from A & Z Pearls; photo by Diamond Graphics.*

A double strand looped together in the front. *Cultured pearls from A & Z Pearls; photo by Diamond Graphics.*

A single strand pinned to the shoulder. *Cultured pearls and oyster clasps from A & Z Pearls; photo by Diamond Graphics.*

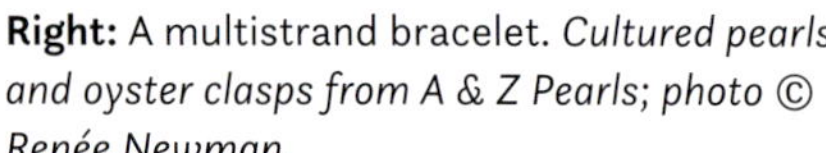

Right: A multistrand bracelet. *Cultured pearls and oyster clasps from A & Z Pearls; photo © Renée Newman.*

An opera-length strand can also be worn as a belt, as a hatband, looped through buttonholes, or in the hair, perhaps wrapped around a chignon or ponytail. These are only some of the ways in which pearls can be worn. Use your imagination and you will discover others!

VERSATILE WAYS TO WEAR PEARL STUDS

Necklaces made with a strand of pearls are not the only type of versatile jewelry. Pearl stud earrings can also be used to create a variety of looks. For example, encircling the studs with removable diamond jackets makes them look dressier. They could also be encircled with jackets set with seed pearls or colored gems.

Custom jewelry designer Cynthia Renée has developed a system that uses cultured pearl studs as the foundation for interchangeable jewelry. Multiple looks can be created with earrings that have a removable post and a drop adapter so that the pearls can be worn as either studs or drops. *"Progressive Pearls" interchangeable pearl system by Cynthia Renée; pearl earring photos by John Parrish; amethyst-and-pearl earring photos by Brian Moghadam/ Rockstone Photography.*

Tahitian cultured pearl studs that can be worn with or without diamond earring jackets. *Earrings from A & Z Pearls; photo by Diamond Graphics.*

CARING FOR YOUR PEARL JEWELRY

The Mohs hardness scale rates the relative hardness of minerals on a scale from 1 to 10. Diamond, at number 10, ranks as the highest, while talc is the lowest, at 1. The intervals between the numbers on the scale are not equal, especially between 9 and 10. Even though ruby and sapphire (corundum) rate 9, diamond is many times harder. Tooth enamel has a hardness of 5 on the Mohs scale, and pearls fall into a range of 2.5 to 4. In other words, pearl is a relatively soft material.

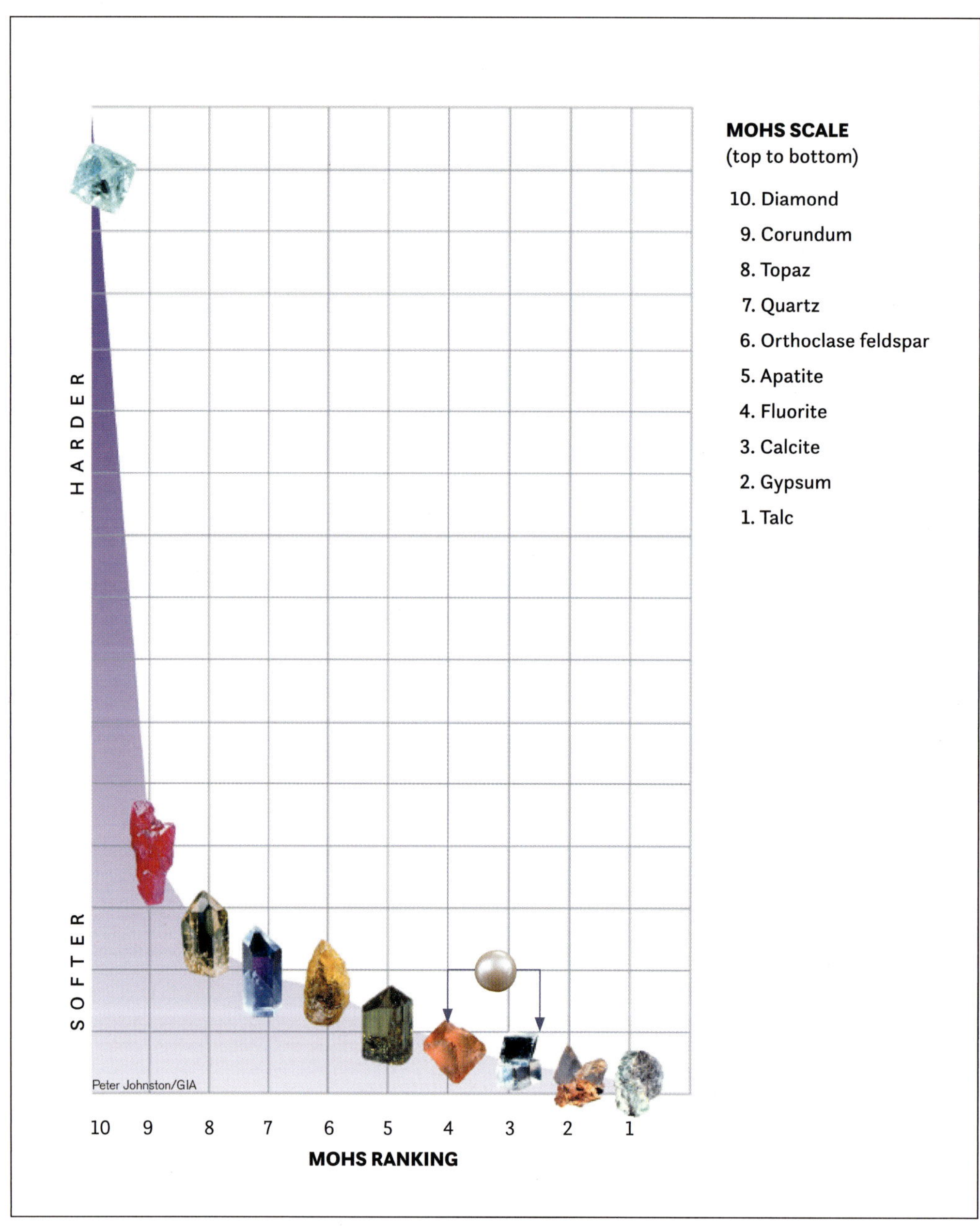

The Mohs hardness scale. *Graphic: Peter Johnston © GIA.*

Knowing how soft they are helps us understand why pearls should not simply be tossed in with other gems in a jewelry box. Knowing that teeth are harder than pearls helps us understand why the "tooth test" for identifying imitations should either be avoided or done very gently. The basic concept of a hardness scale is that a harder material will scratch one that is softer.

Besides being soft, pearls are easily damaged by chemicals and can be eaten away by acids such as vinegar and lemon juice. Heat can turn them brown or dry them out and make them crack.

One advantage of pearls is that, in spite of their softness, they are still fairly tough. In his book *Pearls*, Alexander Farn relates how jewelers and pearl merchants of old would separate imitation pearls from real ones by having footmen stomp on them. The ones that were crushed were imitation, while the natural pearls would normally resist such blows. Cultured pearls, especially those with thin nacre, are not so durable, so avoid dropping or crushing them.

Cleaning Your Pearls

The softness of pearls and their low resistance to heat and chemicals mean that special precautions must be taken when cleaning them. Keep in mind the following guidelines:

- Do not use a commercial jewelry cleaner unless the label says it is safe for pearls. Many of these cleaners contain ammonia, which will cause deterioration.
- Never use an ultrasonic cleaner to clean pearls. It can damage them and also wash away the color if the pearls have been dyed.
- Never steam-clean pearls. Heat can harm them.
- Never use detergents, bleaches, powdered cleansers, baking soda or ammonia-based cleaners on pearls.
- Do not use a toothbrush, scouring pads or other abrasive materials to clean pearls, as they can scratch the surface. If a speck of dirt cannot be rubbed off with a soft cloth, try using your fingernail—fingernails have a Mohs hardness of only 2.5 or less.
- Do not leave jewelry pieces containing pearls soaking in water for more than a few minutes. Pearls set into jewelry are usually cemented to a precious-metal post with glue or epoxy. Liquids, even water, may begin to loosen the cement that is holding the pearl in place.
- Clean your pearls and other jewelry on a regular basis. Then they will not get so dirty that you have to turn to risky procedures later.

Beadless freshwater cultured pearls lying on a soft cleaning cloth provided by a jewelry supply store. The knots between the pearls protect them from rubbing against each other and from scattering if the string breaks. *Photo © Renée Newman.*

Cleaning pearls is not all that complicated. After you have worn them, just wipe them off with a soft cloth or chamois, which can be either dry or damp. This will prevent dirt from accumulating and prevent perspiration—which is slightly acidic—from eating away at the pearl nacre.

If pearls have not been cleaned regularly and are very dirty, they can be cleaned by your jeweler, or they can be washed in water with a mild dish soap such as Ivory or Lux liquid. (Note that some liquid dish soaps, such as Dawn, can damage pearls, so check before using to make sure the soap is mild enough.) Clean the pearls with a soft cloth, paying attention to the areas around the drill holes, where dirt tends to collect.

After washing the pearls, lay them flat on a kitchen towel to dry. Once the towel is dry, the pearls should also be dry. Do not wear pearls when the string is wet; wet string stretches and attracts dirt that is hard to remove. Likewise, do not hang pearls to dry.

Pouches like these are ideal for storing and protecting pearl jewelry. They are closed with drawstrings, snaps or snaps plus zippers. *Photo © Renée Newman.*

Storing Your Pearls

Pearls are composed of about 2 to 4 percent water, along with calcium carbonate and an organic binder. If they become dehydrated, they can get brittle and crack. Consequently, they should not be kept near a heat source or exposed to strong sunlight, such as on a window sill. Jewelers should not place them in sunny display windows.

A safe-deposit box can be an unusually dry environment, so if you ever store pearls in one, place a small open container of water in the box with them, or try to take them out occasionally and expose them to higher humidity. Sealed plastic bags are not the best place for pearls either, especially for long periods, as the plastic can keep them from getting sufficient moisture.

Since pearls are soft, they should be stored in something that will protect them from scratches. Jewelry pouches or cloth bags are ideal. Pearls can also be wrapped in a soft material and kept wherever convenient.

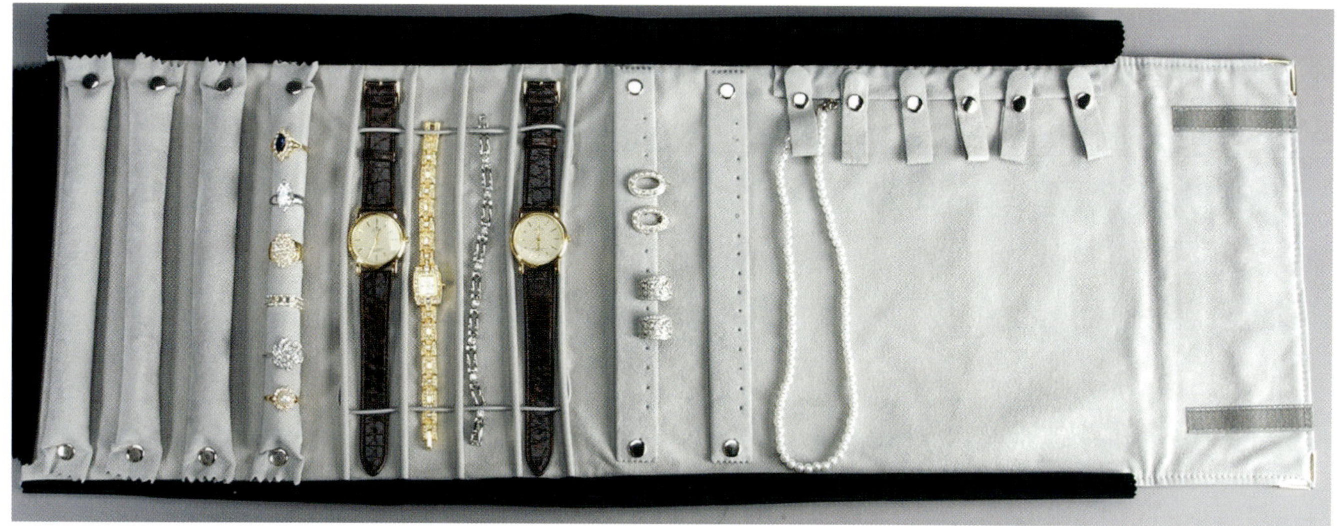

A jewelry roll made of Italian suede with a wide display area. *Roll and photo from A & A Jewelry Supply.*

Jewelry rolls that open up to display their contents have the advantage of letting you see a lot of pieces at once without having to open up individual pouches. Jewelry boxes may be handy, but they are also the first place burglars look!

Having Your Pearls Strung

Pearl necklaces can stretch with time and the string can become dirty and weak. Thus, they should be restrung periodically, preferably by a trained professional about once a year, but the frequency depends on how often they are worn. Fine pearls should be strung with silk and with knots tied between each pearl. The knots prevent them from rubbing against one another and from scattering if the string should break.

Occasionally pearls are strung with gold beads. However, according to a Los Angeles pearl stringer, gold discolors pearls. Therefore, it is not advisable to string expensive pearls with gold beads.

Miscellaneous Tips

- Take your pearls off when applying cosmetics, hair spray and perfume. These beauty aids are made of chemicals and acids that can harm your pearls.
- Take your pearls off when showering or swimming. It is not good to get the string wet, and chlorine and soap can damage the pearls. Pearl rings should be taken off when washing your hands or doing the dishes. Put your ring in a protective container or a safe spot where it will not accidentally fall into the drain or get lost.

An Edwardian natural-pearl-and-diamond bib necklace that is still beautiful after more than 100 years because it received proper care. *LangAntiques.com; photo by Cole Bybee.*

- When selecting pearl jewelry, check to see if the pearl is mounted securely. Preferably it will have been drilled and glued to a post on the mounting, especially if the piece is a ring; otherwise, the pearl may come loose. If a pearl is flawless, a drill hole could lower its value. In such a case it would be better to set the undrilled pearl in a pin, pendant or earring rather than a ring. Another possibility is a 950 platinum/ruthenium setting, which can hold a pearl more securely than gold, silver or some other platinum alloys and does not require a post when set properly.
- If possible, avoid wearing pearls and other jewelry while participating in contact sports or doing housework, gardening, repairs, etc. The mounting, pearls and other gems can be damaged.
- When taking off a pearl ring, grasp the shank or a metal part rather than the pearl. This will prevent the pearl from being loosened or coming into contact with the natural oils on your hands.
- Take a photo of your pearls and other jewelry. Simply lay them out on a table for the photo. If they are ever lost or stolen, you will have documentation to help you remember and to prove what you had. Expensive jewelry should be documented and appraised by a professional jewelry appraiser.
- About every six months, have a jewelry professional verify that the pearls in your jewelry are securely mounted or that the string is still in good condition. Many jewelers will do this free of charge, and they will be happy to answer your questions regarding the care of your jewelry.

Your pearls are very special, just like the person wearing them. So treasure them and take good care of them. If you do, they can bring you and your loved ones a lifetime or more of enjoyment.

Opposite page: Autore South Sea pearl farm, Java, Indonesia. *Photo courtesy of Autore Pearls.*

APPENDIX

CHEMICAL, PHYSICAL AND OPTICAL CHARACTERISTICS OF PEARLS

The information below is based primarily on the following four sources:

Gempedia: A Comprehensive Glossary for Gemstones and Gemmology by Rui Galopim de Carvalho
Gems: Their Sources, Descriptions and Identification by Robert Webster
GIA Gem Reference Guide by Gemological Institute of America
Color Encyclopedia of Gemstones by Joel E. Arem

Chemical composition: $CaCO_3$ (most is aragonite, the rest calcite) 82 to 92 percent; organic material: 4 to 14 percent; H_2O: 2 to 4 percent.

Mohs hardness: 2.5 to 4.0

Specific gravity:
White natural saltwater pearls: 2.66 to 2.78, except for some
Australian pearls: may be as high as 2.78
Black natural saltwater pearls (Gulf of California): 2.61 to 2.69
Conch pearls: 2.85
Natural freshwater pearls: 2.66 to 2.78
Japanese akoya cultured pearls: 2.72 to 2.78 or more
Mantle tissue–nucleated *cultured pearls*: 2.67 to 2.70

Toughness: Usually good, but variable. Old, dehydrated or excessively bleached pearls are not as resistant to breakage and cracking.

Cleavage: None.

Fracture: Uneven.

Streak: White.

Crystal character: An aggregate composed mostly of tiny orthorhombic (pseudo hexagonal) aragonite crystals and sometimes hexagonal calcite crystals. The organic binding material is noncrystalline.

Optic character: AGG, if not opaque (also listed as doubly refractive).

Refractive index: 1.530 to 1.685

Birefringence (double refraction): 0.155

Dispersion: None.

Luster: Dull to almost metallic. Fractures may look pearly to dull.

Phenomena: Orient. Varies from almost none to very noticeable.

Pleochroism: None.

Chelsea-filter reaction: None.

Absorption spectra: Varies greatly, not diagnostic.

Ultraviolet fluorescence: None to strong light blue, yellow, green or pink under both LW and SW.
Natural color black pearls: none to moderate red to orangey red under LW.
Pteria sterna pearls: a distinctive red fluorescence, which can be strong.

Reaction to heat: Can burn, split, crack or turn brown in excessive heat, such as an open flame. Prolonged heat may cause dehydration, which may cause nacre to crack.

Reaction to chemicals: Attacked by all acids. Lotions, cosmetics, perspiration and perfumes can also damage the nacre.

Stability to light: Stable except for some dyed pearls.

Effect of irradiation: Darkens color.

Transparency to X-rays: Semitransparent.

X-ray fluorescence:
Natural saltwater pearls: inert except for a few white Australian pearls, which fluoresce faintly.
Cultured saltwater pearls: moderately strong to very weak greenish yellow depending on nacre thickness.
Freshwater pearls: moderate to strong yellowish white.

X-radiograph:
Cultured pearls usually show a clear separation between core and nacre, and their core normally looks lighter than the nacre coating. A mantle tissue nucleus will look like a very dark, irregularly shaped void. Natural pearls show a more or less concentric structure, and they tend to have the same tone throughout or get darker in the center.

GLOSSARY

Abu Dhabi Pearl: the oldest Gulf pearl on record found in 2017 at an archaeological site on Marawah Island, United Arab Emirates.

Akoya cultured pearl: a beaded cultured pearl cultivated in the *Pinctada fucata (martensii)* oyster.

Akoya keshi cultured pearl: a trade term for a non-beaded cultured pearl grown in a *Pinctada fucata (martensii)* oyster that is a by-product of the culturing process.

Arabian Gulf: an area between Iran and the Arabian Peninsula, also known as the Persian Gulf. It is an extension of the Indian Ocean.

Arabian (Persian) Gulf pearl: a natural pearl produced by the *Pinctada radiata* oyster (World Jewellery Confederation [CIBJO] definition).

Aragonite: a form of crystallized calcium carbonate ($CaCO_3$) that is a primary component of mother-of-pearl, pearl nacre and ammolite. It is also a gemstone that is usually colorless to yellow but can also be pink, white, orange, blue or brown.

Atypical bead-cultured pearl: a cultured pearl with a nucleus that is another pearl or that is made of a different material than shell, e.g., coral or synthetic turquoise.

Baroque pearl: an asymmetrical, irregularly shaped natural or cultured pearl.

Basra pearl: a natural pearl from the Persian Gulf, produced by the *Pinctada radiata* oyster.

Bead (for culturing pearls): a sphere or other shape formed by cutting and polishing a nacreous shell, usually from a freshwater mussel, that forms the center of a beaded cultured pearl. If the bead is a different material, such as turquoise or another cultured pearl, the resulting pearl is called an atypical bead-cultured pearl.

Beaded cultured pearl: cultured pearls with a bead nucleus, usually made from the shell of a freshwater mollusk.

Bivalve: a mollusk with a two-part shell, e.g., clam, mussel, oyster and scallop.

Biwa cultured pearl: a freshwater beaded or non-beaded cultured pearl produced in Lake Biwa, Japan, using the freshwater bivalve mollusk *Hyriopsis schlegelii.*

Black cultured pearl: a natural-color pearl cultured in a *Pinctada margaritifera, Pinctada mazatlanica* or *Pteria sterna* pearl oyster.

Black-lipped oyster: the *Pinctada margaritifera* oyster.

Bleaching: a process that whitens pearls with chemical agents and/or light.

Blister (also known as shell blister): a natural or cultured dome-shaped formation that grows attached to the inner surface of a mollusk shell. When cut from the shell, one side is left flat with no pearly coating. In the American trade, this is commonly called a "blister pearl," but the World Jewellery Confederation (CIBJO) calls it a "blister."

Body color: the dominant, overall color of a natural or cultured pearl.

Buffing: the removal of organic residues from the surfaces of natural and cultured pearls following harvest.

Button shape: a symmetrical dome shape, with or without a flattish bottom. The vertical axis of a button pearl is always shorter than its horizontal axis.

Carat: a unit of weight equaling 200 milligrams (⅕ gram).

Carved: engraved on the surface.

Chaw: a system of converting weight into volume. Pearls in the Persian Gulf and India are often sold by chaw. The formula for calculating the weight in chaw is as follows: multiply the carat weight by itself and then multiply by 0.6518 (World Jewellery Confederation [CIBJO] definition).

Chocolate pearl: a trade name for a brown Tahitian cultured pearl colored with a treatment process developed by the Ballerina Pearl Company. Dyes can produce similar-looking pearls.

Choker: a 35 to 40 centimeter (14 to 16 inch) necklace whose central pearl normally lies in the hollow of the throat or just below.

CIBJO: the World Jewellery Confederation. CIBJO is the initialism for the *Conféderation Internationale de la Bijouterie, Joaillerie, Orfèvrerie des Diamants, Perles et Pierres.* It sets trade standards for nomenclature, treatment disclosure, and responsible and ethical business practices.

Circle(d) pearl: a pearl with one or more parallel grooves or rings around the circumference.

Coin pearl: a trade name for a flat, mantle-grown, beaded pearl produced in the first harvest of a freshwater mussel.

Conch pearl: a non-nacreous pearl found especially in the queen conch sea snail (*Aliger gigas*, formerly *Strombus gigas*) and the horse conch sea snail (*Triplofusus giganteus*), both of which are found in tropical waters from southeastern Florida to the West Indies and the Caribbean Sea.

Cortez Pearl: a trade name for a beaded pearl cultured in the *Pteria sterna* oyster in the Sea of Cortez, also known as the Gulf of California in Mexico.

Cultivated pearl: another term for a cultured pearl.

Cultured blister: a dome-shaped formation that grows attached to the inner surface of a mollusk shell when a bead or other object is inserted between the shell and the mantle. This is a different growing process than that of whole pearls, which form in a pearl sac in the connective tissue of the mantle.

Cultured blister pearl: a cultured pearl that has perforated the mantle (freshwater) or the gonad cavity of the mollusk and has adhered to the inner wall of the shell through layers of nacreous or non-nacreous secretions applied by the mollusk. The subsequently formed layers of nacreous or non-nacreous material are continuous with those of the inner wall of the shell (World Jewellery Confederation [CIBJO] definition). Many trade members also identify cultured blisters as cultured blister pearls.

Cultured pearl: a pearl that is formed with human intervention by inserting a mantle tissue graft from a donor mollusk into a live mollusk with or without a bead.

Cyst pearl: a pearl that occurs in a pearl sac and is not in direct contact with the shell of a pearl-producing mollusk. It is also called a free pearl, loose pearl or whole pearl.

DANAT: the Bahrain Institute for Pearls and Gemstones. The organization was founded in 2017 to support a national plan to revive the natural pearl sector. Its functions include testing and certifying pearls and offering hands-on pearl grading education.

Drop shape: rounded at one end and elongated or pointed at the opposite end, like a teardrop.

Essence of orient: a solution of powdered fish scales mixed with varnish, resin or another coating material, used to make imitation pearls. Also called pearl essence or *essence d'orient.*

Faux pearl: an imitation pearl. *Faux* is the French word for "false" or "fake."

Fiji cultured pearl: a cultured pearl produced in the Fiji Islands in the *Pinctada margaritifera typica* oyster.

Fireball pearl: a trade name for a mantle-grown beaded pearl that is produced in the second harvest of a freshwater mussel and resembles fire or flames.

Flame pearl: another name for a fireball pearl.

Fluorescence: the emission of visible light (a glowing effect) by a material when it is stimulated by ultraviolet light, X-rays or other forms of electromagnetic radiation.

Freshwater pearl: a pearl that grows in mollusks found in rivers, lakes and streams. It can be natural or cultured.

Gonad: the sex or reproductive organ.

Gonad-grown cultured pearl: a cultured pearl grown in the gonad of a mollusk.

Graft: a piece of epithelial tissue cut from the mantle of a nacre-producing mollusk that is inserted into the body of another nacre-producing mollusk (usually of the same species), to initiate the growth of a cultured pearl sac and a cultured pearl (World Jewellery Confederation [CIBJO] definition).

Grafting: the act of introducing tissue cut from the mantle of a nacre-producing mollusk into the body of another nacre-producing mollusk (usually of the same species), to initiate the growth of a cultured pearl sac and, thereafter, a cultured pearl (World Jewellery Confederation [CIBJO] definition).

Grain: a unit of weight equaling 0.25 carats that is often used in the trade to approximate the weight of a natural pearl.

Gram: 1/1,000 of a kilogram, or 5 carats.

Gulf cultured pearl: a cultured pearl from the Persian Gulf, produced in the *Pinctada radiata* oyster.

Gulf pearl: a natural pearl from the Persian Gulf, produced in the *Pinctada radiata* oyster.

Half pearl: a whole pearl that has been ground or sawed on one side, usually to remove blemishes. Historically, the term was a misnomer for blisters and mabe pearls.

Hinge pearl: a natural pearl of irregular and usually elongated shape, found near the hinge of a bivalve mollusk, not cut from the shell (World Jewellery Confederation [CIBJO] definition).

Imitation pearl: a product that simulates the appearance of a natural or cultured pearl.

Japan Kasumi pearl: a trade name for a Japanese beaded cultured freshwater pearl produced in Lake Kasumigaura, Japan.

Kan: a unit of weight for cultured pearls equaling 1,000 momme or 3.75 kilograms.

Keshi: the Japanese word for "poppy seed" that was originally used for seed-sized natural pearls from the akoya oyster in Japan. The meaning of the word has changed to include non-beaded cultured saltwater pearls of any size formed accidentally during the culturing process. Freshwater pearl sellers have also used it to refer to second-harvest non-beaded cultured pearls.

Lion's paw pearls: a trade name for non-nacreous pearls from the *Nodipecten subnodosus* scallop, which has a shell that resembles a lion's paw.

Luster: the surface brilliancy and glow from within a pearl when light is reflected off the internal layers of pearl nacre.

Mabe pearl: a trade term for an assembled cultured blister. It is composed of a shell blister; a wax, resin or paste filling in the blister cavity; and a backing, usually made of mother-of-pearl. "Mabe pearl" can also refer more specifically to an assembled pearl from the *Pteria penguin* oyster, also known by the Japanese name *mabe gai*.

Maeshori treatment: a proprietary nacre-tightening and luster-improvement treatment process involving heating and cooling and sometimes chemicals. The effects are not always permanent.

Majorica (or Mallorca) pearl: an imitation glass pearl that is coated with pearl essence or another substance.

Mantle: a tissue that lines the inner shell surface and encloses the soft inner body of the mollusk. Displaced external mantle cells trigger the formation of a pearl sac and the creation of a pearl within the sac.

Matinee: a 50 to 66 centimeter (20 to 26 inch) necklace.

Momme: a Japanese unit of weight for cultured pearls equaling 0.13 ounces or 3.75 grams. One thousand momme equals 1 kan.

Mother-of-pearl: the smooth, hard, iridescent coating on the inner shell surface of some mollusks.

Nacre: a natural iridescent substance secreted by some mollusks. It is called mother-of-pearl when it is lining the inside of the mollusk's shell and nacre when it is a component of pearls.

Natural pearl: an organic gem formed inside the pearl sac of a wild saltwater or freshwater mollusk without human intervention.

Optical brightening: a treatment process using chemicals to generate a blue fluorescence that masks yellow and brightens pearls by absorbing light in the ultraviolet and violet regions of the electromagnetic spectrum and emitting light in the blue region as fluorescence.

Organic substance: a natural product of plant or animal origin, such as mother-of-pearl.

Orient: a term used for pearl iridescence—an optical phenomenon caused by the interference and diffraction of light from within the surface of some nacreous pearls.

Oriental pearl: historically this term referred to any natural saltwater pearl, but today it usually means natural Persian Gulf pearls.

Overtone: the one or more colors that overlie the body color, usually pink, green, blue or silver.

Pearl: an organic gem formed inside a one-shelled or two-shelled living mollusk.

Pearl essence: a solution of powdered fish scales mixed with varnish, resin or another coating material, used to make imitation pearls. Also called essence of orient or *essence d'orient.*

Pearl sac: an enclosure in which pearls grow, formed from cells from the epithelium of the mantle. The epithelial cells of the pearl sac secrete mainly nacre in the case of pearl oysters.

Persian Gulf: an area between Iran and the Arabian Peninsula, also known as the Arabian Gulf. It is an extension of the Indian Ocean.

Petal pearl: a trade name for a mantle-grown, beadless cultured pearl that is produced in the second harvest of a freshwater mussel and resembles a thin flower petal.

Pipi pearl: a natural pearl produced in the *Pinctada maculata* pearl oyster in the Indo-Pacific region, especially French Polynesia and the Cook Islands.

Princess: a 40 to 50 centimeter (16 to 20 inch) necklace.

Quahog pearl: a pearl from the *Mercenaria mercenaria* clam, named after the Algonquian word for the mollusk. These pearls are found along the North Atlantic coast.

Rainbow pearl: a trade name for a pearl from the rainbow-lipped *Pteria sterna* oyster.

Rope: a necklace measuring 1 meter (40 inches) or longer.

Seed pearl: a tiny natural pearl less than 2 millimeters in diameter. Some trade members today also identify tiny cultured pearls as seed pearls.

Shell blister: a natural or cultured dome-shaped formation that grows attached to the inner surface of a mollusk shell.

Shell pearl: an imitation pearl made from the shell of a mollusk.

Simulated pearl: another name for an imitation pearl.

Soufflé cultured pearl: a trade name for a baroque freshwater cultured pearl that forms around "mud" inserted into an existing cultured pearl sac after the first harvest in some Chinese mussels. When drilled the interior usually drains out and becomes hollow.

South Sea cultured pearl: a pearl from the silver-lipped or gold-lipped *Pinctada maxima* oyster. These types of pearls are cultivated in Australia, Indonesia, the Philippines, Myanmar and Thailand.

Spat: young oysters or mussels; the name is given to pearl mollusk larvae after they permanently attach to a surface.

Tahitian cultured pearl: a pearl from the black-lipped *Pinctada margaritifera* oyster that is cultivated in French Polynesia. These types of pearls are marketed in Tahiti.

Torsade: a multi-strand necklace formed by twisting strands around each other. This is a popular way to wear freshwater pearl strands.

Treated pearl: a pearl that has been altered to change its appearance, composition and/or durability by methods other than what are considered normal procedures.

Whole pearl: a pearl that occurs in a pearl sac and is not in direct contact with the shell of a pearl-producing mollusk. It is also called a free pearl, loose pearl or cyst pearl.

BIBLIOGRAPHY

BOOKS AND BOOKLETS

Ahrens, Joan and Malloy, Ruth. *Hong Kong Gems & Jewelry*. Hong Kong: Delta Dragon, 1986.

Anderson, Basil W. *Gem Testing*. Verplanck, NY: Emerson Books, 1985.

Arem, Joel. *Gems & Jewelry*. New York: Bantam, 1986.

Bari, Hubert and Lam, David. *Pearls*. Milan, Italy: Skira, 2009.

Bauer, Max. *Precious Stones*. Rutland, VT, and Tokyo, Japan: Charles E. Tuttle, 1969.

Bingham, Anne. *Buying Jewelry*. New York: McGraw Hill, 1989.

Blakemore, Kenneth. *The Retail Jeweller's Guide*. London, UK: Butterworths, 1988.

Bloom, Stephen G. *Tears of Mermaids*. New York: St. Martin's Press, 2009.

Branellec, Jacques. *The Ultimate Orient: The Quest for the Perfect Pearl*. Manila, Philippines: Asiatype, 2013.

Bruton, Eric. *Legendary Gems or Gems that Made History*. Radnor, PA: Chilton, 1986.

Ciprani, Curzio and Borelli, Alessandro. *Simon & Schuster's Guide to Gems and Precious Stones*. New York: Simon and Schuster, 1986.

Dawson, Marge. *Pearls of Creation. A–Z of Pearls, 2nd Edition*. Pearls of Creation LLC, 2011.

Dickinson, Joan Younger. *The Book of Pearls*. New York: Crown Publishers, 1968.

Dirlam, Dona and Weldon, Robert. *Splendour & Science of Pearls*. Carlsbad, CA: Gemological Institute of America, 2013.

Farn, Alexander E. *Pearls: Natural, Cultured and Imitation*. London, UK: Butterworths, 1986.

Farrington, Oliver Cummings. *Gems and Gem Minerals*. Chicago, IL: A.W. Mumford, 1903.

Federman, David and Bari, Hubert. *The Pink Pearl: A Natural Treasure of the Caribbean*. Milan, Italy: Skira, 2007.

Federman, David and Hammid, Tino. *Consumer Guide to Colored Gemstones*. Shawnee Mission, KS: Modern Jeweler, 1989.

Freeman, Michael. *Light*. New York: Amphoto, 1988.

Galopim de Carvalho, Rui. *Gempedia*. Bangkok, Thailand: Asian Institute of Gemological Sciences Co. Ltd., 2024.

Gemological Institute of America. *Gem Reference Guide*. Santa Monica, CA: GIA, 1988.

Gemological Institute of America. *The GIA Jeweler's Manual*. Santa Monica, CA: GIA, 1989.

Gemological Institute of America. Proceedings of the International Gemological Symposium, 1991. GIA, 1992.

Graham, Wendy. *Pearls: A Practical Guide*. Ramsbury, UK: Crowood Press, 2021.

Greenbaum, Walter W. *The Gemstone Identifier*. New York: Prentice Hall Press, 1988.

Hackney, Ki and Edkins, Diana. *People & Pearls: The Magic Endures*. New York: HarperCollins, 2000.

Hall, Cally. *Gemstones, Eyewitness Handbooks*. London, UK: Dorling Kindersley, 1994.

Hodgkinson, Alan. *Gem Testing Techniques*. Scotland, UK: Valerie Hodgkinson, 2015.

Idaka, Kimiko. *Pearls of the World*. Tokyo, Japan: Shinsoshoku Co., 1985.

Jackson, Carole. *Color Me Beautiful*. New York: Ballantine, 1985.

Japan Pearl Exporters' Association. *Cultured Pearls*. Japan Pearl Exporters' Association.

Jewelers of America. *The Gemstone Enhancement Manual*. New York: Jewelers of America, 1990.

Joyce, Kristin and Addison, Shellei. *Pearls: Ornament & Obsession*. New York: Simon & Schuster, 1993.

Kunz, George Frederick. *The Curious Lore of Precious Stones*. New York: Bell, 1989.

Kunz, George and Stephenson, Charles. *The Book of the Pearl*. New York: Century Co., 1908.

Landman, Neil, Mikkelsen, Pula, Bieler, Rudiger and Bronson, Bennet. *Pearls: A Natural History*. New York: Harry N. Abrams, 2001.

Liddicoat, Richard T. *Handbook of Gem Identification*. Santa Monica, CA: GIA, 1993.

Lintilhac, Jean-Paul. *Black Pearls of Tahiti*. Papeete, Tahiti: Royal Tahitian Pearl Book, 1985.

Marcum, David. *The Dow Jones-Irwin Guide to Fine Gems and Jewelry*. Homewood, IL: Dow Jones-Irwin, 1986.

Matlins, Antoinette L. and Bonanno, A. *The Pearl Book: 4th Edition*. South Woodstock, VT: Gemstone Press, 2008.

Miguel, Jorge. *Jewelry, How to Create Your Image*. Dallas, TX: Taylor Publishing, 1986.

Miller, Anna M. *Gems and Jewelry Appraising*. New York: Van Nostrand Reinhold Company, 1988.

Muller, Andy. *Pearls*. Kobe, Japan: Golay Buchel, Japan, 1990.
Muller, Andy. *Cultured Pearls: The First Hundred Years*. Kobe, Japan: Golay Buchel, Japan, 1997.
Nadelhoffer, Hans. *Cartier Jewels Extraordinary*. New York: Harry Abrams, 1984.
Nassau, Kurt. *Gemstone Enhancement, Second Edition*. London, UK: Butterworths, 1994.
Newman, Renée. *Exotic Gems, Volume 4*. Los Angeles, CA: Intl. Jewelry Publications, 2016.
Newman, Renée. *Pearl Buying Guide*. Los Angeles, CA: Intl. Jewelry Publications, 2017.
O'Donoghue, Michael. *Identifying Man-made Gems*. London, UK: N.A.G. Press, 1983.
O'Donoghue, Michael and Joyner, Louise. *Identification of Gemstones*. Oxford, UK: Butterworth-Heinemann, 2003.
Powley, Tammy. *Making Designer Gemstone & Pearl Jewelry*. Gloucester, MA: Rockport Publishers, 2003.
Preston, William S. *Guides for the Jewelry Industry*. New York: Jewelers Vigilance Committee, Inc., 1986.
Resnick, Lynda and Wilkinson, Francis. *Rubies in the Orchard: How to Uncover the Hidden Gems in Your Business*. New York: Doubleday, 2009.
Romero, Christie. *Warman's Jewelry*. Iola, WI: Krause Publications, 2002.
Rosenthal, Leonard. *The Pearl Hunter*. New York: Henry Schuman, 1952.
Rosenthal, Leonard. *The Pearl and I*. New York: Vantage Press, 1955.
Salomon, Paule. *The Magic of the Black Pearl*. Papeete, Tahiti: Tahiti Perles, 1986.
Sampson, Beatriz and Bari, Hubert. *Pearls*. London, UK: V&A Publishing, 2013.
Schumann, Walter. *Gemstones of the World*. New York: Sterling, 2013.
Shen, Fiona Lindsay. *Pearl: Nature's Perfect Gem*. London, UK: Reaktion Books, 2022.
Shirai, Shohei. *Pearls*. Okinawa, Japan: Marine Planning, 1981.
Smith, George Frederick Herbert. *Gemstones*. London, UK: Pitman, 1949.
Strack, Elisabeth. *Pearls*. Stuttgart, Germany: Rühle-Diebener-Verlag, 2006.
Taburiaux, Jean. *Pearls: Their Origin, Treatment, and Identification*. Radnor, PA: Chilton, 1985.
Ward, Fred. *Pearls*. Bethesda, MD: Gem Book Publishers, 2002.
Webster, Robert. *Practical Gemmology*. Ipswich, UK: N.A.G. Press, 1976.
Webster, Robert. *Gemmologists' Compendium*. New York: Van Nostrand Reinhold, 1979.
Webster, Robert. *Gems*. London, UK: Butterworths, 1983.

PERIODICALS

Auction Market Resource for Gems & Jewelry. Rego Park, NY: Auction Market Resource.
Australian Gemmologist. Brisbane, Australia: Gemmological Association of Australia.
Canadian Gemmologist. Toronto, Canada: Canadian Gemmological Association.
Gems and Gemology. Santa Monica, CA: Gemological Institute of America.
Gems & Jewellery. London, UK: Gemmological Association of Great Britain.
The GemGuide. Glenview, IL: Gemworld International, Inc.
InColor. New York: ICA (International Colored Gemstone Association)
Jewelers Circular Keystone. New York: Reed Elsevier, Inc.
Jewelry Business. Richmond Hill, ON: Kennilworth Media Inc.
Jewelry News Asia. Hong Kong: UBM Asia Ltd.
Journal of Gemmology. London, UK: Gemmological Association Great Britain.
Lapidary Journal Jewelry Artist. Fort Collins, CO: Interweave Press.
National Jeweler. New York: National Business Media.
Pacific Coast Archaeological Society Quarterly, Vol. 53, No. 2 & 3. Costa Mesa, CA: Pacific Coast Archaeological Society.
Pearl World. Phoenix, AZ: Haggis House, Inc.
Rock & Gem. Ventura, CA: Miller Magazines, Inc.
SSEF Facette. Basel, Switzerland: Swiss Gemmological Institute.
Southern Jewelry News. Greensboro, NC: Southern Jewelry News.

MISCELLANEOUS—COURSES, LEAFLETS, CATALOGS, ETC.

Gemological Institute of America: Gem Identification Course. Santa Monica, CA.

Gemological Institute of America: Pearls Course, 1990.

Gemological Institute of America: Pearl Description System Manual, 2000.

Gemological Institute of America: Pearl Report folder with current grading definitions.

"Hints to select your cultured pearls." Hong Kong: Rio Pearl.

"I am a pearl." New York: Mastoloni Pearls.

"Natural Pearls and Cultured Pearls: A basic concept and its variations" by Prof. Dr. H.A. Hänni" in the Third Quarter 2012 issue of the *Australian Gemmologist.*

"Pearls as One" online course. New York: Cultured Pearl Association of America, 2016.

WEBSITES

assael.com
australiansouthseapearls.com
autorepearls.com.au
burmajars.com
cpaa.org
christies.com
conchpearls.com
forbes.com
gem-a.com
gemmologisches-institut-hamburg.de
gemsociety.org
gia.edu
ha.com
homeofpearls.com
karipearls.com
kojimapearl.com
naturalpearsociety.org
palagems.com
paspaley.com
pearl-guide.com
pearlsasone.org
pearlparadise.com
pearlsofaustralia.com
pearlwise.pro
purepearls.com
sinjuken.co.jp
sothebys.com
ssef.ch/research-publications/facette/
thecultureofpearls.com
thejewelleryeditor.com
theworldofpearl.com
winterson.co.uk/blog/fascinated-by-pearls-william-saville-kent/

INDEX

Page numbers in *italics* refer to illustrations.

NUMBERS

10-times magnification, 37, 54–56, 61, 83, 94, 164–67, 174, 180

A

abalone pearls, *45*, *53*, 138–42, *202*, *215*
agate and pearl jewelry, *212*, *214*
akoya pearl jewelry, 71, *83*, 199, *215*
akoya pearls
- beaded cultured pearl(s), 22–23, 31, *34*, 38–*39*, *41*, 130, 199
- beadless pearl(s), *34*
- culture, 72–75, *76–77*, 92t
- defined, 72
- gonad-grown pearls, *72*, 130, 132
- Hanadama pearls, 83
- history of, 72–75
- identification, 38, *110*
- keshi pearls, *34*, 41, 78–79
- nacre, 59–60, 64, 100, 136–37

American freshwater pearls, 23, 64, *119–20*
American mussel shells, 23–25, 60, 73, 118
American Pearl Company, 25, 79, 120
amethyst and pearl jewelry, *182*, 184, *186*, *190*, 196, *203–4*, *210*, *221*
aragonite, 26–27, 29, 143, *143*
archaeological pearl artifacts, *15–16*, 22, 155
archaeological shell artifacts, 161
Art Nouveau jewelry, 24, 183t, 192–94
Assael (jeweler), *59*, 89, 104–5, *107*, *200*
Australia, 22, 31, 42, 77, 88–89, 150, *201*
Autore (jeweler), *85–86*, 93–99, *209*, *226*

B

Bahrain, 9–11, 29, 42–44
Baja California pearls, 16–17, 44, 102–3, 108–9, 181
Baja California sea snail pearls, 138–40, 153
Bari, Hubert, 29, 146, 161
baroque pearls, 121, 129, 139, 144, 148, 152, 155
baroque pearls jewelry, *15*, *21*, *58–59*, *217*
beaded (bead-nucleated) pearls
- culture, 25, 31, *33–34*, 73, 89, 120, 128, 130, 133, 142
- defined, 32
- quality testing, 37, 40, *40*, 163, 177
- second harvest (fireballs), 129, 133t, *174*
- shape, 80, 128

beadless pearls
- conch, 145–46
- culture, *33–34*, *39*, *78–79*, 92, 121, 123, 125, 127–28, 130, 145–46
- defined, 32
- keshi pearls, 78–79, 92
- quality testing, 37–38, 40, *136*
- second harvest, *78–79*, 128

Biwa pearls, 23, *34*, 120–22, 126, 130, 133t
black pearls
- culture, 64, 104–6, 108–10
- defined, 102–3
- history of, 108–9
- jewelry, 111, *213*
- pen pearls, 111
- quality testing, 40, 110

blemishes, 49–55, 83, 93–*94*, 111, 135, 164, *174*, 180
blisters, shell
- abalone, 140
- Buddha, *18*, *30*–31
- defined, 14, 26
- formation, 23, 27–29, 72–74
- history, 23, 30–31, 45, 88, 90, 117–18, 123
- jewelry, *107*, *189*
- nautilus, *161*

Bougainville, Louis Antoine de, 103
Branellec, Jacques, 90, 104
Brouillet, Jean-Claude, 104–5
button-shaped pearls, 94–*96*, 98, 112, 144, 152, *157*, *216*
by-product
- agricultural, 21, 23, 116
- scallop harvesting, 122, 152

C

calcite, 26–27, 29, 37–39, 143, 222
Caribbean Sea, 144, 146, 150, 159
Cartier (jeweler), 11, 15, 90, 105, 144, 186, 196–97
Cassis pearl. *see* helmet pearls
Chanel, Coco, 171
Chaumet (jeweler), 196–97, *199*
China
- akoya pearls, 75, 77
- beaded cultured pearl(s), 129–30, *131*, 133
- beadless cultured pearls, *38–39*, 78–79, 123, 127, 135
- blister pearls, 18, 30–31, 123
- freshwater pearls, *63*, 116, 123–*24*, 126, 137, *204*, *208*, *213*
- history of pearls in, 18, 123–26
- pearl economy, 137
- treated pearls, 172, 175

citrine and pearl jewelry, *198*, *200*, *208*, *213*
clam pearls, 102–3, 111, *155–59*, 171, 200, *211*, *214*
clams, 156, 158, 171
clams (*Atrina* spp.)
- flag pen shell clams (*A. vexillum*), 102, 159
- stiff pen shell clams (*A. rigida*), 102–3, 111

clasps
- hinged, *218–20*
- magnetic, *216*
- "mystery," 68
- ornate, 32, *119*, *217*
- pearl and oyster, *220*
- single, 69

color, 62–66, 135–36
Cook Islands, 45, 102, 107–8
Cortés, Hernán, 16, 44, 108
cross sections, *26–27*, *29*, *36*, *39*
cultured blisters, *18*, 22, 30–31, 72–73, 84, 88. *see also* mabe pearls
Cultured Pearl Association of America, 60, 74, 91
cultured pearl jewelry
- bolo necktie, *213*

bracelet, *92, 105, 188, 201*
brooch, *192–93, 195, 197–98, 202, 204, 208–9, 213*
clasp, *32*
cuff, *201*
earrings, *63, 111, 200, 204–5, 207, 210, 212, 214–15, 221*
necklace, *22, 25, 83, 85, 88, 97, 103, 107, 114, 122, 203, 206, 216–17*
pendant, 113, *203, 208–*10
pin, *217*
ring, *53, 63, 111, 197, 200*
suite, *199*
cultured pearls
conch, 145–46
cultivation, 32, 34, 41–43, 45, 104, *146*
defined, 14, 26, 30–32
earrings, *58–59*
formation, 32, 34
freshwater pearls, 32, 34
history, 22–25
identification, *36*–41
saltwater pearls, 34
scallop pearls, 153

D

diamond
La Peregrina, 15
and pearl bolo necktie, *213*
and pearl bracelet, *92, 201*
and pearl brooch, *109, 189–92, 195, 197–98, 202, 204, 209, 213–14*
and pearl earrings, *204, 207, 210, 212, 214, 221*
and pearl necklace, *41, 44, 119, 131, 196, 226*
and pearl pendant, *44, 187, 190, 194–96, 215*
and pearl pin, *197, 202*
and pearl ring, *185, 197, 200–201, 205*
and pearl suite, *199*
and wedding jewelry, 12
Diana, Princess of Wales, 21–22
Domard, Jean-Marie, 104

E

Edison pearls, 34, 130, 133t, *136*
Elizabeth I, Queen, *21*, 216
emerald and pearl jewelry, *190, 192, 199*
Empress Eugénie, 24, *44*, 109,
Europe, history of pearls in, 19–22, 116–18

F

fake pearls. *see* imitation pearls
Fiji, 45, 102, 106–7, 108, *112, 200, 206*
fireball pearls, *129*, 133t, *174*
fishing bans, 12, 17, 42, 44, 109, 144
flaws, 51–56, 93–94, 101, 111, 115, 130, 135
fluorescence, 40–41, 110, 172–73, 178, 181
fluorescent lights and pearl luster, 50, 57, 65–66
freediving, 16, 42, 140
French Polynesia, 12–106, 114
freshwater pearl jewelry
bracelet, *189*
brooch, *120–21, 213*
brooch/pendant, *204*
earrings, *63, 119, 124, 132, 204, 207, 215*
necklace, *119, 122, 124, 129, 131, 196, 203*
pin, *120, 217*
freshwater pearls
abalone, 142
bleaching, 172
coating, 175
cross section, *39*
culture methods, 32, 34, 92, 127–30, 133t
defined, 14, 116
dyeing, *176*
geographic distribution, 116–32
history of, 18–19, 21, 23–25, 30, 116–18, 120–23, 125–30, 133
melo pearls, 148
seed pearls, 78–79
soufflé pearls, *132–33*
treatments, 172–73, 175–77

G

garnet and pearl jewelry, *185–86, 190–91, 193–94, 196, 199, 202, 205, 211*
Gemological Institute of America (GIA)
pearl cultivation history, 18
pearl formation, 29
pearl grading, 52, 54, 70, 94
pearl industry, 24–25
pearl luster categories, 48
pearl testing, 142, 145–46, 173, 175, 179
on quahog pearls, 156
Gems & Gemology (journal)
akoya pearls, 77
fireball pearls, 129
helmet pearls, 150
mussel pearls, 122, 125–26
pearl treatments, 172–73, 175, 177–79, 181
pen pearls, 159
pipi pearls, 45
quality testing, 110, 168
scallop pearls, 153
gender and pearls, 24–25, 192
Georgian jewelry, 183t, *184–85*
gold, 15–16, 31, 73, 184, 186, 192, 196–99, 225
golden South Sea pearls, 225
gonad-grown pearls. *see* beaded (bead-nucleated) pearls; beadless pearls; cultured pearls
grafting. *see* beaded (bead-nucleated) pearls; beadless pearls; cultured pearls
Gulf of California, 16, 102, 109, 111

H

Hänni, Henry, 92, 133t, 143
Hepburn, Audrey, 171
Humbert, Josh, 64, *114*
Hunter, Justin, 106, 108

I

imitation pearls, 162–71
testing for, 163–68
types of, 162–63
India, 12–*13*, 41, 126, 161
Indigenous peoples, 15, 22, 108, 140, 150, 156
Inter World Trading Co. Inc., 78
International Jewelers' Congress, 74
iridescence, 27, 47, 62–64, 82–83, 113–14
irradiation. *see* pearl treatments

J

Japan, 23–25, 31, 97, 120–22
jasper and pearl jewelry, *200, 214*

K

Kamoka Pearls, 64, *114*
Kasumi pearls, 34, 122, 126, 130, 135

Kennedy, Jackie, 168–71
keshi pearls, *34, 78–79,* 92, *202, 215*
keshi-type pearls, 79, 128
King's Ransom, *81, 129–30, 136, 177*
Kojima company, *44, 65, 110, 122, 146, 153–54, 160*
Kunz, George, 8, 19, 24, 118

L

La Peregrina (pearl), *15,* 57
Lake Biwa pearls, 23, 120–21
Lam, David, 29, 146, 161
lapis lazuli and pearl jewelry, *187, 203, 212*
Latendresse, John, 25, 120
Lintilhac, Jean-Pierre, 103, 115
luster, 109, 111, 133–34, 136, 139, 173, 175, 179

M

mabe pearls
- culture of, 84, 88, 109–*10*
- defined, 14, 30–31
- history, 45, 73, 123
- jewelry, *53, 140,* 203, *214*
- luster, 50

mantle, 14, 26–27, 29, 32
- defined, 14

mantle-grown freshwater pearls
- coin pearls, *128*
- second harvest pearls, *128*

Marie Antoinette, Queen, *20–21*
mass-production, 23, 31, 73, 186, 196
matching, 37, *44,* 69–71, 167
melo pearls, *148–49, 205*
Mexico, 16–17, 44, 102–3, 108–10, 152–53, 159
Mid-Century jewelry, 183t, 199
Mikimoto (jeweler), *32, 68, 83,* 90, *145*
Mikimoto, Kokichi, 18, 22–*23,* 31–32, 42, 60, *75,* 84, 104
Mise, Tatsuhei, 23, 31
Modern jewelry, 183t
Mohs hardness, 144, 222–23
moonstone and pearl jewelry, *201–2, 209, 213*
mother-of-pearl, 14, 22, 24, 26, 163, *184, 196, 207, 214*
mussels, *18,* 116–17, 123
mussels (*Hyriopsis* spp.), 121–23, 125–26
mussels (*Modiolus* spp.), 160
mussels (*Unio* spp.), 23, 60, 116–18

N

nacre
- blemishes, 52–53
- composition, 23, 26–27, 29, *143*
- defined, 14
- deposition, 75, 127
- quality, 46–47, 164–65, 181
- thickness, 36–38, 46, 55–57, 59–62, 93–94, 100–101, 110, 136–37

Native Americans, 23, 163
natural pearl jewelry
- brooch, *109, 184, 188, 190, 192, 214*
- earrings, *214*
- mourning suite, *191*
- necklace, *15–16, 21, 41, 45, 187, 226*
- parure, *184*
- pendant, *20, 44, 182, 186–87, 190, 194–95, 215*
- pin, *45, 197, 202*
- ring, *184, 211*

natural pearls
- color, 64
- cultivation, 88, 109, 117
- defined, 14, 29, 78
- history, 9, 11–12, 15–19, 21–25, 77, 89, 103, 108–10, 116–17, 120
- and period jewelry, 194, 197, 199
- quality and identity testing, 36–38, 40–41, 110, 163–64, 168, 175
- sea snail pearls, 148
- shape, *41,* 57
- source, 41–45
- structure, *26–27*
- value, 11, 21, 24, 67, 71, 115

near round pearls
- cultured pearls, 57, 59, 125, *135*
- natural pearls, 45
- sea snail pearls, 148, 155

Nishikawa, Tokichi, 23, 31
non-nacreous pearls
- clam pearls, 102, 111, 152, 158–59
- defined, 143
- identification, 171
- nautilus pearls, 161
- scallop pearls, 152–53
- sea snail pearls, 139, 144, 146, 148–50

O

opal and pearl jewelry, *204, 206, 210, 213, 217*
orient. see iridescence
oriental pearls, 14, 24
overtone. *see* color
oysters (*Malleus* spp.), *28*
oysters (*Pinctada* spp.)
- akoya pearl oyster (*P. fucata martensii*), 31, 47–*48,* 72–73
- black-lipped pearl oyster (*P. margaritifera*), 105, 108
- Fijian black-lipped pearl oyster (*P. margaritifera typica*), 45, 64, 102, 106
- Gulf pearl oyster (*P. radiata*), 9, 27, 77
- Mazatlan pearl oysters (*P. mazatlanica*), 17, *31,* 102, 108–9
- silver- or gold-lipped pearl oyster (*P. maxima*), 22, *33, 40,* 45, *84,* 86, 88–89, 98–99
- spotted pearl oyster (*P. maculata*), 45

oysters (*Pteria* spp.), *18, 31, 40–41, 44–45,* 47, 102–3, 108–9

P

Pacific Coast Pearls, *17,* 152, *155,* 159–60
Pacific Pearls, 122, *128,* 130
pearl and gem jewelry, 182–215. *see also* listings for individual gems
pearl care
- cleaning, 223–24
- maintenance, 225–26
- storage, 224–25

pearl essence (essence of orient), 162–63
pearl farming, 35, *125*
pearl fishing, 42, 44, 109, 117–18, 137
Pearl Geodes, *132–*33
pearl identity and quality tests, 36–37, 40, 163–71, 179–81, 223
pearl sac, 29, *33,* 78–79, 92, 118, 127, 129, 178
Pearl Science Laboratory (PSL), 83, 94, 114
pearl shapes, 34, *96–98,* 138–40, 148, 155
pearl-grading, 11, 43, 52, 54–56, 59, 66, 70–71, 82–83, 93, 134, 136
pearls, symbolism of, 8, 19, 21, 23
Peña, Lider, *150, 211*
period jewelry, 183–96, 198–215

Persian Gulf, 9–11, 24, 41
Philippines, 90–91, 158, 160, 171, 200
pricing pearls. *see* value factors

Q

quahog pearls, *156–57*, *211*

R

Rainforest Design, *150*, *211*
Resnick, Lynda, 168–69
ruby and pearl jewelry, 15, *183–84*, *187–88*, *190*, *193*, *197–98*, *201–2*, *206*, *208*, *210*
Russia, 116–17, 186, 196

S

saltwater pearls. *see also* akoya pearls *and* South Sea pearls
  culture, 22, 32, 34, 88, 92
  defined, 14, 72, 84
  geographic distribution, 18, 137
  jewelry, 21, *214*
  value factors, 59, 134–35
sapphire
  and Georgian jewelry, 184
  and pearl bracelet, *188–89*, *201*
  and pearl brooch, *188*, 190, *195*, *202*, *204*, *209*, *213*
  and pearl earrings, *204–5*, *207*, *215*
  and pearl necklace, *206*
  and pearl pendant, *187*, *190*, *195–96*, *203*, *215*
  and pearl pin, *197*
  and pearl ring, *200–201*
Saville-Kent, William, 22, 31, 88
scallop, giant lion's paw (*Nodipecten subnodosus*), 152–53
scallop pearls, 152--55
Sea Hunt Pearls, *128*, 132
Sea of Cortez pearls, 16, 44, 102–3, 109, 153
sea snails
  bailer shell (*Melo melo*), 138, 148–49
  horned helmet (*Cassis cornuta*), 138, 150–51
  horse conch (*Triplofusus giganteus*), 146
  queen conch (*Aliger gigas*), 144–46
  queen helmet (*Cassis madagascariensis*), *211*
  trapezium horse conch (*Pleuroploca trapezium*), 146–47
seed pearls, *184–85*, *187*, *190–91*, *196*, *214*
Shepherd, Jeremy, 81, *83*, *132*, 171, *176*
silver, 16, 31, *39*, 73, *110*, 177, 180–81, 184, 192, 196, 226
size, 66–69, 136
smoothness, 135
soufflé pearls, *132–33*
South Sea cultured blisters, *84*
South Sea pearls
  cultured pearls, 45
  defined, 14, 84
  dyeing, 176
  geographic distribution, 85–91
  jewelry, *22*, *85*, *88*, 92, *131*, *208–9*, *217*
  keshi pearls, 92
  treatments, 172, 177
spat (oyster larvae), 12, 35, 75, 86, 106, *108*
spectrometry, 16, 173, 176, 181
Stevenson, Charles, 8, 15, *18–19*, 24, 87, 118
Strack, Elizabeth, 18, 23–24, 29, 31, 86, 88–90, 116–17, 120–21, 123, 159, 173
styling
  pearl studs, 221
  strand of pearls, 216–20
surface quality, 51–57, 135
Swiss Gemmological Institute (SSEF), 15, 22, 40, 79, 143, 158, 171

T

Tahitian pearls
  color variability, *114*
  defined, 14
  imitation, 175–76
  jewelry, *59*, *63*, *92*, *103*, *105*, *111–12*, *131*, *208–10*, *212*
  luster, 93
  nacre thickness, 60
  overtone, *63*
  pearl economy, 104–5, 114, 200
  shape, 57, *112*
  X-ray, *38*
Takashima, Kikiro, 87
Taylor, Elizabeth, 15
Tiffany & Co., 24, 105, 118, 186, 196–97
tourmaline and pearl jewelry, *202*, *205*, *207–8*, *210–11*, *215*
tsavorite and pearl jewelry, *201*, *205*, *207*

U

United Arab Emirates (UAE), *9–10*, 77
United States
  California, 108–9, 152–53
  Florida, 144–45, 150, 159
  Iowa, 24
  Nashville, 25, 120
  New Jersey, 24
  Ohio River, 64
  Rhode Island, 156
  Texas, 118, 159
  Wisconsin, 118
units of pearl weight, 15, 37, 43, 67, 115, 139, 144, 148

V

value factors, 46–57, 59–71, 93–101, 111–15, 134–37
Victorian jewelry, 183t, 186–*91*
Vietnam, 14, 72, *76–77*, 81, 148
Voll, Fuji, 122, *128*, 130

W

Wan, Robert, *103–5*, *114*
whole pearls, 29, 32, 34, 36, 84, 88, 110
World Jewellery Confederation (CIBJO), 26, 30, 79, 128
World War I, 183t, 194, 196
World War II, 42, 74, 85, 89, 121

X

X-ray, 29, 38, 83, 146, 175

Y

Yoko London, 92, *131*, *204*, *207*

ALSO BY RENÉE NEWMAN

"**It would not be hyperbole to call this book the bible for diamond knowledge.** The coffee-table-size volume takes the reader on a fascinating journey covering the symbolic power of diamonds through the ages, the various mining levels, provenance, the evolution of cutting, and jewelry styles. It also tackles issues such as pricing, ethics and lab-grown diamonds. And to make sure she's left no stone unturned, she closes her exhaustive guide with the emotional significance of these sparkling gems. ***Diamonds* is the gift every newcomer to the industry should receive or buy for themselves. It's also an essential read for consumers who want to make informed choices.**"

Rapaport Magazine, reviewed by Sonia Esther Soltani, Editor-in-Chief

"All in all, this splendid volume is **comprehensive, with a treasure trove of up-to-date data**, and is easily readable. It will appeal to many different kinds of readers, from diamond loving laypersons to professionals in the diamond trade to scientists. And, it is sold for a moderate price. I concur with the sentiments of another reviewer of this book (Peter Indorf): 'If you are a jeweler, gemologist, designer, appraiser, buy or sell diamonds, love or hate diamonds, buy this book, period.'"

Journal of Gemmology, reviewed by Dr. Rolf Tatje, Duisburg, Germany

"**This book stands out for two reasons: the exceptional quality of photography and the depth of research.** This book is a must for jewellery lovers and collectors."

Australian Gemmologist (A G Journal), reviewed by Garry Holloway Bsc FGAA

"**Although many books on diamonds have appeared during the past 40 years, *Diamonds* is perhaps the best from the standpoint of inclusiveness, understandability and illustrations.** There is something here for everyone, and mineral collectors will especially like the sorting tray illustrations on pages 94 and 95. This wonderful book is, of course, well edited, printed and bound. I strongly recommend it for a place on your bookshelf."

Rocks & Minerals, reviewed by Dr. Robert B. Cook, Auburn University, Auburn, Alabama

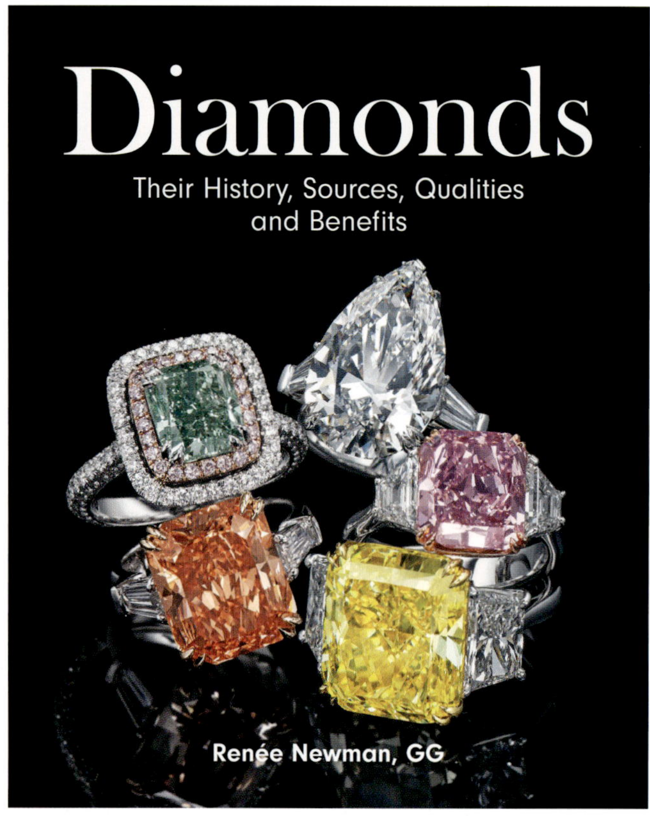

"***Diamonds: Their History, Sources, Qualities and Benefits* is a beautiful book, both in its many photographs and illustrations and in its content. It gives the reader an excellent overview of the many facets of diamonds: historical, technical, industrial, decorative, and symbolic.** The accessible text provides a bounty of information to the novice and fresh insights to the expert, all while working its nimble way from topic to topic. Renée Newman's impressive body of work boasts a brand new star in this lovely book!"

The Jewelry Appraiser (published by National Association of Jewelry Appraisers), reviewed by Caitlin St John, GIA GG

"**The writing is crystal clear, the numerous illustrations are superb, and the information provided is absolutely up-to-the-minute.** Whether your interest in diamonds is casual or intense, you need this book."

ASJRA (Association for the Study of Jewelry & Related Arts) Newsletter, reviewed by Eric J. Hoffman